日本まるごと
Q&A

Everything You Should Know about Japan

Abe Naobumi
安部直文=著

Michael Brase
マイケル・ブレーズ=訳

装　　幀 = 寄藤文平、杉山健太郎
本文イラスト = テッド高橋

本書の英語訳は、日本語からの逐語訳ではありません。日本についての知識があ
まりない外国の方のために、日本語にはない説明も英語では加えてあります

はじめに

　日本には年間およそ1340万人の外国人が訪れ、2020年には２度目の東京オリンピック・パラリンピックが開催されます。一方、戦後70年を経た日本は、これからどんな国をめざすべきかが問われています。そうした節目に当たって、日本とはどんな国なのかを再考する一助として本書を編みました。

　外国人が興味を持つのは、その国独自の文化です。したがって自国の文化と、その歴史的背景を知ること、すなわち「教養」が大事になります。Q & A形式にしたのは、外国の方に質問された場合を想定してのことですが、同時にその問いは日本人が自国を改めて認識するための入り口でもあります。ここから更に知識を広げ、思索を深めていただければ幸いです。

　本書が、日本の読者の「教養」の幅を広げる英語学習の手引きとして、更には外国の方々にとって日本語の勉強、さらには日本への理解を深める入門書として役立つことを、大いに期待しています。

2015年7月　著者

まえがき

日本にはいつ人が住むようになったのか？
日本という国はいつできたのか？
天皇とはどんな人で皇室とはどういったものなのか？
いわゆる、裸祭りや命がけの奇祭とはどんなものなのか？
一番人気のお土産は何か？
最も人気のある温泉地はどこか？
日本が最近直面している問題とは何か？

　上にあげたのは、日本についてよく聞かれる事柄の一例ですが、もっと多くのことが本書の中で説明されています。読者のみなさまが日本という国や日本人について、それも過去から現代に至るまで、多くのことを理解できることでしょう。日本はこれまでもよく、文化的にガラパゴス諸島であるとたとえられてきました。世界中の国々とはかけ離れ、独自の方向で文化的な進化を遂げてきたのです。しかし、そういった文化の発展がいまの日本のバックボーンを形作り、人々の関心を引き寄せているのです。たとえば、武道や生花などは世界的に注目されています。現代の日本はいまもなお文化的な革新を続けており、マンガ、アニメ、温かい便座など数多くの文化を生み出しています。

　今の日本は、過去と現代が複雑に絡み合い、解読するのは必ずしも容易ではありません。本書は日本の全貌を、できるだけシンプルにみなさまに理解していただけるようにつくられました。観光客として来日するときでも、椅子に座って日本のことを空想するときにでも、是非、楽しんでください！

マイケル・ブレーズ

Introduction

When was Japan first inhabited? When did it become a nation? Who is the emperor and the imperial family?
What are the so-called naked and life-risking "bizarre" festivals?
What are the most popular souvenirs?
Which are the most famous hot springs? What modern-day problems is Japan facing?

These questions, and many more, will be answered in this book, providing you with a greater appreciation for the country and its people, both modern and historical. Historically, Japan has often been a kind of cultural Galápagos, cut off from the rest of the world and evolving in its own unique direction. The culture developed then still forms the backbone of modern Japan and is well-worth being acquainted with, especially given the global spread of Japanese martial arts, flower arranging, and much more. Modern Japan has continued this tradition of cultural innovation, producing manga, anime, and heated toilet seats, to mention only a few.

Present-day Japan is an intricate mixture of the modern and the traditional, a convoluted complication that is not always easy to decipher. This book, as simple as it is, will help you enjoy Japan to the fullest, whether as a visiting tourist or as an armchair traveler. Enjoy!

Michael Brase

目次

第1章 自然と成り立ち

1 自然

- **Q:** 地球上のどこにあるの? *30*
- **Q:** 国の大きさは? *30*
- **Q:** 島はいくつあるの? *32*
- **Q:** 地形の特徴は? *32*
- **Q:** 一番高い山は? *34*
- **Q:** 地震が多いのはなぜ? *34*
- **Q:** 気候の特徴は? *38*
- **Q:** 台風はいつ頃やってくるの? *42*

2 成り立ち

- **Q:** 日本人のルーツは? *42*
- **Q:** 国家の誕生はいつ? *44*
- **Q:** 国名の由来は? *44*
- **Q:** 「ニホン」か「ニッポン」か? *46*
- **Q:** 国旗・国歌はいつ制定されたの? *46*
- **Q:** 日本語の起源は? *48*
- **Q:** 日本語の特徴は? *50*
- **Q:** 使っている漢字の数は? *52*
- **Q:** 平仮名と片仮名はどう使い分けるの? *52*
- **Q:** 「縦書き」と「横書き」どちらが多いの? *54*

- **Q:** 元号はどのように決めるの? *56*
- **Q:** 天皇はどんな仕事をしているの? *56*
- **Q:** 女性も天皇になれるの? *58*
- **Q:** 天皇家のルーツは? *58*
- **Q:** 皇族にはどんな人がいるの? *60*

Contents

Chapter 1 Geography and Basic Information

1 Geography

Q: Where is Japan on the world map? *31*
Q: How big is Japan? *31*
Q: How many islands does Japan have? *33*
Q: What are Japan's principal geographical features? *33*
Q: Japan's tallest mountain? *35*
Q: Why are earthquakes so frequent? *35*
Q: The Climate *39*
Q: When is typhoon season? *43*

2 Basic Information

Q: Where did the Japanese people come from? *43*
Q: When did the Japanese nation come into being? *45*
Q: What is the Japanese name for Japan? *45*
Q: Is it "Nippon" or "Nihon"? *47*
Q: When was the national flag officially adopted? *47*
Q: What is the origin of the Japanese language? *49*
Q: What are the chief features of the Japanese language? *51*
Q: How many Chinese characters (*kanji*) are used in writing Japanese? *53*
Q: How are *katakana* and *hiragana* used? *53*
Q: Japanese can be written vertically or horizontally. Which is more common? *55*
Q: How are era names decided? *57*
Q: What does the emperor do? *57*
Q: Can women ascend the imperial throne? *59*
Q: What are the roots of the imperial family? *59*
Q: Who exactly belongs to the imperial family? *61*

第2章 歴史

歴史

- **Q:** 日本の始まりは？ *62*
- **Q:** 縄文時代とは？ *64*
- **Q:** 弥生時代とは？ *64*
- **Q:** 古墳時代とは？ *66*
- **Q:** 飛鳥時代とは？ *66*
- **Q:** 奈良時代とは？ *68*
- **Q:** 平安時代とは？ *70*
- **Q:** 鎌倉時代とは？ *72*
- **Q:** 室町時代とは？ *74*
- **Q:** 安土桃山時代とは？ *74*
- **Q:** 江戸時代とは？ *76*
- **Q:** 明治時代とは？ *80*
- **Q:** 大正時代とは？ *82*
- **Q:** 敗戦までの昭和時代とは？ *84*

- **Q:** 戦後の日本は？ *88*

第3章 政治・行政

1 政治

- **Q:** 政治体制はどうなっているの？ *98*
- **Q:** 日本国憲法の特色は？ *98*
- **Q:** 憲法は改正できるの？ *100*
- **Q:** 国会のしくみは？ *102*
- **Q:** 国会議員はどのように選ぶの？ *104*
- **Q:** 国会議員の特権は？ *104*
- **Q:** 総理大臣の権限は？ *106*
- **Q:** 大臣は何人いるの？ *108*

Contents

 Chapter **2** History

History

Q: What is Japanese history? *63*

Q: What is the Jomon period? *65*

Q: What is the Yayoi period? *65*

Q: What is the Kofun (Burial Mound) period? *67*

Q: What is the Asuka period? *67*

Q: What is the Nara period? *69*

Q: What is the Heian period? *71*

Q: What is the Kamakura period? *73*

Q: What is the Muromachi period? *75*

Q: What is the Azuchi-Momoyama period? *75*

Q: What is the Edo period? *77*

Q: What is the Meiji Period? *81*

Q: What is the Taisho period? *83*

Q: What is the early Showa period (from 1926 to the end of World War II)? *85*

Q: What happened in postwar Japan? *89*

 Chapter **3** Politics and Government

1 Politics

Q: What is Japan's political system? *99*

Q: What features does the Japanese constitution possess? *99*

Q: Can the constitution be revised? *101*

Q: What is the Diet? *103*

Q: How are Diet members elected? *105*

Q: What special privileges to Diet members enjoy? *105*

Q: What are the powers of the prime minister? *107*

Q: How many ministers are there? *109*

9

Q: 政党とは？ *108*

2 行政

Q: 行政区分はどうなっているの？ *110*
Q: 公務員はどれくらいいるの？ *112*
Q: キャリアとノンキャリアの違いは？ *114*

Q: 防災対策はどのようにしているの？ *114*
Q: 地震予知はどこまで可能なの？ *116*
Q: 緊急地震速報はどのように出すの？ *116*
Q: 巨大地震発生の可能性が高い地域は？ *118*

3 税制

Q: 税金にはどんなものがあるの？ *120*
Q: 国家予算はどのように決められるの？ *120*
Q: 国家予算の規模と中身は？ *122*
Q: 政府が発行する国債とは？ *124*
Q: 財政破綻は本当なの？ *124*
Q: 消費税はまだ上がるの？ *126*

第4章 司法・治安

1 司法

Q: 司法制度はどうなっているの？ *128*
Q: どんな裁判所があるの？ *128*
Q: 裁判官になるには？ *128*
Q: 検察官の役割は？ *128*
Q: 弁護士の仕事は？ *128*
Q: 裁判の種類は？ *132*
Q: 裁判員制度って、なに？ *132*
Q: どんな罰則があるの？ *134*
Q: 死刑は行われているの？ *136*

Contents

Q: What is a political party? *109*

2 Administrative Divisions

Q: What are the administrative divisions? *111*

Q: How many civil servants are there? *113*

Q: What is the difference between a career and non-career civil servant? *115*

Q: What is the state of disaster prevention? *115*

Q: To what extent can earthquakes be forecast? *117*

Q: How are earthquake warnings issued? *117*

Q: Which areas are prone to massive earthquakes? *119*

3 Tax Administration

Q: What kinds of taxes are levied? *121*

Q: How is the national budget decided? *121*

Q: What is the size of the national budget? *123*

Q: What are government bonds? *125*

Q: Is financial collapse possible? *125*

Q: Is the consumption tax going to be raised again? *127*

Chapter 4 Law and Order

1 The Law

Q: What is the legal system? *129*

Q: What kind of courts does Japan have? *129*

Q: How does one become a judge? *131*

Q: What is the function of a public prosecutor? *131*

Q: What is the function of a lawyer? *131*

Q: What kinds of trials are there? *133*

Q: What is the lay judge system? *133*

Q: What kinds of punishment are carried out? *135*

Q: Is the death penalty imposed? *137*

2 警察

- **Q:** 警察機構はどうなっているの? *136*
- **Q:** 警察官の階級は? *138*
- **Q:** 逮捕されるとどうなるの? *138*
- **Q:** 受刑者はどこに収容されるの? *138*
- **Q:** どんな犯罪が多いの? *140*

3 防衛

- **Q:** 自衛隊は軍隊ではないの? *140*
- **Q:** シビリアンコントロールとは? *142*
- **Q:** 自衛隊の組織はどうなっているの? *142*
- **Q:** 自衛官には女性もいるの? *144*
- **Q:** 自衛隊の主な装備はどうなっているの? *144*
- **Q:** 海上自衛官と海上保安官の違いは? *146*

第5章 社会保障・医療

1 社会保障

- **Q:** 社会保障制度はどうなっているの? *148*
- **Q:** 年金保険のしくみは? *150*
- **Q:** 年金はいくらもらえるの? *150*
- **Q:** 日本人の平均寿命は? *152*
- **Q:** 日本一の長寿県はどこ? *152*
- **Q:** 介護保険とは? *154*
- **Q:** どんな介護施設があるの? *154*

2 医療

- **Q:** 医療制度の特徴は? *156*
- **Q:** 混合診療とは? *156*
- **Q:** 窓口負担とは? *158*
- **Q:** 病院はなぜ待ち時間が長いの? *158*
- **Q:** 薬の値段はどのように決めているの? *160*

Contents

2 The Police

- **Q:** How is the police organized? *137*
- **Q:** What are the ranks of police officers? *139*
- **Q:** What happens if you are arrested? *139*
- **Q:** Where are convicted criminals incarcerated? *139*
- **Q:** What are the most common crimes? *141*

3 Defense

- **Q:** Is not the so-called Self-Defense Force in fact an army? *141*
- **Q:** Is the Self-Defense Force under civilian control? *143*
- **Q:** What is the structure of the Self-Defense Force? *143*
- **Q:** Do women serve in the Self-Defense Force? *145*
- **Q:** How is the Self-Defense Force equipped? *145*
- **Q:** What is the difference between the Maritime Self-Defense Force and the Japan Coast Guard? *147*

Chapter 5 Social Security and Healthcare

1 Social Security

- **Q:** How is social security organized? *149*
- **Q:** How does the pension system work? *151*
- **Q:** How much can one receive from pension funds? *151*
- **Q:** What is the average life expectancy of a Japanese? *153*
- **Q:** What prefecture has the longest life expectancy? *153*
- **Q:** What is nursing care insurance? *155*
- **Q:** What kinds of nursing care facilities exist? *155*

2 Healthcare

- **Q:** What are the principal features of the healthcare system? *157*
- **Q:** What is mixed treatment? *157*
- **Q:** What does "pay on the spot" mean? *159*
- **Q:** Why is waiting time at hospitals so long? *159*
- **Q:** How is the price of medicine decided? *161*

- **Q:** 大衆薬とは？ *160*
- **Q:** 日本人に多い病気は？ *162*
- **Q:** 生活習慣病とは？ *162*
- **Q:** メタボ健診とは？ *164*
- **Q:** 在宅医療とは？ *164*
- **Q:** 終末期医療とは？ *166*
- **Q:** 脳死判定とは？ *166*

第6章 経済・労働

1 経済

- **Q:** 戦後の日本が経済復興できた理由は？ *168*
- **Q:** 日本銀行の役割は？ *170*
- **Q:** 金融機関の種類は？ *172*
- **Q:** 景気は何を基準に判断するの？ *172*
- **Q:** 日本経済の伸びは期待できるの？ *174*
- **Q:** どんなものを輸出しているの？ *174*
- **Q:** どんなものを輸入しているの？ *176*
- **Q:** 貿易収支はどうなっているの？ *178*

2 産業

- **Q:** 日本の産業構造の特徴は？ *178*
- **Q:** 主要産業は？ *180*
- **Q:** 産業の空洞化はなぜ起きたの？ *180*
- **Q:** 自給率4割って、本当なの？ *182*
- **Q:** 農業はどんな問題を抱えているの？ *182*
- **Q:** 漁業はどんな問題を抱えているの？ *184*
- **Q:** 捕鯨はいつから始まったの？ *184*
- **Q:** サービス業はどんな問題を抱えているの？ *186*
- **Q:** エネルギー問題はどうなるの？ *186*
- **Q:** 原子力発電所はどうなるの？ *188*
- **Q:** 核廃棄物はどうするの？ *188*

Contents

Q: What is "medicine for the masses"? *161*
Q: What kind of illnesses are Japanese susceptible to? *163*
Q: What are lifestyle-related diseases? *163*
Q: What is metabolic screening? *165*
Q: What is home healthcare? *165*
Q: What is the state of end-of-life care? *167*
Q: What determines brain death? *167*

Chapter 6 Economy and Labor Force

1 The Economy

Q: How did the postwar economy recover so quickly? *169*
Q: What is the role of the Bank of Japan? *171*
Q: How many different types of financial institutions are there? *173*
Q: What are the criteria for judging economic conditions? *173*
Q: Can further growth be expected from the Japanese economy? *175*
Q: What are the principal exports? *175*
Q: What are the principal imports? *177*
Q: What is the state of the balance of trade? *179*

2 Industry

Q: How is Japanese industry structured? *179*
Q: What are the principal industries? *181*
Q: How did the hollowing out of industry take place? *181*
Q: The food self-sufficiency ratio is only 40%? *183*
Q: What are the problems facing agriculture? *183*
Q: What kind of challenges is the fishing industry facing? *185*
Q: When did whaling start? *185*
Q: What problems is the service industry facing? *187*
Q: What energy problems does Japan face? *187*
Q: What is the future of nuclear power? *189*
Q: How is nuclear waste being handled? *189*

3 労働

- **Q:** 企業の雇用形態は？ *190*
- **Q:** 失業率は？ *190*
- **Q:** 労働時間は？ *192*
- **Q:** 休日は？ *192*
- **Q:** 賃金は？ *194*
- **Q:** 労働者の年収は？ *194*
- **Q:** 定年は何歳？ *194*
- **Q:** 男女機会均等法とは？ *196*
- **Q:** 女性が多い職場は？ *196*
- **Q:** 単身赴任が多いのは、なぜ？ *198*

- **Q:** 外国人が働くために必要なことは？ *200*
- **Q:** 企業が社員を解雇できるのは、どんな時？ *200*
- **Q:** ブラック企業とは？ *202*
- **Q:** 過労死って、なに？ *202*
- **Q:** 名刺はどんな時に必要なの？ *204*
- **Q:** 印鑑はどんな時に必要なの？ *204*

第7章 外交

1 国際関係

- **Q:** 外交関係がある国は、いくつ？ *208*
- **Q:** 国連に加盟したのは、いつ？ *208*
- **Q:** 国連の分担金は、いくら？ *210*
- **Q:** 常任理事国になれないのは、なぜ？ *210*

- **Q:** ODAとは、なに？ *212*
- **Q:** 日本もPKOに参加しているの？ *212*
- **Q:** 日本が加盟している国際経済機構は？ *214*

- **Q:** TPPとは、なに？ *214*

3 The Work Force

Q: How is corporate employment structured? *191*

Q: What is the unemployment rate? *191*

Q: What are the working hours? *193*

Q: What about paid vacation? *193*

Q: How are wages paid? *195*

Q: How much is average annual income? *195*

Q: What is the age of retirement? *195*

Q: What is the Equal Employment Opportunity Law? *197*

Q: In what occupations are women most prevalent? *197*

Q: Why are so many business people assigned to branch offices unaccompanied by their families? *199*

Q: What is needed for a foreigner to work in Japan? *201*

Q: When can an employee be fired? *201*

Q: What is a "black company"? *203*

Q: What does "death from overwork" mean? *203*

Q: How are business cards used? *205*

Q: When are seals necessary? *205*

Chapter 7 Diplomacy

1 International Relations

Q: How many countries does Japan have diplomatic relations with? *209*

Q: When did Japan join the United Nations? *209*

Q: How is UN funding shared? *211*

Q: Why can't Japan become a permanent member of the UN Security Council? *211*

Q: What is Japan's contribution to ODA? *213*

Q: Is Japan participating in UN Peacekeeping Operations? *213*

Q: What international economic organizations does Japan belong to? *215*

Q: What is the Trans-Pacific Partnership? *215*

2 外交課題

- **Q:** 米国とは、どんな問題があるの？ *216*
- **Q:** 中国とは、どんな問題があるの？ *218*
- **Q:** ロシアとは、どんな問題があるの？ *218*
- **Q:** 韓国とは、どんな問題があるの？ *220*
- **Q:** 北朝鮮とは、どんな問題があるの？ *220*
- **Q:** 中東諸国とは、どんな問題があるの？ *222*

第8章 暮らし

1 日本人の特質

- **Q:** 日本人って、どんな民族なの？ *226*
- **Q:** イエス、ノーをはっきり言わないのは、なぜ？ *228*
- **Q:** 日本人の特性とは？ *228*

2 衣

- **Q:** 洋服はいつから着るようになったの？ *230*
- **Q:** 和服はどんな時に着るの？ *232*
- **Q:** 男性の和服の正装は？ *232*
- **Q:** 女性の和服の正装は？ *232*

3 食

- **Q:** 和食の特徴は *234*
- **Q:** 日本人の一般的な食事習慣は？ *236*
- **Q:** よく食べる魚料理にはどんなものがあるの？ *236*
- **Q:** 醤油・味噌はいつから使うようになったの？ *238*
- **Q:** うどん、そばの違いは？ *238*
- **Q:** すきやきって、なに？ *240*
- **Q:** 寿司はいつから食べるようになったの？ *240*
- **Q:** うなぎはいつから食べるようになったの？ *242*
- **Q:** 改まった席で出される料理とは？ *244*
- **Q:** 食器の正しい置き方は？ *244*

Contents

2 Diplomatic Issues

Q: What kinds of issues are there with the United States? *217*

Q: What kinds of problems exist with China? *219*

Q: What problems exist with Russia? *219*

Q: What issues exist with South Korea? *221*

Q: What issues exist with North Korea? *221*

Q: What issues are there with Middle Eastern countries? *223*

Chapter 8 Everyday Life

1 What Characterizes the Japanese People?

Q: What kind of people are the Japanese? *227*

Q: Why can't Japanese give a clear yes or no answer? *229*

Q: What are the outstanding Japanese cultural traits? *229*

2 Clothing

Q: When did Western clothing become common? *231*

Q: When is Japanese clothing worn? *233*

Q: What does formal Japanese wear for men consist of? *233*

Q: What does formal attire for women consist of? *233*

3 Food

Q: What is Japanese cuisine (*washoku*)? *235*

Q: What is the usual meal like? *237*

Q: How is fish most often eaten? *237*

Q: When did soy sauce and miso come to be used? *239*

Q: What is the difference between udon and soba? *239*

Q: What is sukiyaki? *241*

Q: When did sushi come into being? *241*

Q: When did grilled eel become a favorite food? *243*

Q: What is the most formal Japanese cuisine? *245*

Q: Is there a fixed order to the placement of tableware? *245*

19

- **Q:** 日本酒の種類は？ *246*
- **Q:** 日本酒の飲み方は？ *248*

4 住

- **Q:** 日本の住宅の特徴は？ *250*
- **Q:** 土地や建物の値段はどのように決めるの？ *250*
- **Q:** 賃貸住宅の契約時にいくら必要？ *252*
- **Q:** しゃがんでするトイレがあるって、本当？ *252*
- **Q:** 寝具の特徴は？ *254*
- **Q:** なぜ、玄関で靴を脱ぐの？ *254*
- **Q:** 畳は、なにでできているの？ *254*
- **Q:** 床の間って、なに？ *256*
- **Q:** 襖と障子の違いは？ *256*

5 冠婚葬祭

- **Q:** 子どもが産まれてすぐしなければならないことは？ *258*
- **Q:** 七五三とは、どんな行事なの？ *258*
- **Q:** 成人式とは、どんな儀式なの？ *260*
- **Q:** 日本人の一般的な結婚式とは？ *262*
- **Q:** 結婚式の費用はいくらかかるの？ *262*
- **Q:** 結婚のお祝いの相場は、いくら？ *264*
- **Q:** 日本人の結婚年齢は、いくつ？ *264*
- **Q:** 外国人との国際結婚は多いのですか？ *266*
- **Q:** 毎年、離婚する人はどれくらいいるの？ *266*
- **Q:** 日本人が祝う記念日にはどんなものがあるの？ *266*
- **Q:** 贈り物で注意しなければならないことは？ *268*
- **Q:** 日本の一般的な葬儀は？ *268*
- **Q:** 仏式の葬儀はどのように行われるの？ *270*
- **Q:** 葬儀の費用はいくらぐらいかかるの？ *270*
- **Q:** 埋葬はどのようにするの？ *272*
- **Q:** 死後の法要はいつまでするの？ *272*

Contents

Q: How many different kinds of saké are there? *247*

Q: Is there a particular way to drink saké? *249*

4 Japanese Housing

Q: What distinguishes Japanese housing? *251*

Q: How is the price of land and houses decided? *251*

Q: What is the initial cost of renting a house or apartment? *253*

Q: Are squat toilets still used? *253*

Q: What does Japanese bedding consist of? *255*

Q: Why are shoes removed in the entryway? *255*

Q: What are tatami mats made of? *255*

Q: What is a *tokonoma*? *257*

Q: What is the difference between a *fusuma* and a *shoji*? *257*

5 Weddings and Other Special Occasions

Q: What is required after the birth of a child? *259*

Q: What does 7-5-3 mean? *259*

Q: What is the coming-of-age ceremony? *261*

Q: What is a typical Japanese wedding? *263*

Q: How much does a wedding cost? *263*

Q: What is the going rate for a wedding gift? *265*

Q: What is the average marriage age? *265*

Q: Are international marriages common? *267*

Q: How many divorces are there a year? *267*

Q: What ages are objects of special commemoration? *267*

Q: Is caution required in presenting a gift? *269*

Q: What is the typical funeral like? *269*

Q: What does a Buddhist funeral consist of? *271*

Q: How much does a funeral cost? *271*

Q: How are the deceased interred? *273*

Q: How long do services for the dead continue? *273*

6 行事

- **Q:** 国民の祝日は？ *274*
- **Q:** お正月は、なにをするの？ *278*
- **Q:** 節分って、どんな行事なの？ *280*
- **Q:** お彼岸とは？ *280*
- **Q:** お節句とは？ *280*
- **Q:** 七夕って、どんな日なの？ *282*
- **Q:** お盆とは？ *284*
- **Q:** お月見って、なに？ *284*
- **Q:** 大晦日には、なにをするの？ *284*
- **Q:** 他に、どんな行事があるの？ *286*

第9章 教育・宗教

1 教育

- **Q:** 日本の教育制度はいつできたの？ *288*
- **Q:** どんな学校があるの？ *288*
- **Q:** 在学者数は？ *290*
- **Q:** 不登校者が増えているって、ほんとう？ *292*
- **Q:** 学習塾や予備校が多いのは、なぜ？ *292*
- **Q:** 進学率は、どれくらい？ *292*

2 資格制度

- **Q:** どんな資格があるの？ *294*
- **Q:** 取得が難しい資格は？ *296*
- **Q:** 職能資格とは、なに？ *296*

3 宗教

- **Q:** 日本人は無宗教の人が多いの？ *298*
- **Q:** 神道は、日本の国教なの？ *300*
- **Q:** 靖国神社とは？ *300*
- **Q:** 神社はお寺とどこが違うの？ *302*

6 Holidays and Special Occasions

Q: What are the national holidays? *275*

Q: What do people do on New Year's Day? *279*

Q: What is *setsubun*? *281*

Q: What is *higan*? *281*

Q: What are *osekku*? *281*

Q: What is Tanabata? *283*

Q: What is Obon? *285*

Q: What does "moon viewing" mean? *285*

Q: What is *omisoka*? *285*

Q: What other special events are there? *287*

Chapter 9 Education and Religion

1 Education

Q: When did the present education system come into being? *289*

Q: What kinds of schools are there? *289*

Q: How many students are there in each type of school? *291*

Q: How many students have school phobia? *293*

Q: Why are there so many cram and prep schools? *293*

Q: How many students go on to higher levels of education? *293*

2 Education through Certification

Q: What kinds of certificates are there? *295*

Q: What kinds of certification are the most difficult to obtain? *297*

Q: What does "competence certification" mean? *297*

3 Religion

Q: Why do so many Japanese say they are not religious? *299*

Q: Is Shinto the state religion of Japan? *301*

Q: What is the significance of Yasukuni Shrine? *301*

Q: What makes a Shinto shrine different from a Buddhist temple? *303*

- **Q:** 神社参拝は、どのように行うの？ *302*
- **Q:** 仏教には、どんな宗派があるの？ *304*
- **Q:** 禅とは、どんな教えなの？ *304*
- **Q:** 僧侶は、なぜ髪を剃っているの？ *306*
- **Q:** お寺での参拝の作法は？ *306*

第10章 文化

1 学芸

- **Q:** 日本人のノーベル賞受賞者は？ *308*
- **Q:** 文化勲章とは？ *310*
- **Q:** 日本の代表的なマンガ家・アニメ作家は？ *310*
- **Q:** 世界的に有名な映画監督は？ *312*
- **Q:** 世界で評価が高い音楽家は？ *312*
- **Q:** 代表的なマスメディアは？ *314*
- **Q:** NHKの経営者は？ *316*
- **Q:** テレビの長寿番組は？ *316*
- **Q:** 日本画は西洋の絵とどう違うの？ *318*

2 伝統技芸

- **Q:** 歌舞伎はいつから始まったの？ *320*
- **Q:** 歌舞伎はどこでやっているの？ *322*
- **Q:** 能と狂言はどんな関係なの？ *322*
- **Q:** 文楽とはどんな芸能なの？ *324*
- **Q:** 落語と講談の違いは？ *324*
- **Q:** 生け花って、なに？ *326*
- **Q:** 日本人は誰でも茶道の心得があるの？ *326*
- **Q:** 家元制度って、なに？ *328*
- **Q:** 陶磁器と漆器の違いは？ *328*
- **Q:** 日本刀の特徴は？ *330*
- **Q:** 人間国宝って、なに？ *332*

Q: What is the proper procedure for praying at a Shinto shrine? *303*
Q: How many Buddhist sects are there? *305*
Q: What is Zen Buddhism? *305*
Q: Why do Buddhist monks shave their heads? *307*
Q: What is the proper procedure for praying at a Buddhist temple? *307*

Chapter 10 Culture

1 Arts and Sciences

Q: How many Japanese have won the Nobel Prize? *309*
Q: What is the Order of Culture? *311*
Q: Who are the most famous Japanese manga and anime artists? *311*
Q: Who is the most famous Japanese film director? *313*
Q: Who are Japan's most acclaimed world musicians? *313*
Q: What are the principal mass media outlets? *315*
Q: What is NHK? *317*
Q: What are the longest running TV programs? *317*
Q: What is the difference between Japanese painting and Western painting? *319*

2 Traditional Theater and Handicrafts

Q: What are the roots of the Kabuki theater? *321*
Q: Where is Kabuki performed? *323*
Q: What is the relationship between Noh and Kyogen? *323*
Q: What is Bunraku? *325*
Q: What is the difference between Rakugo and Kodan? *325*
Q: What is ikebana? *327*
Q: Is every Japanese familiar with the principles of the Way of Tea? *327*
Q: What is the *iemoto* system? *329*
Q: What is the difference between ceramic ware and lacquer ware? *329*
Q: What are the outstanding characteristics of a Japanese sword? *331*
Q: What is a Living National Treasure? *333*

- **Q:** 大相撲はいつから始まったの？ *332*
- **Q:** 大相撲はいつ、どこでやっているの？ *332*
- **Q:** 力士になるには？ *334*
- **Q:** 柔道と空手の違いは？ *334*
- **Q:** 剣道の勝負はどうつけるの？ *336*
- **Q:** アーチェリーと弓道の違いは？ *338*

- **Q:** 囲碁、将棋のプロ棋士とは？ *338*
- **Q:** 競技かるたは、どんなゲームなの？ *340*
- **Q:** けん玉って、なに？ *342*

3 芸能

- **Q:** 人気が高い芸能は？ *342*
- **Q:** 演歌って、なに？ *344*
- **Q:** 宝塚歌劇団とは？ *344*
- **Q:** 民間テレビ局の広告収入は、いくら？ *346*
- **Q:** タレントの出演料の相場は？ *346*

4 現代の文化の特徴

- **Q:** 今の日本文化の特徴は？ *348*
- **Q:** 日本人はコメを食べなくなったの？ *348*
- **Q:** コンビニはいくつあるの？ *350*
- **Q:** スマホって、なに？ *350*

第11章 レジャー・スポーツ

1 レジャー

- **Q:** 日本人の余暇の過ごし方は？ *354*
- **Q:** 海外旅行で人気がある国は？ *356*
- **Q:** 日本独特のレジャー施設は？ *356*
- **Q:** ゲームや漫画に熱中する大人がいるって、ほんとう？ *356*

- **Q:** カラオケはいつからブームになったの？ *358*

Contents

Q: When was the first sumo bout? *333*

Q: When and where are sumo tournaments held? *333*

Q: What are the requirements for becoming a sumo wrestler? *335*

Q: What is the difference between judo and karate? *335*

Q: How is the winner decided in kendo? *337*

Q: What is the difference between Japanese archery (*kyudo*) and Western archery? *339*

Q: What does it take to become a professional go or shogi player? *339*

Q: What is competitive *karuta*? *341*

Q: What is *kendama*? *343*

3 Performing Arts

Q: What are the most popular performing arts? *343*

Q: What is *enka*? *345*

Q: What is the Takarazuka Revue? *345*

Q: What is the advertising revenue of commercial TV stations? *347*

Q: What is the going appearance fee for TV performers? *347*

4 Modern-day Culture

Q: What are the features of Japanese culture today? *349*

Q: Is rice no longer eaten? *349*

Q: How many convenience stores are there? *351*

Q: What is a *sumaho*? *351*

Chapter 11 Leisure and Sports

1 Leisure

Q: How do Japanese spend their free time? *355*

Q: What are the most popular destinations for foreign travel? *357*

Q: Are there any uniquely Japanese leisure facilities? *357*

Q: Is it true that mature adults are just as enthusiastic about comics and video games as young people? *357*

Q: When did karaoke begin to boom? *359*

- **Q:** パチンコはどんな遊技なの？ *358*

2 スポーツ

- **Q:** 日本人がよくするスポーツは？ *360*
- **Q:** 観戦するのが好きなスポーツは？ *362*
- **Q:** プロ野球のチームは、いくつあるの？ *362*
- **Q:** プロサッカーチームは、いくつあるの？ *362*
- **Q:** サッカーくじって、なに？ *364*

第12章 観光・イベント

1 観光

- **Q:** 日本への観光客が多い国は？ *366*
- **Q:** 外国人に人気がある観光地は？ *368*
- **Q:** 宿泊施設にはどんなものがあるの？ *368*
- **Q:** 世界遺産に登録されているのは、どこ？ *370*
- **Q:** 温泉って、なに？ *372*
- **Q:** 有名な温泉地は、どこ？ *374*
- **Q:** 日本のおみやげで人気があるのは？ *376*
- **Q:** 国宝って、どのように決めるの？ *378*
- **Q:** 仏像にはどんな種類があるの？ *378*
- **Q:** お城は、いくつあるの？ *380*

2 イベント

- **Q:** 有名な祭りは？ *382*
- **Q:** 祭りは、なんのためにやるの？ *382*
- **Q:** 花火大会は、いつから始まったの？ *384*
- **Q:** 灯篭流しって、なに？ *386*
- **Q:** かまくらって、なに？ *388*
- **Q:** 学芸会って、なにをするの？ *388*
- **Q:** 運動会って、どんな行事なの？ *390*

Q: What is pachinko? *359*

2 Sports

Q: Which sports are most actively engaged in? *361*
Q: What sports are the most watched? *363*
Q: How many professional baseball teams are there? *363*
Q: How many professional soccer teams are there? *363*
Q: What is the soccer lottery? *365*

Chapter 12 Tourism and Special Events

1 Tourism

Q: What countries send the most visitors to Japan? *367*
Q: What are the most popular tourist sites? *369*
Q: What kinds of accommodations are there for tourists? *369*
Q: How many World Heritage Sites are there? *371*
Q: What distinguishes Japanese hot springs? *373*
Q: Which hot spring areas are the most well-known? *375*
Q: What are the most popular souvenirs? *377*
Q: How is a National Treasure designated? *379*
Q: What kinds of Buddhist sculpture are there? *379*
Q: How many castles are there? *381*

2 Special Events

Q: What are the most famous festivals? *383*
Q: What is the purpose of a festival? *383*
Q: When did fireworks displays first begin? *385*
Q: What is lantern floating? *387*
Q: What is a *kamakura*? *389*
Q: What is "performance day"? *389*
Q: What is "sports day"? *391*

第1章

自然と成り立ち
Geography and Basic Information

1 自 然

Q: 地球上のどこにあるの?

　　日本は、イギリスと同様に島国です。地球上での位置は、東経123度〜154度、北緯20度〜46度の間を日本列島が南北に連なっています。日本の標準子午線は東経135度で、経度0度のロンドンとは時差が約9時間あります。

Q: 国の大きさは?

　　日本の国土面積は約38万平方kmで、イギリスの約1.5倍です。しかしアメリカと比べると約25分の1しかなく、カリフォルニア州(約41万平方km)よりも小さいのです。

● 同じくらいの国
Countries of approximately the same size

377,812 km²

Germany
ドイツ

357,000 km²

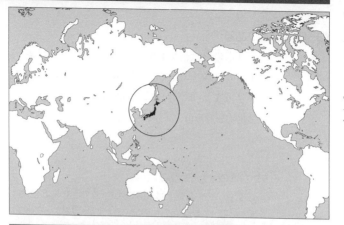

1 Geography

Q: Where is Japan on the world map?

Like the United Kingdom, Japan is an island country. It stretches out from north to south between latitudes 20° and 46°N and longitudes 123° and 154°E. At 135th meridian east, Japan Standard Time gains 9 hours from Greenwich Mean Time, with London at zero degrees longitude.

Q: How big is Japan?

The area of Japan is some 380,000 square kilometers, about 1.5 times that of the United Kingdom. However, it is only 1/25 of the United States, even smaller than California's 410,000 square kilometers.

● アメリカと比べると
Compared to the United States

U.S.A.
アメリカ

9,373,000 km²

第1章 自然と成り立ち

Q: 島はいくつあるの？

日本列島は、北海道、本州、四国、九州という4つの大きな島と、約6800の小さな島々から成り立っています。全体では弓のような形をし、南北約3500km、海岸線の総延長は約3万4000kmです。

▶日本の領土と問題点

現在の日本の領土は、第二次世界大戦で敗戦国となった1945年以来のものです。ただし沖縄諸島はアメリカの施政下に置かれ、1972年に日本の領土として復帰しました。島をめぐって、周辺国と領土問題が起きています。ロシアとの間では北方四島（国後島、択捉島、歯舞諸島、色丹島）の日本返還交渉問題があり、韓国とは竹島（韓国名は独島）の領有問題、さらに尖閣諸島（中国名は釣魚島）をめぐって中国が領有権を主張しています。

尖閣島

Q: 地形の特徴は？

日本の地形の特徴は、山が多いことです。国土の67％が山地で、そこから海に流れ落ちる川が谷を作り、国土の地形にさまざまな変化を与えています。

たくさんの人が暮らせる平野は国土の13％し

● 人口密度が高い国
Most Densely Populated Countries (people per square kilometer)

数字は1平方kmあたりの人口数

1位
バングラディシュ
Bangladesh

985人

2位
台湾
Taiwan

643人

32

Q: How many islands does Japan have?

Japan is composed of four large islands—Hokkaido, Honshu, Shikoku, and Kyushu—and some 6,800 smaller islands. It stretches in an arc from north to south over 3,500 kilometers, and its coastline is 34,000 kilometers long.

> ▶ **Questions concerning the territory of Japan**
> The territory of present-day Japan was established in 1945 after its defeat in World War II. However, the Okinawa Islands remained under American administration until their return to Japan in 1972. There are disputes with neighboring countries over the ownership of certain islands. There are ongoing negotiations with Russia concerning the return of the northern islands (called the Northern Territories) of Kunashiri, Etorofu, Habomai, and Shikotan. With South Korea there is a dispute over the rightful possession of the Takeshima islets (called Dokdo in Korean). The Japan-administered Senkaku Islands (Diaoyutai in Chinese) are also claimed by China.

Q: What are Japan's principal geographical features?

Mountains are the principal geographical feature of Japan. Sixty-seven percent of the country is occupied by mountains, and the rivers that run off these mountains into the sea create valleys and lend variety to the landscape.

Inhabitable flatland composes only 13% of the country's

かなく、このことから世界有数の人口密度の高い国とされます。

Q: 一番高い山は?

富士山です。高さは3776mで、古くから国内外で日本を象徴する山として有名でした。2013年にはユネスコが登録する世界文化遺産になりましたが、自然遺産にならなかったのは日本における信仰や芸術の対象としての富士山の歴史的評価によるものです。

富士山

富士山はなだらかな稜線をもち、その姿の美しさからも「日本一の山」とされてきましたが、本来は火山です。記録に残されている限りでは781年を最初として、1707年までに16回にわたって噴火をし、その後は休火山となっています。しかし今後、噴火の可能性がまったくないわけではありません。

▶ 火山国・日本

日本列島の下には7つの火山帯が走っていて、現在も活動中の活火山が98ほど存在します。世界には800もの活火山があるとされるので、その12％が日本に集中していることになります。2013年11月には、小笠原諸島(東京都)で海底火山の噴火による新島が誕生しました。

Q: 地震が多いのはなぜ?

火山活動も地震を引き起こす原因の一つですが、大地震の多くは日本列島の下にあるプレートの移動によるものです。日本列島は北米プレー

area, making Japan one of the most densely populated countries in the world.

Q: Japan's tallest mountain?

Without a doubt, Mt. Fuji at 3,776 meters. From olden times Mt. Fuji has been considered the symbol of Japan, both in Japan and abroad. In 2013 he was registered as a cultural World Heritage Site. It was not registered as a natural site due to the historical role it has played in Japanese art and religion.

Due to the beautiful lines presented by its slopes, Mt. Fuji has always been considered as Japan's paramount mountain, but in actual fact it is a volcano. Its earliest documented eruption occurred in 781, and between that date and 1707 it has erupted a total of 16 times. Subsequently Mt. Fuji has been dormant, but future eruptions are not inconceivable.

> ▶ **A Land of volcanoes**
> There are seven volcanic belts beneath the islands of Japan, and at present there are 98 active volcanoes. Since there are 800 volcanoes active worldwide, 12% of that total are concentrated in Japan. In November 2013 a submarine eruption near the Ogasawara Islands (Tokyo Metropolis) resulted in the creation of a new island.

Q: Why are earthquakes so frequent?

While volcanic activity is one of the causes of earthquakes, most large earthquakes are brought about by the movement of tectonic plates. Japan sits on the North American and

トとユーラシアプレートの上に乗っていますが、これらの下に太平洋プレートとフィリピン海プレートが潜りこもうとしてきた結果、地震が起きるのです。2011年3月11日に起きた東北地方太平洋沖地震（マグニチュード9.0）はプレート移動が原因とされ、2万人超もの死者・行方不明者を出した東日本大震災をもたらしました。

また、日本列島を形成する地層には、1000年に一度くらい動くといわれる活断層が随所に走っています。1995年1月7日に起きた兵庫県南部地震（マグニチュード7.3）は活断層が動いたことによる直下型地震で、この地震による阪神・淡路大震災では6500人近くの死者が出ました。

津波（東日本大震災）

▶津波

東日本大震災で多くの死者や行方不明者が出てしまったのは、津波が原因でした。東北地方の海岸には陸地の奥まで食い込んだ小さな湾が点在していて、地震によって起きた津波が海底の地形の影響で湾内に入ってきた時には、数倍の高さになるのです。高さ10m超もの津波に襲われたら、ひとたまりもありません。津波対策は、いざという時にすぐ避難できる高台を決めておくことが大事です。「TSUNAMI」は今では、世界共通語になっています。

● 日本列島とプレート
Tectonic Plates around Japan

▶秋の日本

9月になると、再び短い雨期がやってきます。これを「秋雨（あきさめ）」とよび、梅雨とは逆に列島の北から南下していきます。秋の気配が深まるにつれ、落葉広葉樹が緑の葉の色を赤・黄・茶色に変え、その色どりを楽しむために山へ「紅葉狩（もみじがり）」に出かける人々もいます。

三国峠

9月の終り頃から11月中旬にかけての日本は、温暖で過ごしやすく、行楽に出かけるのに最も適した時期といえます。

▶冬の日本

亜熱帯の沖縄諸島などは例外として、日本列島では冬になると雪が降ります。特に西の日本海側は大陸から吹きつける季節風が山岳地帯にさえぎられ、北海道から本州中部にかけて豪雪をもたらします。

さっぽろ雪まつり

なかでも「雪国」として知られる新潟県では、山岳部で8mもの高さの積雪記録が残っています。新潟県や秋田県で冬に行われるのが、雪でつくった家で正月を迎える伝統行事の「かまくら」。北海道では2月上旬に巨大な氷の彫刻が立ち並ぶ「さっぽろ雪まつり」が開催されます。

Q: The Climate

Japan is a long archipelago stretching from north to south, with the north being subarctic and the south subtropical. Overall, the climate is temperate, and the change in seasons from spring, summer, fall, to winter is distinctly defined, forming the most prominent climatic characteristic. Spring is from March to May, summer from June to August, fall from September to November, and winter from December to February.

▶ Spring

Spring is the most eagerly awaited season in Japan. The coming of warm weather is epitomized by the blooming of the cherry trees, which form a "cherry blossom front" that moves from south to north from March to May. During the one week in which the cherries blossom, it is customary for people to enjoy "flower viewing" by taking walks among the opulent trees, holding picnics with family, friends, or colleagues, and so forth.

Spring is also the season for new starts in life, as students move on to higher levels of education and new graduates take up for their first positions of employment.

▶ Summer

In June, which marks the changing of the seasons from spring to summer, Japan is visited by a rainy season. This rainy interlude progresses from south to north, but it doesn't quite reach Hokkaido.

Rain continues to the middle of July, and when it ceases, summer has arrived. This period is marked by subtropical high pressure in the North Pacific Ocean, which brings a great deal of moist air to Japan, making the summers very humid.

Q: 気候の特徴は?

南北に長い列島ということから南は亜熱帯、北は亜寒帯という極端な気候分布が特徴ですが、全般的には温帯で春、夏、秋、冬という四季の移り変わりがはっきりしていることが最大の特徴です。ちなみに春は3月〜5月、夏は6月〜8月、秋は9月〜11月、冬は12月〜2月とされています。

花見

▶ 春の日本

日本人にとって春は待望の季節。暖かな春の訪れを実感させるのが桜の開花で、3月〜5月にかけて列島の南から北上する「桜前線」の位置で開花時期が変ってきます。桜が咲いている1週間ほどの間、人々は満開の桜の下を散策したり、家族や職場ごとに宴席を設けるなどして「お花見」を楽しむ習慣があります。

また春は、入学式や入社式など、学生や新社会人にとって新しい門出を祝う季節です。

海水浴

▶ 夏の日本

春から夏への季節の変り目の6月には、「梅雨」とよばれる雨期があります。梅雨も列島の南から北上しますが、北海道だけは例外的に梅雨がありません。

梅雨は7月中旬頃まで続きますが、これが明けると季節は夏。この時期は北太平洋の熱帯性高気圧が、暖かい空気に大量の湿気を含んでやってくるため、とても蒸し暑くなります。

Eurasian plates, and the Pacific and Philippine Sea plates are attempting to move beneath them, resulting in earthquakes. The earthquake that occurred off the Pacific coast of Tohoku, with a magnitude of 9.0, on March 11, 2011, was caused by the movement of such tectonic plates and resulted in over 20,000 dead and missing.

The geological makeup of Japan consists of innumerable active faults that are said to move every thousand years or so. The earthquake that occurred in the southern part of Hyogo prefecture on January 7, 1995, with a magnitude of 7.3, was the result of the movement of a fault directly under a populous area and resulted in the loss of life of nearly 6,500 people.

▶ TSUNAMI

The reason that so many lives were lost in the Great East Japan Earthquake was due to the tsunami. The Tohoku coastline is characterized by many small bays that stretch far inland, and when tsunami waves are led into these bays following submarine geological formations, they reach heights of multiple proportions. There is no escape from waves towering over 10 meters tall. The only recourse is to seek refuge on higher ground. Incidentally, the word *tsunami* (Japanese for "harbor wave") is now an internationally recognized term.

▶ Fall

In September another short rainy season makes its appearance. Different from the summer rainy season, it descends from north to south. As the season deepens, the leaves of deciduous broadleaved trees change in color from green to red, yellow, and brown, and many people go out on "maple hunting" excursions to take in this chromatic display.

From the time around the end of September to the middle of November, the weather is comfortably mild and imminently suited for outings of any sort.

▶ Winter

With the exception of areas like subtropical Okinawa, the coming of winter is marked by snowfall. Particularly in the western part of the country that faces the Sea of Japan, seasonal winds from the Asian continent are block by Japanese mountain ranges and release their heavy snow in the area from Hokkaido down to the middle of Honshu.

Particularly well-known in this respect is Niigata prefecture, aptly called Snow Country, which has recorded heights of eight meters of snowfall in its mountainous regions. In Niigata as well as Akita prefecture, the New Year is greeted with the building of igloo-like structures known as *kamakura*. In Hokkaido, early February sees the Sapporo Snow Festival, which features a good number of monumental ice sculptures.

Q: 台風はいつ頃やってくるの？

　　日本列島に上陸して被害をもたらす台風は、夏から秋にかけてやってきます。北西太平洋や南シナ海に発生する熱帯性低気圧のうち中心付近の最大風速が約34ノット以上のものを台風といいますが、冬や春に発生する台風は貿易風に乗って西へ向い、日本へはやってきません。

　　台風は地域によって呼びかたが変り、太平洋北東・北中部で発生したものは「ハリケーン」、太平洋南部の場合は「サイクロン」といいます。日本にやってくることが予想される台風には、気象庁が発生順に台風番号をつけています。

2　成り立ち

Q: 日本人のルーツは？

　　日本人の祖先については諸説ありますが、現在の研究では身体的特徴から、いくつかの種族の混血といわれています。人類学上はモンゴロイドの一種とされ、南アジアから渡来した先住民（縄文人）とその後に北アジアから渡来した種族（弥生人）に大別されます。縄文人は狩猟や植物の採取など自然に依存した生活をしていましたが、弥生人は稲作などの栽培技術によって安定した食糧確保ができるようになったことで定住化を果たし、それが発展した形で統一国家を形成するに至りました。

Q: When is typhoon season?

Typhoons, which bring so much havoc to Japan, make their appearance in late summer and early fall. A typhoon is a subtropical low pressure zone occurring in the northwestern Pacific Ocean or the South China Sea with a wind velocity of over 34 knots at its center. Typhoons developing in winter and spring are carried west by the trade winds and miss Japan.

Typhoons are called by different names according to their region of origin. Those from the northeastern and north-central Pacific are called hurricanes, those from the southern Pacific cyclones. Typhoons expected to reach Japan are assigned an ordinal number by the Meteorological Agency.

2 Basic Information

Q: Where did the Japanese people come from?

While there are a number of theories about the origin of the Japanese people, modern research suggests a mixture of peoples, based on physical characteristics. Anthropologically, the original inhabitants of Japan can be broadly divided into the Jomon people, a Mongoloid type who arrived from South Asia, and later immigrants (the Yayoi people) who arrived via North Asia. The Jomon people were hunter-gatherers, living a life close to nature, while the Yayoi people possessed the technology for rice cultivation and hence a stable food supply, leading to life in fixed settlements and eventually to the formation of a nation state.

アイヌの人

▶ **アイヌ民族**

今から約1000年前、樺太、千島列島、北海道および本州北部に広がる擦文文化圏を形成していたのがアイヌ民族で、18世紀には「和人」の支配下におかれていました。国が、その文化を復興し保存することになったのは、1997年でした。

Q: 国家の誕生はいつ？

たしかなことはわかっていませんが、中国の記録では西暦57年に邪馬台国という国があって、その王が使節を寄こした、とあります。また、その国には卑弥呼という女王がいて、30ほどの国々をまとめていたとも記されています。邪馬台国の場所については、もっぱら北九州説と近畿説が有力ですが、それを裏づけるのは卑弥呼の墓の存在で、まだ決定的な証拠はありません。

いずれにしても、日本では5世紀以前の文献上の記録が存在しないために中国の記録に頼らざるをえないのですが、西暦266年から413年にかけて日本を指す「倭国」の記述がないため「空白の4世紀」とも呼ばれています。3世紀半ばから6世紀末までを古墳時代といいますが、統一国家としての大和政権ができあがったのは、古墳時代の終末期の7世紀頃ではないかというのが定説になっています。

Q: 国名の由来は？

交流があった中国や韓国では「倭国」と呼んで

> **▶ The Ainu**
>
> About a thousand years ago, Sakhalin, the Kuril Islands, Hokkaido, and northern Honshu were part of the cultural sphere known as Satsumon culture, which was a product of the Ainu people. By the 18th century the Ainu had come under Japanese subjugation. In 1997 the central government took steps to preserve and protect this culture.

Q: When did the Japanese nation come into being?

While there is no definitive answer to this question, it is true that, according to Chinese records, in AD 57 there was a country in Japan called Yamatai that sent envoys to China. Furthermore, some 30 countries were said to be under the control of a queen named Himiko. The two strongest theories as to the location of this country point to northern Kyushu and the Kinki region (now encompassing Kyoto, Osaka, and Nara). Himiko's tomb would definitively settle the matter, but it has yet to be found.

In any case, since there is no Japanese documentation preceding the 5th century, Chinese records must be relied on. However, there is no Chinese mention of Japan from 266 to 413. The period from the middle of the 3rd century to the end of the sixth is called the Kofun (Burial Mound) period, and it is now accepted that the country came under the rule of the Yamato court in the 7th century, toward the end of the Kofun period.

Q: What is the Japanese name for Japan?

In ancient times Japan was referred to as *Wa* (倭) in

いました。日本人はのちに倭をヤマトと発音し、「大和」という漢字をあてるようになりました。

7世紀の初めの中国の書物に「日本」という国名が登場します。それから約一世紀後に著された『日本書紀』は、日本という国名が定着したことを象徴しています。

英語の国名「JAPAN」は、マルコ・ポーロが13世紀末頃に発表した『東方見聞録』に登場する黄金の国ジパング（ZIPANGU）が語源とされています。

Q: 「ニホン」か「ニッポン」か？

正式な呼びかたは「ニッポン」で、1934年に文部省の臨時国語審議会が決定しました。オリンピックなどの国際競技のユニフォームに「NIPPON」と表記されるのはそのためです。とはいえ「ニホン」という呼びかたも一般的に通用しているので間違いではありません。

Q: 国旗・国歌はいつ制定されたの？

白地に赤い円を描いた国旗は1999年8月に成立した法律（国旗国歌法）によって制定されました。デザインは19世紀半ば、徳川幕府が外国船と区別するために船の旗印として取り入れたもので、必ずしも日本の国旗というわけではあり

diplomatic exchanges with China and Korea. Japanese later began to pronounce this Chinese character as "*Yamato,*" referring to the Yamato court, and even later applied entirely different Chinese characters (大和) to produce the reading "Great Yamato."

At the beginning of the 7th century, the word "Nihon" (日本) appears in Chinese documents for the first time. In Japan's second oldest book, *Chronicles of Japan*, written a century later, "Nihon" has apparently become fixed as the name of the country.

The word "Japan" apparently has its origins in Marco Polo's *Book of the Marvels of the World* (ca. 1300), in which Japan is referred to as *Zipangu* (Japan) and described as a land rich in silver and gold.

Q: Is it "Nippon" or "Nihon"?

The official nomenclature for Japan is "Nippon," which was decided in 1934 at an extraordinary meeting of the Japanese Language Council. That is why, at the Olympics and other international sporting events, the uniforms of Japanese athletes bear the name Nippon. On the other hand, "Nihon," written with the same Chinese characters, is also commonly used and cannot be considered wrong.

Q: When was the national flag officially adopted?

The national flag, a red disc on a white background, was officially decided in August 1999 with the passage of the Act on the National Flag and Anthem. Flags with this design were used by the Tokugawa shogunate in the middle of the 19th century to distinguish Japanese ships from foreign

ませんでした。

しかし、明治時代以降は軍国主義の旗印として宣揚されたため、敗戦後は「日の丸」の国旗を掲げることに抵抗する人々もいます。

Q: 日本語の起源は？

日本語はウラル・アルタイ語族の一つではないか、マライ・ポリネシア語族ではないか、タミル語と同系ではないかなど、その起源をめぐっ

● 日本の国旗 The Japanese Flag

正式には「日章旗」といい、旗の形は縦が横の3分の2の長方形で白色、日章の直径は縦の5分の3で旗の中心に位置し紅色、と規定されています。緑地に赤い円を描いたバングラディシュの国旗は、日の丸を参考にしたとされます。

日の丸

Officially called the *Nisshoki* (Sun Mark Flag), the length and height is set at a ratio of 3 to 2, and the red disc is 3/5 of the length of the flag, positioned exactly in the center. The flag of Bangladesh, with a red disc on a green background, is said to have been modeled on the Japanese flag.

● 日本の国花 The National Flower

法律で定められてはいませんが、国民に広く親しまれている桜、皇室の紋章に使われている菊の二つが事実上の「国の花」として扱われています。

菊

While not established in law, the cherry blossom, widely beloved by the Japanese people, and the chrysanthemum, which appears on the crest of the imperial family, are the de facto flowers of Japan.

vessels, but they were not necessarily considered the national flag of Japan.

However, from the Meiji period onward, this flag was employed as a symbol of Japanese nationalism, and following World War II many people were averse to its use as the national flag.

Q: What is the origin of the Japanese language?

Some propose that Japanese is a member of the Ural–Altaic language family, others that it is Malayo-Polynesian, and still others that it is a Tamil language. The number and variety

● 日本の国歌 The National Anthem

19世紀末、イギリス人のフェントンの提唱で国歌を作ることになり、日本古来の和歌から引用した歌詞に、雅楽の旋律をアレンジした曲をつけ完成しました。

「君が代」を天皇賛美の歌とした時代もありましたが、民主主義の今は「国民の代」という意味です。

Toward the end of the 19th century, at the suggestion of the Irishman John Fenton, a national anthem was created with the lyrics taken from a 10th century poem and the melody from classical Japanese court music.

The word Kimigayo was once interpreted as "Your majesty's reign," but now, in our democratic era, it is taken to mean "the people's reign."

てさまざまな説があります。また、文法的には主語・目的語・述語の並びかたが同じ朝鮮語に近いとされます。これらのことから、アジアの国々の言葉に強く影響を受けていることは想像できるのですが、いずれも起源という点で決定的といえるものではありません。

しかし、文字という面からみれば、古くからの中国との文化交流を通して、中国語の語彙を取り入れ、さらに漢字の中国字音から平仮名や片仮名を作り出すなどして、漢字と仮名で構成される日本語が創られてきたことは特筆すべきでしょう。

Q: 日本語の特徴は？

日本語の発音は、基本的に「ん」以外の一つの音は、母音だけ、あるいは子音+母音で表わされます。

(例) 私　　→　wa – ta – ku – shi
　　 天気　→　ten – ki

アクセントは、英語のような強弱アクセントでなく、高低アクセントが特徴です。

(例) 横浜　→　yoko – hama
　　 yoは低く、ko – hamaは少し高く

しかし、アクセントは全国一律というわけでなく、関東や関西というように地域によって異なる場合があります。

文章は、基本的に

of theories abound. Japanese is also seen to be close to Korean in the grammatical order of subject, object, and verb. From this we can imagine that Japanese has been strongly influenced by Asian languages, but still there is no definitive answer as to its origins.

However, from the point of view of the written language, it should be noted that through long cultural exchange with China, the Japanese language has incorporated a great deal of vocabulary from Chinese, developed phonetic letters (*kana*) based on Chinese characters, and has come today to be written with a combination of Chinese characters and *kana*.

Q: What are the chief features of the Japanese language?

Japanese pronunciation (with the exception of *n*) consists of one vowel or of one consonant with a vowel.

> ▶ Examples: I = *wa-ta-ku-shi*
> weather = *ten-ki*

Japanese employs pitch accent rather than the stress accent seen in English.

> ▶ Example: Yokohama (city name) = *yoko hama*
> Yo has a lower pitch, ko-hama a slightly higher pitch.

However, accent is not the same throughout the country but varies according to region—eastern Kanto and western Kansai being cases in point.

Sentence structure is basically as follows:

① 主語＋補語＋述語動詞
（例）　私は＋学生＋です。

② 主語＋目的語＋述語動詞
（例）　彼は＋ランチを＋食べた。

という形をしていますが、述語は文末に、修飾語は被修飾語の前に、を原則にする以外の語順は比較的自由です。

英語などに比べて特徴的なのは、敬語が高度に発達していること、会話では男性語と女性語の区別がはっきりしていることなどです。

Q: 使っている漢字の数は？

漢字は10万字もあるとされますが、日本人が日常、一般的に使用するための目安として「常用漢字」（2136字、2010年）が選定されています。日本語の場合、一つの漢字に多くの異なる発音があることが多く、中国語起源の音読み、日本独自の訓読みに大別されます。

Q: 平仮名と片仮名はどう使い分けるの？

仮名は、漢字の読み方（発音）を簡単な形にしたもので、日本独自の文字として作られました。その一例を下に記しましたが（次ページ）、漢字が平仮名や片仮名に変えられてゆく姿がわかるはずです。

漢字をくずした平仮名は8世紀中ごろに作ら

1. Subject + complement + verb
   ▶ Example:
   Watakushi (I) *wa* + *gakusei* (student) + *desu* (am).
2. Subject + object + verb
   ▶ Example:
   Kare (He) *wa* + *ranchi* (lunch) *o* + *tabeta* (ate).

Aside from the basic rule that verbs come at the end of the sentence and modifiers precede what they modify, the order of words is fairly free.

Compared to English, two outstanding features are the high development of polite language and the fact that masculine and feminine speech are distinct.

Q: How many Chinese characters (*kanji*) are used in writing Japanese?

The total number of *kanji* is said to be 100,000, but the number designated for everyday use (*Joyo Kanji*) is 2,136. As used in Japanese a single *kanji* may have several readings or pronunciations, and these readings are broadly divided into those of Chinese origin (*on-yomi*) and those of Japanese origin (*kun-yomi*).

Q: How are *katakana* and *hiragana* used?

Kana (*hiragana* and *katakana*) were developed originally in Japan as simplified forms of *kanji* to make it easier to read them. One example has been given here to show how this transformation took place (see next page).

The cursive *hiragana* was developed from simplified *kanji*

れて書簡文や物語文に、漢字の一部を使った片仮名は9世紀初頭ごろに登場して漢文の難しい文字の読みや注釈に使われました。現代では平仮名は漢字と一緒に、片仮名は外来語の表記などにも使われています。

Q:「縦書き」と「横書き」どちらが多いの？

　日本の歴史的文献は、すべてが縦書きです。漢字や仮名は本来、縦書きを前提に作られています。しかし、西洋の文献が盛んに入ってくるにつれ、アルファベットや数式の表記上、縦書きは不都合になってきました。

　例えば教科書では、国語や古文以外はすべて横書きです。新聞や雑誌類が若者に読まれなくなっているのは、縦書きだからではないかという説もあります。パソコンなどの普及で書類は横書きが一般的で、年齢が下るほど横書きになじんでいます。これらのことから、日本人は「横書き派」が主流になりつつあるといえるでしょう。

● 漢字と仮名の関係
The Connection between *Kanji* and *Kana*

あ ← あ ← 安
い ← い ← 以

forms in mid 8th century for use in writing letters and works of fiction. The gothic *katakana*, making use of one part of *kanji* followed at the beginning of the 9th century as a means of noting the pronunciations of difficult *kanji* and adding explanatory notes. Today ordinary Japanese is written with a combination of *kanji* and *hiragana*, with *katakana* reserved for foreign words and other special uses.

Q: Japanese can be written vertically or horizontally. Which is more common?

Historical documents are all written vertically. In fact, *kanji* and the two forms of *kana* were originally created to be written from top to bottom. However, with the increasing appearance of Western alphabets and mathematical formulas, vertical writing proved inconvenient.

Now, aside from Japanese language classes and classical literature, almost all textbooks are written horizontally. The fact that younger Japanese don't read magazines and newspapers as much as they used to is attributed to these publications' vertical format. With the standardization of horizontal writing on computers, younger Japanese have become increasingly accustomed to that format. Hence it can be fairly said that horizontal writing is rapidly becoming the mainstream.

う ← ウ ← 宇
え ← 衤 ← 衣　　ア ← 阿
お ← 扵 ← 於　　イ ← 伊

Q: 元号はどのように決めるの?

元号とは日本独自の年号表記で、昔は天皇が即位する場合だけでなく、天変地異や疫病の流行などの災いを避けたり、人心を刷新しようという意味合いで新しい元号を採用（改元）することも多かったようです。しかし、江戸幕府から政権を奪還した明治天皇は「元号は在位から崩御まで」と定め、これが現在にも受け継がれています。

小渕官房長官の記者発表

▶平成という元号

1989年（昭和64年）1月7日、昭和天皇の崩御をうけて内閣は協議の結果「平成」と決定し、翌日に改元されました。元号は中国の古典から二文字を選んで命名する慣わしで、内閣が決めた最初のケースでした。

Q: 天皇はどんな仕事をしているの?

敗戦後の1946年11月に公布された日本国憲法で、天皇は「日本国の象徴」という存在になり、その行いは「内閣の承認のもとでの国事行為」に限るとされました。

具体的には、総理大臣・最高裁判所長官などの任免、国会の開会・解散の告示、法令の公布、国民的行事への出席などです。さらに日本を訪れた賓客や外国の大・公使の着任時の接遇も重要な公務とされ、「皇室外交」といわれます。一方、

Q: How are era names decided?

The assigning of era names is a particular Japanese practice. In the past as now, a new era name was announced when a new emperor assumed the throne, but that is not all. New eras were also formulated in order to ward off natural disasters, the spread of contagious diseases and other calamities as well as to unite the people in some important endeavor. However, when Emperor Meiji assumed the throne in 1868, it was decided that the era name would remain the same throughout the reign of a particular emperor (for example, the reign of the emperor Hirohito is known as the Showa era or period, 1926-89). This practice has remained in effect until the present day.

▶ From Showa to Heisei
With the passing of Emperor Showa on January 7, 1989, the cabinet decided after due deliberation that the new era name would be *Heisei*, which decision was put into effect the following day. Following the established practice of choosing two characters from Chinese classics, *Heisei* was the first era name to be chosen by the cabinet.

Q: What does the emperor do?

In accordance with the postwar Japanese constitution promulgated in November 1946, the emperor is the symbol of the state, and all imperial acts in matters of state are subject to the approval of the cabinet.

In practical terms, this means that the emperor appoints the prime minister and the chief justice of the supreme court, convokes and dissolves the Diet, attests laws, and participates in national events, all as designated by the parliament (the Diet). Among other important official duties are the reception of

私的には天皇家の伝統祭祀を主宰する立場なので、天皇の日常は公私にわたって多忙です。

皇居

> ▶ **皇居**
>
> 天皇の住居は、旧・江戸城址で「皇居」といいます。ここには宮内庁という役所が置かれ、警備や皇族の護衛をする皇宮警察官が勤務しています。宮内庁には長官以下約1000名の公務員と、天皇家が私的に雇う職員25名ほどが働いています。

Q: 女性も天皇になれるの？

記録に残る歴代天皇のうち推古帝(592–628)を初めとして後桜町帝(1762–70)まで、10代(8名のうち2名が重複)が女性天皇なので、必ずしも男性限定ではありませんでした。しかし、その後は主に政治的理由などから女性に皇位継承権を認めず、現行の法律(皇室典範)でも「男子に限る」と定めているので、法改正をしない限り女性は天皇になれません。

Q: 天皇家のルーツは？

『日本書紀』や『古事記』には、初代天皇を紀元前660年頃に登場した神武帝としていますが、これらの史書は8世紀になって著されたものな

important foreign guests and foreign ministers and ambassadors when they assume their posts, a function often referred to as imperial diplomacy. On a personal level, the emperor also conducts traditional ceremonial functions pertaining to the imperial family. All in all, the emperor leads a busy life.

> ### ▶ The Imperial Palace
>
> The residence of the emperor is located where Edo castle once stood and is called the Imperial Palace. The headquarters of the Imperial Household Agency, in charge of state matters concerning the imperial family, is located there, serving as the office of the Imperial Palace Police, which functions as escorts to the imperial family and as security guards. Under the Grand Steward there are 1,000 civil servants working in the Agency, in addition to 25 employees hired privately by the imperial family.

Q: Can women ascend the imperial throne?

From Empress Suiko (r. 592-628) to Go-Sakuramachi (r. 1762-70) there were ten empresses (two serving twice), and so succession to the throne was not limited to the male line. Later, however, principally for political reasons, female succession was not recognized. Under present law (the Imperial Household Law) succession is limited to male descendants of the imperial line. Hence, barring revision of the present law, women cannot ascend the imperial throne.

Q: What are the roots of the imperial family?

According to the *Chronicles of Japan* and the *Record of Ancient Matters*, Japan's two oldest histories, the first emperor was Jimmu, who ascended the throne around 660 BC. However,

ので、天皇家の正統性を強調するための神話として創作されたという説が有力です。とはいえ神話をすべて架空の物語として無視はできません。ギリシャ神話に登場する都市国家トロイアの発掘に成功したドイツ人のハインリッヒ・シュリーマンの例のように、神話は信じる者に扉を開く場合があるからです。

今日、実在の可能性が高いのは第10代の崇神帝からとされ、記録上は前述の推古帝以降で、平成時代の天皇（在位中は今上天皇と呼ぶ）を第125代とするのは、神武帝から数えた場合です。

Q: 皇族にはどんな人がいるの？

天皇の直系の子孫を「皇族」といい、「宮」の称号が与えられます。今上天皇の第一皇子の称号は浩宮、第二皇子は結婚を機に秋篠宮として宮家を創設、皇女・紀宮は一般人と結婚したため皇族でなくなりました。他に今上天皇の弟・常陸宮家、昭和天皇の弟・三笠宮家と親族が皇族となっていますが、総数18名で、うち男性が5名（2014年12月現在）。

浩宮は皇太子として皇位継承順位第一位ですが、皇太子妃との間に男子が生れないことで、女性天皇を認めていない現時点では、皇太子の後の皇位を継承するのは秋篠宮家の長男・悠仁親王にならざるをえないのではないかともいわれます。

since these works came into being in the 8th century to emphasize the legitimacy of the imperial line, they are now considered to be mythological. On the other hand, mythology cannot always be dismissed as being entirely fictional. This was demonstrated by the German Heinrich Schliemann who excavated the city of Troy, until then thought to exist only in Greek mythology. For those who believe, mythology can open new doors.

Today the emperors thought to have a high possibility of existence date from the tenth emperor, Sujin, onward. When the present emperor is described as being the 125th in the imperial line, this is counting from Emperor Jimmu.

Q: Who exactly belongs to the imperial family?

Direct descendants of the emperor are members of the imperial family and given the title of *miya* (prince or princess). The first son of the present emperor is known as Hiro no Miya. The second son, upon marriage, became known as Akishino no Miya and was allowed to establish a new branch of the imperial family. The present emperor's one and only daughter, Nori no Miya, married a commoner and therefore was removed from the imperial family. Otherwise, there is the present emperor's younger brother, Hitachi no Miya, Emperor Showa's younger brother, Mikasa no Miya, and other relatives, for a total of 18 (of which 5 are male; as of December 2014).

The crown prince is Hiro no Miya and therefore first in line to succeed to the throne, but since the crown princess has not given birth to a son, under the present law the next to succeed to the throne after the crown prince would be the son of Akishino no Miya, Hisahito.

第2章 歴史

第2章
歴史
History

葛飾北斎『富嶽三十六景』の「神奈川沖浪裏」▶

歴 史

Q: 日本の始まりは?

日本列島は太古には、ユーラシア、アジア、北アメリカの各大陸と地続きでしたが、度重なる地殻変動で約1万年前に完全な島国になりました。各大陸から渡って来た人々の生活の痕跡が各地に残っていて、それらを起点にして日本の歴史の流れを読み取ることができます。

歴史をおおざっぱに「有史以前」と「有史以後」とに分ける見方がありますが、この区分の境界にあるのは稲作に象徴される「農耕」です。日本で農耕社会が形成される以前の紀元前3世紀頃

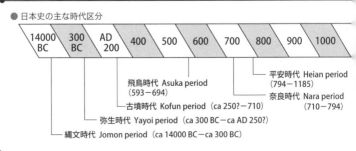

● 日本史の主な時代区分

| 14000 BC | 300 BC | AD 200 | 400 | 500 | 600 | 700 | 800 | 900 | 1000 |

- 平安時代 Heian period (794−1185)
- 奈良時代 Nara period (710−794)
- 飛鳥時代 Asuka period (593−694)
- 古墳時代 Kofun period (ca 250?−710)
- 弥生時代 Yayoi period (ca 300 BC−ca AD 250?)
- 縄文時代 Jomon period (ca 14000 BC−ca 300 BC)

History

Q: What is Japanese history?

In the very distant past Japan was connected by land to the Eurasian, Asian, and North American continents, but due to repeated movements in the earth's crust, it became a conglomeration of islands about 10,000 years ago. The archeological remains of people who immigrated to Japan can still be found throughout the country, and taking these as a starting point, we can begin to read the flow of Japanese history.

In general, history can be divided into prehistory and recorded history, with the dividing line between these two periods being the appearance of agriculture or, in Japan, the cultivation of rice. Japan before rice, that is, until about the

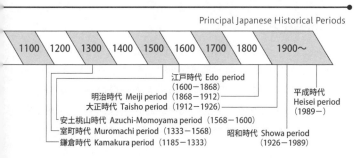

Principal Japanese Historical Periods

までに存在していた縄文人は、原始的で野蛮とみなされがちでしたが、例えば青森県の三内丸山遺跡の発掘調査で5000年前の縄文人が豊かで文化的な暮らしをしていたことがわかってきました。このことで稲作を始めた弥生人とそれ以前の縄文人との間に、はっきりとした歴史的区分がつけにくいというのが定説になりつつあります。

Q: 縄文時代とは？

縄文土器

紀元前14000年〜紀元前300年の間の、ほぼ1万年強の期間で、それ以前は旧石器時代とか先土器時代と呼ばれます。遺跡から発掘された土器（写真）に縄状の紋様が描かれていることから、縄文時代と呼ばれるようになりました。遺跡は全国各地にあり、集落間の交流があったこともわかっています。山でイノシシやシカを、海や川で魚貝を捕って食べていたことも、貝塚の存在ではっきりしています。土器はクルミやクリなどの木の実、魚の保存のために使っていました。縄文時代の後期には、稲作が普及し始めていました。

Q: 弥生時代とは？

紀元前300年〜西暦300年までというのが定説ですが、紀元前900年にさかのぼるという説もあります。この時代の最大の特徴は稲作が本格的に普及したことです。時代名は、当時の土器が発見された東京の弥生町にちなんだもの。弥

3rd century BC, was inhabited by the Jomon people, who until recently were thought to be a primitive and backward folk. However, with the excavation of the Sannai-Maruyama site in Aomori prefecture, it became clear that the Jomon people of 5,000 years ago lived a rich cultural life. As a consequence, historians are now finding it difficult to draw a clear line between the Jomon people and the rice-growing Yayoi people who followed them.

Q: What is the Jomon period?

The Jomon period refers to the time span from about 14,000 BC to 300 BC, covering a little more than 10,000 years. The age preceding this period is called the Paleolithic or pre-pottery period. From Jomon archeological sites, pottery has been found bearing cord patterns (*jomon*), from which the period takes its name. Such sites are found throughout the country, and it is known that there was traffic between the villages. From shell middens it is also know that the inhabitants subsisted on boar and deer meat from the mountains and fish and shellfish from the sea and rivers. Pottery was used for the storage and preservation of walnuts, chestnuts, and fish. Toward the end of the period, rice began to be cultivated.

Q: What is the Yayoi period?

The Yayoi period is generally considered to cover the years from 300 BC to AD 300, although some theories trace it back as far as 900 BC. The chief characteristic of this period is the intense cultivation of rice. The period takes its name from Yayoi-cho in Tokyo, where pottery from this period was first

生人は南方からやって来て、先住の縄文人を金属製の武器で駆逐したともいわれます。渡来系弥生人は水田耕作の技術と金属器の文化をもたらし、人々の生活は大きく変化しました。

Q: 古墳時代とは？

はにわ

古墳は大規模な墓のことで、各地に豪族が出現して権勢を誇った時代です。盛んに造られるようになったのは4世紀から7世紀末にかけてです。小山のように土を盛り上げ、周囲に埴輪（写真）と呼ばれる土製の人物や馬などを飾り、内部には遺体の他に鏡・装身具などの副葬品を入れた石室があります。現天皇家の直系先祖といわれる大和政権が確立した時代なので、巨大古墳は天皇の墓とみられています。

Q: 飛鳥時代とは？

法隆寺夢殿

推古天皇（女帝）が即位した時（593年）から、持統天皇（女帝）が藤原京（奈良県橿原市）に都を移した時（694年）までの約102年間。時代名は推古帝が飛鳥京（奈良県明日香村）を都としていたことにちなんだもの。

推古帝は政務の補佐役として甥の厩戸皇子（聖徳太子）を摂政に任じ、皇子は幅広い層から人材をつのる行政改革や日本初の成文法の「憲法十七条」を制定するなど、天皇を中心とした中央集権につとめました。また、中国の皇帝との

discovered. It is said that the Yayoi people, arriving in Japan from the south with iron weapons, gradually supplanted the Jomon people. With the arrival of rice-growing technology and metallurgy, life on the islands underwent a drastic change.

Q: What is the Kofun (Burial Mound) period?

Kofun are large manmade mounds of earth serving as tombs, and they began appearing around the country with the rise of powerful local clans. They were most actively made from the 4th to the end of the 7th century. Around these hill-like mounds were placed pottery figurines of human beings, horses, and so forth, and within the mounds was a stone crypt with, besides the body of the deceased, such funeral furnishings as mirrors and body accessories. This was about the time of the appearance of the Yamato court, the direct predecessors of the present imperial line, and therefore the larger mounds are thought to be those of emperors.

Q: What is the Asuka period?

The Asuka period refers to the 102 years from the succession of Empress Suiko in 593 to 694, when Empress Jito relocated the capital to Fujiwara (present-day Kashiwara city, Nara prefecture). The period takes its name from Asuka village, the site of Empress Suiko's capital.

Empress Suiko appointed her nephew, Prince Shotoku (572-622), as her political advisor, and he gathered around him people from various walks of life to initiate administrative reforms, create the first Japanese written law (the 17 Article Constitution), and successfully establish a centralized

対等な付き合いを目的とした遣隋使を派遣する一方、中国から伝わった仏教の国教化にも熱心で、法隆寺をはじめとする寺院がたくさん建立され、飛鳥文化や白鳳文化が花開きました。しかし、中央集権の反作用としての権力闘争が激化し、時の天皇は、そのつど都を移らなければなりませんでした。

Q: 奈良時代とは？

元明天皇が平城京（奈良市、大和郡山市）に都を移した710年から約84年間です。平城京は、中国の首都・長安を参考にした都市計画にもとづく大規模工事で造営された都でした。仏教はこの時代も国家に保護され、大いに栄えました。現存する銅製の仏像では世界最大の東大寺の大仏が造られ、仏教を基調とした天平文化が爛熟しました。また、遣唐使を度々派遣するなど、外国との交流も盛んに行われ、朝鮮半島やインドなどの文物が輸入されました。

大仏（東大寺）

平城京への移転の9年前、「大宝律令」が制定されています。「律」は刑罰法、「令」は行政法で、法治国家としての体制が整ったことを意味します。平城京には中央政府が置かれ、国内は五畿内と七道の行政区に大別されて、その下に国・郡・里を設け、中央政府が派遣した国司が地方

government focused on the empress. He also sent envoys to the Sui dynasty in China in an attempt to establish an equal relationship. He was eager to make Buddhism, which had been introduced into Japan via China, the state religion. Many Buddhist temples were built during his time, including Horyu-ji, leading to the flowering of what is generally known as the Asuka and Hakuho cultural periods. However, as a reaction to the concentration of power in imperial hands, heated political struggles broke out, forcing the empress to relocate the capital to escape them.

Q: What is the Nara period?

The Nara period refers to the 84 years following Empress Genmei's establishment of the Heijo capital in 710 (in present-day Yamato Koriyama city and Nara city). Heijo was modeled after the Chinese capital of Chang'an and was a huge architectural undertaking. Buddhism came under the protection of the state and made remarkable advances. The world's largest bronze Buddhist statue was created at Todai-ji, and the Buddhist-based culture period known as the Tempyo era came into full bloom. Envoys were sent to the Tang dynasty of China, and energetic international exchange took place. Cultural artifacts were imported from India and Korea.

Nine years before the move to Heijo, an administrative reform known as the Taiho Code was enacted, making Japan a country ruled by law. The central government was located in the capital, with the rest of the country divided into five provinces and seven circuits, under which were prefectures, counties, and villages. The central government appointed

豪族から任命した郡司以下を支配しました。役人は位階で、人民は良と賤というように、公的差別をつけるようになったのも、奈良時代からです。

Q: 平安時代とは？

桓武天皇が都を京都に移したのが794年で、平安京と呼ばれました。これ以降、明治維新の江戸城への入城までの約1000年間、天皇は京都以外に都を移したことはありません。その名の通り、平安の世は約400年間続きました。この時代は、王朝貴族が政治に関わり、奈良時代に定着した位階が家格を決めていました。男性は低い位の家に生まれると、貴族といえども出世はできない差別社会でした。その反面、女性には自らの才能を伸ばす機会が与えられていたようです。これは、貴族社会が自由恋愛を認めていたことと無縁ではありません。

源氏物語

▶ 王朝文学

恋の駆け引きに男女の間で和歌が交わされ、女文字とされた仮名が日常的に使われ出すと、創作の筆をとる女性が現われました。世界に知られる紫式部の『源氏物語』、清少納言の『枕草子』が著されたのも、この時代です。

provincial governors from powerful local clans to oversee the counties and villages. Government officials were classified according to a system of rankings, and commoners were divided into the worthy and the humble, setting up a system of official discrimination. This was put into effect during the Nara period.

Q: What is the Heian period?

Emperor Kanmu relocated the capital to what is now Kyoto in 794, naming it the Heian capital and marking the beginning of the Heian period (794-1185). For the next approximately 1,000 years, until the emperor took up residence in Edo castle in 1868 during the Meiji Restoration, Kyoto remained the capital. The "peace" of this period (lit., *heian*) continued for 400 years. The court aristocracy played an active role in politics, but their individual status remained what had been determined by the rankings established in the Nara period. For aristocratic men born into a low-ranking family, their status remained unchanged, regardless of talent or ability. On the other hand, women were given the opportunity to expand upon their natural talents. This is probably not entirely unrelated to the fact that aristocratic society permitted freedom among the sexes.

▶ Courtly Literature

As the exchange of poetry between aristocratic men and women became part of the interplay between the sexes, and as writing became easier with the introduction of *kana*, creative women writers appeared on the scene. This period gave birth to Murasaki Shikibu's *Tale of Genji* and Sei Shonagon's *Pillow Book*.

> ▶ **末法思想**
>
> 仏教では釈迦滅後2001年目から末法といって仏力が失われる時代に入るとの予言があり、1052年がその年に当りました。関白・藤原頼通は宇治の別荘に阿弥陀堂（鳳凰堂）を建て、地上の極楽として救済を願いました。

宇治平等院鳳凰堂

Q: 鎌倉時代とは？

鎌倉八幡宮

平安時代に貴族の護衛役として雇われていた武士の中から、やがて武力を背景に貴族となり、終には政治の実権を握ってしまったのが平清盛（1118－1181）を棟梁とする平家一門でした。その平家を滅ぼしたのが、同じく武門出身の源頼朝（1147－1199）でした。源氏の棟梁として頼朝は、鎌倉（神奈川県鎌倉市）に拠点を定め、守護・地頭を任命して諸国に配置し、勢力を固めました。そして、1192年に征夷大将軍になると鎌倉幕府を設置して、武家政治を断行したのです。その結果、京都の公家と鎌倉の武家の二元支配となりましたが、後鳥羽上皇が幕府打倒の兵を起こして敗北した1221年からは、武家が政治の主導権を握る時代が続きました。頼朝の死後、妻の政子の一族の北条氏が執権として権力をもつ時代が1333年の後醍醐天皇による幕府討伐まで続きました。

この時代の出来事として特筆すべきは、中国大陸からフビライ・ハンの蒙古軍が大船団で攻

> **Dharma-ending Philosophy**
> In the 2,001st year after the passing of the Buddha, Buddhism was prophesized to enter a period of decline, a period called the end of the Buddhist law (dharma). That year would correspond to 1052. As a means of humble supplication, the then regent to the emperor, Fujiwara no Yorimichi, built the Amida Hall renowned Phoenix Hall in his rural villa, as an earthly representation of the Pure Land.

Q: What is the Kamakura period?

During the Heian period, the aristocrats hired warriors (samurai or *bushi*) to provide security and protection, and over time these military clans seized political power and became aristocrats themselves. This was first done by Taira no Kiyomori (1118-81) of the Heike clan. The Heike clan, however, was eventually defeated by another military clan, the Genji, led by Minamoto no Yoritomo (1147-99). Taking Kamakura (present-day Kamakura city, Kanagawa prefecture) as his base, Yoritomo sent governors and stewards to the provinces to solidify his power. In 1192 he was appointed shogun by the emperor, established the Kamakura shogunate, and assumed political control of the country. At first the aristocrats and the samurai shared political control, but in 1221 the retired emperor Go-Toba was defeated when he attempted to overthrow the shogunate, and political control fell fully into the hands of the shogun. After the death of Yoritomo, the family of his wife Masako, the Hojo, was appointed regent and assumed effective control of the shogunate until it was toppled by Emperor Go-Daigo in 1333.

Particularly noteworthy events in this period include the attempts by the Mongolian emperor Kublai Khan to invade

め込んで来たことです。しかも、1274年と1284年の2度にわたる来襲でしたが、運良く2度とも大嵐になり撤退しました。

Q: 室町(むろまち)時代とは?

後醍醐天皇と共に鎌倉幕府を倒した足利尊氏(あしかがたかうじ)は、新たに光明(こうみょう)天皇をかついで1336年に京都(室町)に幕府を置きました。後醍醐帝が亡くなると、足利一族は全国支配に乗り出しますが、地方の実力武将である守護(しゅご)(大名)の領国支配の上に成り立っていたため、幕府は領地をめぐる裁判や武家の監視・取締りなどの警察機構を強化することで政権維持を図らなければなりませんでした。幕府の実権は将軍の補佐役の管領(かんれい)が握っていました。

1467年、将軍家の相続問題から応仁の乱が起き、10年以上もの内乱を経て幕府の権威は失墜し、その後は100年にも及ぶ戦国時代が続くことになりました。

Q: 安土桃山(あづちももやま)時代とは?

地方豪族が覇権を争う戦国の世で「天下統一」へ、いち早く頭角を現したのが織田(おだ)信長(のぶなが)(1534 – 1582)でした。信長はそれまでの武将たちとは異質で、外国の文物を好み、常識にとらわれない発想で政治を行いました。

織田信長

and conquer Japan in 1274 and 1284. Fortunately for the Japanese, the large Mongolian fleets had to withdraw in the face of violent storms on both occasions.

Q: What is the Muromachi period?

The warrior Ashikaga Takauji, who with Emperor Go-Daigo had toppled the Kamakura shogunate, set up the pretender Komyo as emperor and established a new shogunate in the Muromachi district of Kyoto in 1336. After the death of Emperor Go-Daigo, the Muromachi shogunate increased its policing activities over provincial estates that local governors (now warlords) depended on for their power. The authority of the shogunate was in effect exercised by a deputy to the shogun with the title of *kanrei*.

In 1467 a dispute over shogunal succession erupted, leading to ten years of civil war, the Onin War, and resulting in the loss of power and authority of the shogunate. This was followed by 100 years of fighting among provincial warlords known as the Warring States period.

Q: What is the Azuchi-Momoyama period?

In the nationwide struggle among feudal lords for dominance, the first to lay claim to hegemony was Oda Nobunaga (1534-82). Nobunaga was unlike other warlords in his fondness for foreign things and in his mold-breaking approach to political maneuvering. After Nobunaga's assassination, the baton for national control was passed on to his foremost general, Toyotomi Hideyoshi (1537-98).

信長の暗殺後、その遺志を受け継ぐ形で「天下統一」を実現したのが豊臣秀吉（1537 - 1598）です。秀吉は貧しい農民の子として生まれ育ち、信長のもとで武将として出世した、当時としては珍しい経歴の持ち主でした。そのため権力維持に莫大な金品を使い、京都に政庁と邸宅を兼ねた聚楽第を建て、豪勢な暮しをすることで権威を保とうとしました。秀吉の時代には、京都を中心に、華やかな桃山文化が花開きました。

豊臣秀吉

秀吉はまた、農地の面積や収穫高を調べる「検地」、農民から武器を取り上げる「刀狩り」という制度を実施しました。これによって、武家中心の封建社会が確立したのです。晩年の秀吉は領地拡大のため朝鮮出兵を試み、失敗しました。

Q: 江戸時代とは？

豊臣家を滅ぼし、1603年に江戸（東京）に幕府を置き、武家による全国支配を果たしたのが徳川家康（1543 - 1616）です。徳川幕府は全国を約300の藩に分け、武士を最上とする士農工商という身分制度を確立し、藩を通じて領地と民衆を支配しました。この幕藩制度によって政権は安定し、260年という長期間、徳川家による全国支配が続きました。

徳川家康

幕府が置かれたことで、小さな村だった江戸は、江戸城を中心にした城下町が形成され、18世紀にはロンドンと並ぶ人口100万都市になりました。江戸時代は外国との

Hideyoshi was unusual in that he was born the son of a poor farmer and achieved success as a warrior under Nobunaga. As a display of his power and authority, he spent huge sums to build the lavish Jurakudai palace in Kyoto, which served both as residence and political headquarters but is no longer extant. The cultural florescence that blossomed in Nobunaga's and Hideyoshi's time is referred to as the Azuchi-Momoyama period.

Hideyoshi carried out surveys of land area and rice production and forbade farmers to own or possess weapons. These and other measures created a feudal society with the samurai at its core. In his latter years, in an effort at territorial expansion, he made an unsuccessful attempt to conquer Korea.

Q: What is the Edo period?

After largely eliminating Hideyoshi's allies, in 1603 the warlord Tokugawa Ieyasu (1543-1616) set up his shogunate in Edo (now Tokyo) and successfully established military control over the whole country. He divided the country into some 300 fiefs, set up a class system consisting of samurai, farmers, craftsmen, and merchants, and exercised control over land and people by means of the fiefs. This arrangement assured political stability and domestic peace for 260 years under Tokugawa rule.

With the establishment of the shogunate, the small village of Edo grew rapidly as a castle town and in the 18th century reached a population of 1,000,000 people, comparable to contemporary London. Since the shogunate forbade contact

交流を禁じた鎖国政策をとっていたため、日本独自の生活や文化が定着しました。

生活のおおもとは、コメに代表される植物利用の暮らしです。木を材料にした建物や乗物、植物から織り出された衣類、薬草を原料にした医薬品、燃料は木材や菜種から採取した油などが使われました。これらは使用後には自然に還元でき、リサイクルが可能でした。

武士は主君から与えられるコメをお金に替えるなどして生活をしていましたが、やがて貨幣経済が発達するとともに、最下位の身分の商人が力を持つようになりました。江戸時代は町民による文化が花開き、中でも17世紀末〜18世紀始めの元禄文化は、人形浄瑠璃や歌舞伎が人気を博し、松尾芭蕉が俳句を大成し、歌麿・北斎・広重などの浮世絵画家が活躍しました。

● 幕末のキーパーソン　People Active at the End of the Edo Period

1853年、ペリー率いるアメリカ軍艦4隻が現われ、幕府に対して開国を迫りました。これをきっかけに国内が、開国派と攘夷派に分かれて武力抗争をするようになりました。抗争はやがて、明治天皇（1867−1912）に政権を返上させる内戦へと発展。

明治天皇

In 1853 a squadron of four vessels under the command of Matthew C. Perry arrived in Japan and demanded that Japan open its doors to foreign trade. This set off an internal armed struggle between those in favor of opening the country and those opposed. The result was the assumption of political power by Emperor Meiji (r. 1867-1912).

西郷隆盛

with foreign countries, Japan evolved its own original lifestyles and culture.

The basis of life was vegetation—rice, first of all. Timber was used for the construction of houses and carts, plant fiber for clothing, herbs for medicine, wood for fuel, and rapeseed for oil. After use, all of these could be returned to nature, making recycling possible.

At first the samurai, at the top of the class system, were paid in rice, which they converted into currency, but with the development of a monetary economy, the merchant class, the lowest ranking class, gained in power and influence. A period of great cultural activity by ordinary townspeople ensued, particularly in the Genroku era at the end of the 17th and beginning of the 18th centuries, which saw the flourishing of the Bunraku puppet and Kabuki theaters as well as the appearance of the haiku poet Matsuo Basho and the ukiyo-e artists Utamaro, Hokusai, Hiroshige, and others.

徳川慶喜

その指揮を取ったのが薩摩藩士・西郷隆盛（1828 -1877）でした。開国をして武家や公家が一緒に政府をつくり新しい日本国を建設しようと夢みて行動した坂本龍馬（1836-1867）は土佐藩の下級武士出身でしたが、その夢が実現する直前に暗殺されてしまいました。

坂本龍馬

The opposition party was led by Saigo Takamori (1828-77) of the Satsuma fief. One of those hoping that the courtly aristocrats and samurai could join forces to create a new government was Sakamoto Ryoma (1836-67), a low-ranking samurai from the Tosa fief. Just before his efforts could bear fruit, however, he fell to the sword of an assassin.

1867年、第15代将軍・徳川慶喜（1837 - 1913）が朝廷に政権を返上し武士の世は終わりました。

Q: 明治（めいじ）時代とは？

明治天皇は京都から東京に遷都し、維新で活躍した人たちが政府要人となり、明治政府を樹立しました。江戸時代と大きく変わったのは、文明開化の名のもとで行われた欧米風の暮らしでした。

藩は県と名称を変え、士農工商の身分制度は廃止され、武士階級以上にしか許されなかった名字を庶民がつけることが許されました。近代化を進めるにあたって、政府は外国から各分野の専門家を招くとともに、多くの留学生を派遣しました。また、フランス流の学校制度が採用され、国民が学校教育を受ける機会が開かれました。

擬洋風の官庁街（山形）

▶ 文明開化

ガス灯や蒸気機関車など科学技術がとり入れられ、西洋風の建物が建てられるようになりました。男性は髪型を変え、洋服を着たり靴を履く人が増えました。東京で流行したのが、洋食店と牛鍋店でした。

In 1867 the 15th Tokugawa shogun, Yoshinobu (1837-1913), handed over political power to the emperor, and the Edo period and the era of the samurai came to an end.

Q: What is the Meiji Period?

The Meiji period opened with the emperor moving from Kyoto to Tokyo and the formation of a new government by those who had brought about the reinstatement of the emperor as a political force. The big difference between the new era and the Edo period was the introduction of Western ways under the motto Civilization and Enlightenment.

The fiefs became prefectures, the class system was abolished, and surnames, until then only permitted to samurai, were vouchsafed to commoners. To spur the modernization of the country, the government employed many foreign technical experts and sent many students to study abroad. Moreover, it set up an educational system modeled on the French, affording all citizens the opportunity to attend school.

▶ Civilization and Enlightenment

Under this slogan, gas lighting, steam locomotives, and Western-style architecture were introduced at the beginning of the Meiji period. Men gave up their Japanese-style hairdos, and some people took to donning Western clothes and wearing shoes rather than Japanese sandals. In Tokyo, particularly popular were restaurants serving Western cuisine and shops specializing in hot-pot beef (meat being traditionally frowned upon due to Buddhist influence).

政府樹立後は、薩摩や長州などの出身者が政治の実権を握っていることに不満を持った旧士族が、各地で自由と権利を主張する運動を起こしたり、反政府の内乱が続きました。1889年、大日本帝国憲法が制定され、天皇が神格化されるとともに全体主義が台頭するようになりました。

しかし、富国強兵のスローガンを掲げ、資本主義経済と軍備増強を図ったことで、諸外国との対立が生じました。中国との日清戦争（1894－95）、ロシアとの日露戦争（1904－05）に勝利し、1895年に台湾、1910年に韓国を併合するなどして領土を拡大。外国との戦争に勝ったことで政府も国民も自信を持ち、それが帝国主義へと傾いて行ったのです。

Q: 大正時代とは？

1912年から26年までの約15年間という短期間でしたが、この時代は近代日本が繁栄とともに、さまざまな矛盾を呈した変動期でもありました。1914年、第一次世界大戦が始まると、日本はドイツに宣戦布告して参戦。大戦は18年にドイツが降伏したことで終わりましたが、その間、戦争による特需景気で日本経済は超高度成長を遂げたのです。ところが、繁栄は長く続かず、20年には戦後恐慌、22年には銀行恐慌、そして23年に起きた関東大震災による恐慌が、社会不安を増幅させました。

全国に波及したコメ騒動（1918年）や労働争

The new government was dominated by former samurai from the Satsuma and Choshu fiefs, which had played a significant role in toppling the shogunate, with the result that disgruntled samurai from other fiefs started movements calling for "liberty and people's right" and stirred up anti-government sentiment. In 1889 a constitution was promulgated, which deified the emperor and showed the first signs of totalitarianism.

Under the slogan "A Rich Country and a Strong Military," capitalism and military spending were emphasized, leading to conflict with foreign powers. Japan emerged victorious in wars with China (1894-95) and Russia (1904-05), and expanded its territory by annexing Taiwan (1895) and Korea (1910). Both the Japanese government and the Japanese people gained confidence from these victories and thus started down the road toward imperialism.

Q: What is the Taisho period?

During this short 15-year period from 1912 to 1926, Japan enjoyed great prosperity but also evinced numerous anomalies. In 1914 World War I broke out, and Japan declared war on Germany. The war ended in 1918 with Germany's surrender, but during the wartime period Japan achieved an extraordinary rate of economic growth due to the demand for military supplies. This period was short-lived, however, and in 1920 there was a postwar financial panic, in 1922 a run on the banks, and in 1923 the Great Kanto Earthquake, further destabilizing the country.

With the rice riots of 1918 and the eruption of labor

議をはじめ、「大正デモクラシー」という言葉に象徴される社会運動が活発に展開されました。

瓦礫と化した浅草寺周辺

▶関東大震災

1923年9月1日に相模湾沖（神奈川県）を震源とするマグニチュード7.9の巨大地震が発生。東京ほか9県の被害建物は約37万棟、被災者190万人（うち死者・行方不明者約10.5万余）で、東京市街地は壊滅状態。

Q: 敗戦までの昭和時代とは？

1926年12月25日に大正天皇が48歳で亡くなり、25歳の皇太子が皇位につくと元号が昭和に改められました。日露戦争後、日本は中国大陸の満州における権益を確保するため関東軍を駐留させていましたが、軍部が一方的に満州国を建国（32年）させ、国際問題となりました。このことで非難を浴びた日本は翌年、国際連盟を脱退し、軍国化をますます強めて行ったのです。

1937年、日本軍と中国軍の戦闘（盧溝橋事件）が起き、それをきっかけに日中戦争が始まりました。

日本軍は中国に進攻しただけでなく、欧米列強国の植民地があった東南アジア一帯にも進出したため、各地で戦闘が繰り広げられました。中でも日本の武力による覇権主義を警戒したア

disputes, socialist movements spread throughout the country, giving rise to the expression "Taisho Democracy."

> ### ▶ The Great Kanto Earthquake
> An earthquake of magnitude 7.9 occurred off Sagami Bay, Kanagawa prefecture, on September 1, 1923. The number of buildings destroyed in Tokyo and nine prefectures reached some 370,000, with 1,900,000 people affected (more than 105,000 dead or missing). The city of Tokyo was virtually destroyed.

Q: What is the early Showa period (from 1926 to the end of World War II)?

On December 25, 1926, Emperor Taisho passed away at the age of 48, and the 25-year-old crown prince, Hirohito, assumed the throne. The era name changed from Taisho to Showa. After the Russo-Japanese War of 1904-1905, Japan had sent the Kwantung Army into China to secure its interests in Manchuria, and subsequently the Army unilaterally created the puppet state of Manchukuo in 1932, causing an international incident. In reaction to strident criticism from abroad, Japan withdrew from the League of Nations and took another step toward militarization.

In 1937 Japanese and Chinese troops clashed at Marco Polo Bridge, setting off the second Sino-Japanese war.

Aside from the invasion of China, Japan also moved against colonies in Southeast Asia held by Western powers, leading to conflict over a wide area. Fearing Japanese military hegemony, the United States prohibited the sale of oil to Japan

メリカは、対日石油輸出を禁止するなど経済制裁を加えましたが、それに反発した日本はドイツ、イタリアとの三国同盟、ソ連との中立条約を締結して孤立化を回避する一方で、アメリカとの戦争準備を進めました。軍部内にも、物量の乏しい日本が、豊かなアメリカに勝てるはずがないという意見もありましたが、神国・日本は明治以来、外国と戦争をして負けたことがないとの「不敗神話」に押し切られたのです。

学校教育などで、国民は神である天皇の子であり臣民であるとの意識が植えつけられるようになったのは、国家総動員法が制定（1938年）されてからで、その後、軍事費は国家予算の4分の3を占めるようになりました。

真珠湾攻撃で炎上するUSSアリゾナ

▶太平洋戦争

1941年12月8日、日本軍がハワイ真珠湾のアメリカ艦隊を奇襲攻撃したことでアメリカが宣戦布告し、開戦。やがて第二次世界大戦に発展するのですが、敗戦までの二国間の戦いを太平洋戦争といいます。

原爆投下

▶敗戦

日本軍が優勢だったのは開戦から半年ほどまでで、1942年6月のミッドウエー海戦で日本海軍は空母4隻を失う大敗北を喫し、戦争の主導権をアメリカに握られてしまいました。その事実を兵士たちや国民に知らせないまま戦争を続けたため、1945年8月に広島と長崎に原爆を落とされたことで敗戦を認めるまでに3年以上もかかりました。太平洋戦争での日本の軍人や民間人の死者は約300万人とされています。

and implemented other economic sanctions. In response, Japan joined the Axis powers and signed a neutrality pact with the Soviet Union, while making preparations for war with the United States. Some within the Japanese army itself thought that resource-poor Japan couldn't hope to defeat resource-rich America, but this opinion was silenced by the myth that Japan was the Country of the Gods and had never lost a foreign war.

It was after the general mobilization of 1938 that the notion that the Japanese people were the subjects of a living god began to be implanted in the minds of students and the general populace. Subsequently, military expenses came to occupy three quarters of the national budget.

▶ The Pacific War

On December 8, 1941, Japan carried out a surprise attack on Pearl Harbor in Hawaii, and the United States declared war on Japan. This would bring the United States into World War II. The theater of fighting in the Pacific and East Asia is called the Pacific War.

▶ Defeat

The Japanese army was in the ascendant for the first six months of the war. In June 1942, however, Japan lost four aircraft carriers in the Battle of Midway, and the United States assumed a dominant position in the war. But this disastrous defeat was not made known to soldiers in general or the people, a state of ignorance that continued until August 1945, when atomic bombs were dropped on Hiroshima and Nagasaki. Japanese casualties among civilians and the military in the Pacific War are said to be about 3,000,000.

Q: 戦後の日本は？

1945年8月15日昼、天皇の言葉がラジオ放送で流されました。それは、国民に対して戦争終結を告げるものでした。

敗戦の結果、日本はアメリカのマッカーサー元帥が最高司令官を務める連合国軍総司令部（GHQ）の占領下に置かれ、新しい憲法の制定、農地改革、教育改革、財閥の解体、華族制度の廃止などが進められました。

昭和天皇とマッカーサー元帥

新しい憲法（日本国憲法）では、国民が主権者であることが明記され、天皇は国の象徴とされました。併せて、天皇は自ら神ではなく人間であることを宣言しました。また憲法（第9条）には、太平洋戦争の反省を込めて、戦争の放棄がうたわれました。

～昭和64年(1989)

戦争で失った国土の復旧と経済復興には困難が伴いましたが、1950年の朝鮮戦争による特需をきっかけに景気が上向き、55年から60年にかけて国民総生産が毎年9％以上の伸びを見せました。また、高度な工業技術によって船舶、自動車、テレビなど多くの製品の生産国となり、70年代から80年代にかけて輸出が増大し、アメリカに次ぐ経済大国になりました。

Q: What happened in postwar Japan?

At noon on August 8, 1945, the emperor delivered a radio announcement to the people, proclaiming the end of the war.

As a result of defeat, Japan was occupied by the Allied powers under the direction of Douglas MacArthur as Supreme Commander, who issued directives from his General Headquarters (GHQ). The changes he effected included the promulgation of a new constitution, agricultural reform, a revamping of the educational system, dismantling of the *zaibatsu* (corporate conglomerates), and abolishment of the peerage system.

Under the new constitution, sovereign power was held by the people, and the emperor was declared "the symbol of the State and the unity of the people." In a separate rescript, the emperor announced that he was not a living god. Article 9 of the constitution outlawed war as a means of settling international disputes.

~1989

Regaining territory lost in the war and economic recovery proved arduous undertakings, but with incoming orders for supplies needed by the American army in the Korean War, the economy turned upward. From 1955 into 1960 the gross national product grew at an annual rate of 9%. Moreover, thanks to advanced industrial technology, Japan became a producer of ships, cars, televisions, and more. From 1970 into the 1980s exports grew to the extent that Japan became the second largest economic power in the world.

▶ 東京五輪

戦争のため1940年のオリンピック夏季大会の開催権を返上していた日本が、ようやく24年後（1964年）に東京で開催することができました。敗戦国・日本が驚異的な復興を果たしたことを世界に示す場となったのです。

東京オリンピック

政治は、自民党がほぼ独占的に権力を握ってきましたが、そのために政治家への献金問題が度々、取り上げられ、中でも造船疑獄（1954年）やリクルート事件（88年）は政・財・官を揺るがす贈収賄事件として昭和史の大汚点となっています。

平成元年(1989)〜

在位63年目にあたる1989年1月7日、昭和天皇が亡くなり、皇太子が55歳で皇位を継承し、平成と元号が改まりました。日本経済は、昭和の終り頃に発生した「バブル経済」で成長を続けていましたが、1991年に入ると一気にしぼみ始めました。地価は下がり、不動産向け融資を拡大し続けた金融機関は膨大な不良債権を抱え込み、銀行や証券会社の倒産が続出しました。

サリンがまかれた日の霞ヶ関駅

▶ 地下鉄サリン事件

90年代になると社会不安を煽るかのような宗教団体・オウム真理教が登場。若い信者たちは教祖の言うがまま、国家転覆のテロ行為に走り、1995年には猛毒ガスの

▶ The Tokyo Olympics

The 1940 Summer Olympics, originally scheduled to be held in Tokyo, were canceled due to the fear of war. It was only 24 years later, in 1964, that the Tokyo Olympics was realized. It proved the perfect opportunity to demonstrate how defeated Japan had achieved a miraculous recovery.

On the political front, one party was virtually unopposed during this time, the Liberal Democratic Party. As a consequence, illegal political contributions and graft were a recurrent problem, such as the shipbuilding bribery case of 1954 and the Recruit scandal of 1988. Such incidents of graft and bribery, involving politics, money, and government bureaucracy, left a black mark on the history of the Showa period.

The Heisei Period (1989~)

January 7, 1989, saw the passing of Emperor Showa in the 63rd year of his reign. The crown prince, then 55, assumed the throne, and the era name became Heisei. Near the end of the Showa period, the Japanese economy, in the midst of an economic "bubble," was still enjoying robust growth. But in 1991 it began suddenly to shrink. Land prices fell sharply, securities took on bad debt from their supplying of credit to the real estate market, and security companies and banks went bankrupt.

▶ Tokyo Subway Sarin Attack

As if to exacerbate already uneasy social conditions, the fanatical religious organization Aum Shinrikyo rose to prominence in the early 1990s. Unquestioningly following the lead of its founder, its goal was to overthrow the government

> サリンを地下鉄に撒き、死者17人、負傷者約6300人の大事件になりました。

　地下鉄サリン事件が起きる2カ月前の1995年1月17日早朝、マグニチュード7.3の兵庫県南部地震が発生。人口密集地域での大地震だったため、被害が甚大でした。この阪神・淡路大震災による死者・行方不明者6434人、負傷者4万3792人、被害を受けた住宅約64万戸、被害総額約10兆円とされています。

　この時の総理大臣は社会党の村山富市で、退潮著しい自民党が野党第一党と手を組むべく、「自・社・さ」連立政権のトップにまつりあげたのです。しかし、村山総理は大震災の対応の遅れや、国会答弁での社会党の主張を覆す発言で党消滅のきっかけを作りました。

　2001年、自民党の古い体質からの脱却を目指した小泉政権が誕生。北朝鮮を電撃訪問し、金総書記に日本人の拉致被害者の存在を認めさせて帰国を実現するなど、国民受けするパフォーマンスを展開し、5年以上の長期政権になりました。2006年9月、52歳の安倍総理にバトンタッチするも1年で政権放棄。その後は毎年のように総理が替わるという不安定な政権が続きました。

> through terrorist activities. In 1995 it carried out a sarin attack on Tokyo subways, resulting in 17 dead and 6,300 injured.

Two months before this attack took place, the Great Hanshin Earthquake with a magnitude of 7.3 occurred on the morning of January 17, 1995. Since the affected area was densely populated, the damage was immense. Dead and missing numbered 6,434, the homeless 43,792, damaged buildings 640,000, and total costs approximately 10 trillion yen.

The then prime minister was Tomiichi Murayama of the Socialist Party, who had been appointed symbolic head of the coalition government consisting of the Socialist Party, the Sakigake Party, and the rapidly declining Liberal Democratic Party. His response to the earthquake was slow, and his remarks in the Diet contradicted Socialist principles and eventually led to the demise of his party.

In 2001 Junichiro Koizumi of the Liberal Democratic Party became prime minister with the aim of renewing the party. He made an unexpected visit to North Korea, met the Supreme Leader Kim Jong-il, and gained from him an admission of past abductions of Japanese citizens. Through this and other crowd-appealing activities, his administration stayed in power for an unprecedented five years. In September 2006 he was succeeded by 52-year-old Shinzo Abe, who resigned after only one year in office. Thereafter, new prime ministers were appointed on almost a yearly basis, producing an atmosphere of political instability.

鳩山政権

▶政権交代

2009年8月の総選挙で、民主党が自民党に圧倒的勝利をおさめ、政権交代が実現。世論は新政権を歓迎しましたが、鳩山総理の沖縄米軍基地をめぐる無責任な発言で支持率が急降下し、またもや不安定な政権になりました。

▶福島原発事故

2011年3月11日に起きたマグニチュード9.0の東北地方太平洋沖地震による大津波で電源を喪失した東京電力・福島第一原発の原子炉4基が爆発を含む事故で放射能を飛散させました。この4基は廃炉になることが決定。

福島原発事故

この東日本大震災では、約2万人の死者・行方不明者が出ました。さらに原発事故による避難者を加えると、25万人以上が故郷を失ったとされます。この年の12月の総選挙で自民党は民主党に大勝し、政権復帰を果たしました。

政府は復興庁を設置し、被災地の復旧・復興の支援を進めていますが、放射能汚染という問題も含め、その歩みは遅々としています。民主党政権が「脱原発」としていた原発問題は、自民党政権になってからは「再稼働」へと180度転換しつつあります。

21世紀の前後25年ほどの間、日本経済は低迷を続け、国家財政は危機に瀕していると言われてきました。不況で消費が落ち込み、その結果、

▶ Changing of the Guard

In the general election of August 2009, the Democratic Party of Japan achieved an overwhelming victory over the Liberal Democratic Party and became the ruling party. The general public welcomed this change, but the prime minister's (Yukio Hatoyama's) irresponsible handling of the American military base issue in Okinawa put a damper on enthusiasm and led to a decline in the party's popularity. The result was once again political instability.

▶ The Fukushima Nuclear Disaster

One result of the 9.0 magnitude earthquake off the coast of Tohoku in March 11, 2011, was the loss of power at the TEPCO Fukushima Daiichi Nuclear Power Plant, causing the meltdown of four of its reactors and the release of radioactive material. It was decided to shutdown these reactors.

In the aftermath of the Great East Japan Earthquake, approximately 20,000 people lost their lives or went missing. Including those who had to evacuate from contaminated areas, over 250,000 people were unable to return to their homes. In December of this same year, the Liberal Democratic Party trounced the Democratic Party in a general election and returned to power.

The government set up the Reconstruction Agency to coordinate reconstruction and revitalization in the affected areas, but progress has been very slow, including the problem of contaminated soil. While the Democratic Party had made denuclearization of part of its platform, the Liberal Democratic Party, in a 180 degree turn-around, opted for re-nuclearization.

For the 25 years on either side of the turn of the 21st century, the economy remained apathetic, and national finances reached a critical state. With ongoing deflation, consumption

物やサービスの価格を下げないと売れない、企業は利益が少なくなるので社員の給料が上らず消費が落ち込む、という悪循環（デフレスパイラル）に陥りました。人件費などのコストが高い国内を避けて、工場を海外に進出させる企業も増えています。国内消費を活性化させるということが、今後の大きな課題です。

　もう一つの大きな課題は、人口問題です。日本の人口は2010年から減り始め、約1.27億人（13年）が30年には約1.16億人に、50年には0.97億人にまで減少すると見込まれています。その一方で高齢者（65歳以上）の割合が増え、4人に1人（2013年）が2035年には3人に1人になるとされます。日本の社会保障制度は経済面で高齢者を若い労働者が支える構造になっているため、超少子高齢化という人口構成は制度の存続を妨げる要因になると指摘されています。また人口減少は、市町村の消滅を促進するとまで言われているのです。

▶ **東京スカイツリー**
　1958年12月に完成した東京タワー（高さ約333m）に代わる電波塔・観光施設として2012年5月に開業。高さ634mは世界一高いタワーとしてギネス世界記録の認定を受ける（2011年11月）。

東京スカイツリー

dropped off, product and service prices had to be lowered, and profitless corporations had to repress wages, which led again to lower consumption—a so-called deflationary spiral. Further, the high cost of domestic labor forced companies to move overseas. Thus, the biggest challenge facing Japan today is how to increase domestic consumption.

Another crucial problem is the dwindling population. The population of Japan has been shrinking since 2010. At the present rate, it is calculated that the 2013 population of 127 million will drop to 116 million by 2030 and to 97 million by 2048. On the other hand, there has been an increase in the elderly (those over 65), from 25% in 2013 to an estimated 33% in 2035. Since the Japanese social security system relies on the young to support the elderly, the shrinking and aging of the population will prove a disruptive factor in its maintenance. It is further pointed out that a shrinking population will escalate the demise of provincial cities and towns.

▶ Tokyo Skytree

In May 2012 the Tokyo Skytree opened to the public, replacing Tokyo Tower (approximately 333 meters high) as a tourist attraction and the principal broadcasting tower for the Kanto region. At 634 meters in height it is the tallest tower of its type in the world and registered in the Guinness book of world records (November 2011).

第3章 政治・行政
Politics and Government

国会議事堂▶

1 政 治

Q: 政治体制はどうなっているの？

多くの民主主義国家と同様に、立法、司法、行政の三権で成り立ち、それぞれの権力分野は独立しています。主権は国民にあり、立法の分野では国民の代表である議員が国や市区町村議会で政策を審議・決定します。決は多数決が原則で、議会で多数を占める政党が優位です。

Q: 日本国憲法の特色は？

憲法は、前文と11章103条で構成されています。主な理念は①国民主権、②基本的人権の尊重、③平和主義です。また、天皇は国および国民統合の象徴という立場であるとされています。

これが世界に類のない憲法とされるのは、戦争放棄を宣言しつつ攻撃のための戦力を保持し

1 Politics

Q: What is Japan's political system?

As with most democratic countries, there are three independent branches of government: the legislative, the judicial, and the executive, each responsible for its own area of influence. Sovereign power is held by the people, and laws are enacted by the people's representatives in assemblies both on the national and municipal level. Final decisions are reached by a majority vote, with the majority political party enjoying precedence.

Q: What features does the Japanese constitution possess?

The constitution consists of a preamble, 11 chapters, and 103 articles. Its main principles are 1) the sovereignty of the people, 2) respect for fundamental human rights, and 3) the realization of peace. In addition, the emperor is declared "the symbol of the State and the unity of the people."

The reason the constitution is considered a unique document lies in article 9, which outlaws the use of force to

ないことを銘記した第9条があるからです。憲法が施行（1947年5月）された7年後に発足した自衛隊は、他国から攻撃された場合にのみ防衛する役割で軍隊ではないとの位置付けですが、国軍を持たないのは自立した国家とは言えないのではないかと主張する声も高まっています。

Q: 憲法は改正できるの？

憲法は国家の最高法規として、他の法律とは別格とされています。したがって改正をする場合は、議会での決議後に国民投票を経なければなりません。そのため改正は事実上不可能とされてきましたが、2010年5月にいわゆる「国民投票法」が施行されたことで、国会内での改正論議が活発になってきています。

そもそも日本国憲法は戦勝国のアメリカに押し付けられたもので、独立国家なら自主憲法を制定すべきというのが、政権与党・自民党の党是です。国会で安定多数の議席をもつ自民党が、憲法改正草案（2012年決定）を発議し強行決議をする可能性がまったくないとは言い切れません。

settle international disputes and the maintenance of armed forces with war potential. The constitution went into effect in May 1947. The Japan Self-Defense Forces, established seven years later, was positioned as an army to be deployed only in case of foreign attack. However, there is an increasing number of Japanese who claim that a country without a national army cannot be called truly independent.

Q: Can the constitution be revised?

The constitution is the primary law of the state, superseding all other laws. Any amendment to the constitution must gain a two-thirds majority in the national assembly (the Diet) and a simple majority in a general referendum. For that reason, amendment has heretofore been thought a virtual impossibility. However, in 2010, with the Constitutional Amendment Procedure Law going into effect, detailing the procedures for amending the constitution, the possibility of amendment has once again become actively debated in the Diet.

It has long been the position of the ruling Liberal Democratic Party (LDP) that the present constitution was forced on Japan by the United States after World War II, and that any self-respecting independent nation should have a constitution of its own creation. In 2012 the LDP produced a draft amendment to the constitution, and since the LDP is the majority party in the lower house, there is every possibility that it may try to force its acceptance at some future date.

▶国民投票

憲法改正のための国民投票は、投票権者は18歳以上（2018年以降）になる予定。在外邦人にも投票権が認められます。投票は賛成か反対かを問うもので、無効票を除く投票総数の過半数の賛成があれば、改正案が成立します。

投票箱

Q: 国会のしくみは？

国会には、衆議院と参議院の二院があります。外国の国会の多くは一院制で、二院制を採用しているのはアメリカ、イギリス、オーストラリアなど少数です。二院制は本来、貴族などの特権階級で構成される上院、大衆の代表である下院という位置付けで、日本の場合も戦前は貴族院と衆議院という名称を用いていました。

国会の議場

民主主義国家となってからは、衆議院は従来通りで貴族院は参議院（第二院）と名称が変わったのです。参議院は衆議院の行き過ぎにブレーキをかける役割が与えられているのですが、衆議院と同様に数の論理で審議・採決する傾向が強くなっているため「無用論」も取沙汰されています。なお、天皇が出席して開催される国会の開会式は参議院議場で行われます。

> **National Referendum**
>
> The national referendum for amendment of the constitution will encompass all enfranchised voters of 18 years or older (from 2018). Votes by Japanese living abroad will be considered valid. The vote will be of the yes or no variety, and with the exception of invalid ballots, a majority is needed to pass the amendment.

Q: What is the Diet?

The legislature (National Diet) of Japan is composed of two houses: a lower house (House of Representatives) and an upper house (House of Councilors). In most countries the legislature is composed of only one house. Those with two houses are in the minority, including the United States, the United Kingdom, and Australia. The original rationale for two houses was that the upper house would consist of privileged classes and the lower house of commoners. Before World War II, the upper house in Japan was called the House of Peers and the lower house, as now, the House of Representatives (or *shugi-in*, with *shu* literally meaning "the masses.")

After the postwar constitution was adopted, while the name of the House of Representatives remained the same, the House of Peers was renamed the House of Councilors (or the second house). The function of the House of Councilors is to objectively see that the lower house doesn't go to extremes, but in actual fact there is a strong tendency for the upper house to adhere to the same political scheme in discussion and voting as the lower house, giving rise to the argument that the upper house is a useless entity. The Diet is convoked by the emperor in a session of the House of Councilors.

Q: 国会議員はどのように選ぶの?

国会議員は国民を代表して立法に関わる職務で、国政選挙によって選ばれます。投票できるのは満20歳(2016年から満18歳)以上の国民および海外で暮らす日本人です。選挙に立候補できるのは日本国籍を持つ人で、衆議院が満20歳以上、参議院が満30歳以上という制限があります。それぞれの院の議員定数は下記の通りです。

なお、参議院議員は任期(6年)内は選挙がありませんが、衆議院議員は任期(4年)の前でも議会解散による総選挙が行われるのが一般的です。

衆議院 House of Representatives

● 小選挙区 Single-member Districts

全国 295 選挙区　定数 295
295 Electoral Districts　295 Seats

● 比例代表 Proportional Representation

全国 11 ブロック　定数 180
11 National Blocks　180 Seats

計 475 議席
Total Seats: 475

Q: 国会議員の特権は?

国会議員になると、一般国民とは異なる特権が与えられます。その第一は、国会会期中は現行犯や所属議院が認めた場合以外は、逮捕されないことです。もう一つは、国会での演説や討

Q: How are Diet members elected?

Diet members are representatives of the people in passing laws and are chosen in a national election. Voters must be Japanese citizens who are 20 years old or older (at least 18 from 2016), including those residing abroad. Candidates standing for election must be Japanese citizens who are 20 years old or older for the House of Representatives and 30 years old or older for the House of Councilors. The number of seats comprising the two houses is given below.

House of Councilor members have a term of six years, and new elections cannot be held until that term has expired. The term for House of Representatives is four years, but a general election is often held before that term has expired.

参議院 House of Councilors

● 選挙区 Election Districts
都道府県ごとに47選挙区　定数146
47 Prefectural Districts　146 Seats

● 比例代表 Proportional Representatives
全国区　定数96
Nationwide　96 Seats

計242議席（半数を3年ごとに改選）
Total Seats: 242 (half are elected every three years)

Q: What special privileges to Diet members enjoy?

Diet members have certain privileges not possessed by ordinary citizens. One is that Diet members cannot be arrested while the Diet is in session unless they are actually caught in the act of committing a crime or if the House to

論の発言内容に関して、一般国民なら名誉棄損で訴えられるようなものでも法律上の責任が問われないという特権です。その他、年額2000万円超の歳費・手当、3名までの公設秘書、国会内事務室の提供、交通機関の無料パス支給、海外旅行の際の出入国審査・税関のチェック不要などが認められています。

Q: 総理大臣の権限は?

日本では議院内閣制を採用しているため、行政府の長である内閣総理大臣（首相）は、国会の指名を受け天皇が親任（任命）した国会議員（衆議院議員）が就任することになっています。

総理大臣には任期の定めがなく、在任中は本人が辞意を表明しない限り、辞めさせるのは非常に困難です。加えて、総理大臣には大臣の任命・罷免の権限、さらには衆議院の解散権という強い権能が与えられています。国会議員になった以上、誰もが総理大臣を目指すと言われますが、その一方では批判や中傷を何とも思わない神経の図太さがなければ務まらない職責です。

中央政府	Central Government
内閣府	Cabinet Office
総務省	Ministry of Internal Affairs and Communications
法務省	Ministry of Justice
外務省	Ministry of Foreign Affairs
財務省	Ministry of Finance
経済産業省	Ministry of Economy, Trade and Industry

which they belong agrees to their arrest. Another is that members are not held legally responsible for statements made in the Diet that could be interpreted as defamation of character if made by an ordinary citizen. In addition, each member is paid a salary of ¥20 million a year, can hire three official secretaries, and is provided with office space within the Diet building and free travel passes. When traveling abroad, they are not required to pass through immigration or customs.

Q: What are the powers of the prime minister?

Since Japan adopts the parliamentary cabinet system, the prime minister is the head of the executive branch, a member of the House of Representatives who has been designated by that House and who has been appointed by the emperor.

The prime minister's term of office is not fixed, and unless he or she resigns, it is extremely difficult to remove the prime minister from office. In addition, the prime minister has the power to appoint and dismiss ministers and to dissolve the House of Representatives. While it is true that any member of the House of Representatives can become prime minister, the position requires a very thick skin to weather the criticism and abuse that comes with the job.

文部科学省	Ministry of Education, Culture, Sports, Science and Technology
厚生労働省	Ministry of Health, Labour and Welfare
農林水産省	Ministry of Agriculture, Forestry and Fisheries
国土交通省	Ministry of Land, Infrastructure, Transport and Tourism
環境省	Ministry of the Environment
防衛省	Ministry of Defense

Q: 大臣は何人いるの？

　　大臣の定数は17です。そのうちの半数以下なら民間人の登用も可能ですが、任命権者の総理大臣が権力基盤の安定を図ろうとするため国会議員で独占されるのが常態化しています。

　中央政府の府省は12あり、そのトップは主任の大臣と呼ばれます。内閣府は総理大臣が兼務し、その補佐役として大臣格の内閣官房長官がいます。それ以外の大臣は無任所大臣、内閣府特命大臣として任命されます。定数が限られているため、いくつもの特命を兼務する大臣が増えているのが近年の傾向です。また各府省には、政権与党の国会議員の中から副大臣（1〜3名）、大臣政務官（1〜3名）が大臣の補佐役としていて、これらに任命されるのは出世の階段を一歩上ったことになります。

Q: 政党とは？

　　政党には一定の条件を充たしたものと、それ以外のものがあります。前者は所属国会議員5名以上、5名未満の場合は直近の国政選挙での得票率が2％以上の政治団体が条件です。法律上の条件を充たしていない政治団体でも、選挙で10名以上の候補者がいれば◯◯党と名乗ることができます。法律上で認められた政党には、国から政党交付金が支出されます。

　政党交付金は1995年に、健全な政治を目的と

Q: How many ministers are there?

There are 17 ministers (Ministers of State). Of this number, half can be non-Diet members, but in fact, in order to consolidate his political base, the prime minister normally appoints ministers from the Diet.

There are 12 ministries in the central government, and each of them is headed by a minister. The prime minister holds the position of minister of the cabinet office, and is assisted in this role by the Chief Cabinet Secretary, whose position is equal to that of a minister. Other cabinet ministers are without portfolio or especially appointed. Since the number of ministers is limited, it is the recent tendency for one minister to have multiple responsibilities. In each ministry there are one to three vice-ministers and one to three parliamentary secretaries assisting the minister, who are appointed from among the ruling party's Diet members. To be appointed to these positions is usually taken as a sign of advancement.

Q: What is a political party?

Political parties can be divided into those that meet certain conditions and those that don't. The former consists of organizations with five members who are Diet representatives or, failing that, organizations that have won 2% of the vote in the most recent general election. Even organizations that fail to meet these conditions can refer to themselves as political parties if they have put up at least 10 candidates for election. Legally recognized parties are eligible to receive a government subsidy.

Political party subsidies were established in 1995 in an

して制度化されたものです。これには国民が一人当り250円を負担することになっていて、政党の議員数に応じた金額が割りふられています。ちなみに与党第一党の自民党には、年間約173億円が支出されます（2015年度見込み）。

自民党本部

> ▶ **自民党**
>
> 正式党名は自由民主党で、1955年11月に自由党と日本民主党が合同して結成。2009年9月に至る54年間、民主党政権が誕生するまで衆議院第一党の座を守り続けました。民主党政権はわずか3年で終わり、2012年12月から政権与党に返り咲きました。

日本では明治時代に政党が結成され、自由党（1881年）、立憲改進党（82年）、立憲帝政党（82年）が当初の政党です。その後、政党の改編・解党や新党の誕生などを経て、戦時中の1940年に全ての政党に解党命令が下され、政治結社としての大政翼賛会に糾合されました。敗戦後の1945年、政党が復活して日本自由党など5つの政党が政治活動を始めました。以来、70年ほどの間に50近くの政党が生れたり消滅したりしています。

2 行 政

Q: 行政区分はどうなっているの？

日本は一都（東京）、一道（北海道）、二府（大阪、京都）、43県という大きな行政区分がされ、この

attempt to create a healthier political environment. The total sum amounts to an outlay of ¥250 per citizen, and the monies are distributed according to the number of Diet members a party possesses. The sum to be paid to the ruling Liberal Democratic Party in 2015 (estimated) is ¥17.3 billion.

> ▶ **The Liberal Democratic Party**
> The Liberal Democratic Party (LDP) was formed in 1955 by a merger of the Liberal Party and the Japan Democratic Party. For the next 54 years the LDP continued as the majority party until September 2009, when it was unseated by the Democratic Party of Japan. The Democratic Party remained in power for a short three years, and then the LDP regained the reins of government in December 2012.

The first political parties were constituted in the Meiji period: namely, the liberal Party of Japan (1881), the Constitutional Reform Party, and the Constitutional Imperial Rule Party (both 1882). Thereafter there was a period in which various parties were newly born, merged, and dissolved, until 1940 when the single-party Imperial Rule Assistance Association absorbed them all. In 1945, following the end of the war, five political parties were formed, including the Japan Liberal Party. In the succeeding 70 years, nearly 50 political parties have been formed and dissolved.

2 Administrative Divisions

Q: What are the administrative divisions?

Administratively, Japan is divided into one metropolis or *to* (Tokyo), one circuit or *do* (Hokkaido), two urban prefectures

下に市区町村という基礎自治体（約1800）があります。

市には人口数によって政令指定都市（50万人以上）、中核市（30万人以上）、特例市（20万人以上）に指定されるケースがありますが、一般的には所定の要件を備えた3万人以上の都市です。政令指定都市は20市あり、市長は県知事とほぼ同格とされています。

東京都は別格として、地方自治体は財源の多くを国に依存しているため「三割自治」などと言われてきました。近年、財政破綻が危ぶまれている自治体も増えています。

Q: 公務員はどれくらいいるの？

国家公務員が約64万人、地方公務員が約277万人です（2013年度）。日本の就業者数がおよそ6300万人なので、その5％が公務員ということになります。ただし国家公務員と地方公務員が重複して行なっていたり、地方公務員に移管できる業務もあるとして、国家公務員削減を主張する声もあります。

公務員の職場はとかく保守的になりがちで、女性を登用することに消極的です。管理職に占める女性の割合は国家公務員が3％、地方公務員が7％（2013年度）で、まだまだ男性上位の職場環境です。

or *fu* (Osaka and Kyoto), and 43 prefectures or *ken*. Beneath these divisions are 1,800 autonomous administrative units: the cities, towns, villages, and wards (*ku*).

Cities can be divided into designated cities with a population of over 500,000 people, core cities with a population exceeding 300,000, and special cities with a population exceeding 200,000. In common parlance, the word "city" refers to appropriate cities with a population of over 30,000. In total, there are 20 designated cities, and the mayor is considered roughly equivalent to a prefectural governor.

With the exception of Tokyo, most local governments rely on the central government for financial support, giving rise to the phrase "30% autonomy" in reference to the ratio of income locally obtained. Recently many local administrative units appear to be teetering on the brink of financial collapse.

Q: How many civil servants are there?

There are approximately 640,000 national civil servants and some 2,770,000 local civil servants (as of 2013). Since the total number of employed workers is about 63,000,000, civil servants account for 5%. However, since the duties of national and local civil servants sometimes overlap, and since some duties of national civil servants could possibly be transferred to the local level, some quarters argue that the size of the national civil service could be substantially reduced.

Since the civil service tends by nature to be conservative, there are few opportunities for women. The percentage of women in managerial positions is only 3% at the national level and 7% at the local (as of 2013). The civil service is still a male stronghold.

Q: キャリアとノンキャリアの違いは？

公務員は、難関試験に合格して採用されたキャリアと、それ以外のノンキャリアに大別されます。中でも国家公務員のキャリアは特別扱いで、例えば財務省の場合は30歳台で地方の税務署長、40歳台で本省課長あるいは出向で県の部長級に昇進します。ちなみに2011年度に国家公務員に採用されたのは約1万6800人で、そのうちキャリアは487人でした。

東京都庁

> ▶首都・東京
>
> 都制が施行されたのは、戦争中の1943年7月。人口約1316万人、財政規模6兆6667億円、公務員数16.5万人は世界最大級の都市（2014年度）。
>
> 金融・ビジネスなどの国際的総合力評価「都市力ランキング」(13年)では、ロンドン、ニューヨーク、パリに次いで第4位。

Q: 防災対策はどのようにしているの？

阪神・淡路大震災（1995年）以後、都市部の防災意識が高まり、公共施設や住宅の耐震化、避難経路や避難場所の確保などの対策が取られてきています。しかし、人口密集地での防災対策は莫大な費用がかかるなどの理由で、必ずしも万全とは言えません。

そのため大都市では、市民に対して万が一、

Q: What is the difference between a career and non-career civil servant?

Civil servants can be divided between the career group who have passed a stringent qualifying exam and those who have not. Those on a career path receive special consideration. For example, a civil servant in the Ministry of Finance will be appointed superintendent at a local tax office in his thirties, a section chief at the Ministry in his forties, or promoted on loan to a local prefectural office with a rank equivalent to a department head. In 2011 there were 16,800 newly hired civil servants, with 487 being on a career path.

▶ The Capital, Tokyo

The Tokyo Metropolis was formed in July 1943 with the merger of the Tokyo urban prefecture and Tokyo city. With a population of approximately 13,160,000, a budget of ¥6.6667 trillion, and 165,000 civil servants, Tokyo was the world's largest city as of 2014.

In an overall international ranking of cities, including finances and business, Tokyo was ranked 4th in the world, following London, New York, and Paris.

Q: What is the state of disaster prevention?

In the wake of the Great Hanshin Earthquake of 1995, more attention has been paid to urban disaster prevention, such as the erection of earthquake-resistant public buildings and private residences and the establishment of evacuation routes and centers. However, given the fact that disaster prevention in densely populated areas can be enormously expensive, progress in this area has been less that perfect.

Consequently, there has been an effort in the larger cities at

大災害が発生した場合は①自助、②共助、③公助の順に行うべきことを啓蒙しています。①については、発生直後の72時間を目安として「自分の身は自らで守ろう」としているのです。72時間というのは、公共機関が派遣する救援隊が到着して助け出すまでのタイムリミットです。ビルや住宅が多い地域では倒れた建物の下敷きになる人が多く、火災発生や道路の通行不能で救援隊が到着するまでに時間がかかります。したがって、市民は72時間を自らで生き延びる心構えをしておく必要があるのです。

Q: 地震予知はどこまで可能なの?

地震の多い日本では、予知に関するさまざまな研究が進んでいますが、それでも現状では予知は不可能と言わざるを得ません。自然の営みは、人知では捉えきれないものがあるからです。結局、人間ができることは、いつ大地震が起きても身の安全を確保できるような備えをしておくことだけなのです。

Q: 緊急地震速報はどのように出すの?

地震波が二つ以上の地震計で観測され、震度6弱以上と予測された場合に「緊急地震速報」が気象庁から発表されます。「○○で地震発生、○

● 震度階級

Earthquake Sizes
(Moment Magnitude Scale)

巨大地震
Great

震度7
7

大地震
Major

震度6強・6弱
strong 6—weak 6

educating the public to give priority to 1) self-help, 2) mutual aid, and 3) public help, in that order. In the case of self-help, the first 72 hours following a disaster should be given over to tending to one's own needs. This limit is set because it is the amount of time required for public relief teams to reach the site of the disaster. In densely populated areas there will be many buildings that have collapsed, blocking roads and obstructing the movement of aid workers. Disaster victims should therefore have sufficient provisions to survive the first 72 hours.

Q: To what extent can earthquakes be forecast?

Given the frequency of earthquakes in Japan, it is only natural that a great deal of research should have been undertaken to predict their occurrence. Still, the present state of affairs is that accurate prediction is a near impossibility. In the end, the workings of nature surpass human knowledge. The most that can be done is to stockpile the provisions and rations needed in case of emergency.

Q: How are earthquake warnings issued?

When seismic waves are detected by two or more earthquake sensors of a magnitude of 6.0 or higher, an emergency earthquake warning is issued by the Meteorological Agency

中地震 Moderate	小地震 Light	微小地震 Minor
震度5強・5弱 strong 5—weak 5	震度4・3 4 or 3	震度2・1 2 or 1

秒後に、震度○の揺れが襲ってきます」というように、テレビやラジオで放送される他、個人向けに携帯電話で入手できます。

地震発生地の自治体は、必要に応じて住民に避難勧告をし、場合によっては強制的な避難命令を出します。地震速報と関連して発表されるのが「津波警報」で、高さが3mを超える津波の場合は「大津波警報」となります。

Q: 巨大地震発生の可能性が高い地域は？

震度7以上の巨大地震が起きる可能性が高いとされているのは、南海トラフと首都圏直下の二つのエリアです。

南海トラフは、太平洋側の駿河湾（静岡県）から九州沖まで続く深さ約4000mの海溝で、東海・東南海・南海という三つの震源域があり、これらが連動して起きると言われています。もし、南海トラフで巨大地震が起きた場合は、死者32万人、経済的被害は東日本大震災の10倍超の220兆円とも推定されます。

もう一つの首都圏直下のエリアで巨大地震が発生した場合、被害はさらに大きくなります。東京湾岸が液状化して建物がことごとく倒壊、交通やライフラインが遮断され、東京で働く数百万人が帰宅困難になります。

as to the earthquake's source, arrival time, and strength. This is broadcast over radio and television and sent to mobile phones.

Local governments near the source of the quake issue evacuation warnings or mandatory evacuation announcements. In association with these warnings are tsunami warnings. Tsunamis of over 3-meters in height are referred to as large-scale tsunami.

Q: Which areas are prone to massive earthquakes?

The two areas likely to see massive earthquakes of over 7.0 in magnitude in the future are the area along the Nankai trough and the area directly beneath Tokyo.

The Nankai trough runs from Suruga Bay on the Pacific Ocean to the southern edge of Kyushu and is about 4,000 meters deep. There are said to be three sources of earthquakes along this trough—the Tokai, Tonankai, and Nankai regions. It is when these three move in combination that a massive earthquake occurs. In the case of a massive Nankai trough earthquake, it is estimated there would be 320,000 fatalities and damage of ¥220 trillion, ten times greater than the Great East Japan Earthquake.

In addition, if a massive earthquake were to occur directly beneath Tokyo, the damage would be even more catastrophic. There would be liquefaction in the reclaimed land along Tokyo Bay, buildings would topple in one fell swoop, transportation lifelines would be cut, and several hundred thousand people would have difficulty getting home.

3 税制

Q: 税金にはどんなものがあるの?

日本の税制は、所得・資産・消費に対する課税を基本としています。国民や企業が負担する税金は国税と地方税に大別され、所得課税分が約51%、資産課税分が約15%、消費課税分が約34%です。

所得税は企業勤務者は給料からの天引き、個人事業者は年1回の確定申告で納付します。資産課税には、不動産に関わる取得税・固定資産税・都市計画税・相続税などがあります。消費課税には、品物やサービスを提供された時にかかる消費税（8%）、酒税、たばこ税、石油ガス税、自動車重量税、関税などがあります。

日本は先進諸国の中では税金が高く、所得税の最高税率が45%、相続税が同じく55%、法人税の実効税率が約36%です。

Q: 国家予算はどのように決められるの?

国家予算は、4月1日から翌年3月31日までの収支をベースに策定されます。予算案は財務省が原案を作り、内閣が編成をした後、国会で審議され決定します。この過程では、各官庁や政治家による予算の分捕り合戦が展開されます。8月頃から財務省と各省庁の間で概算要求の検討が行われ、12月末までに財務省原案ができ、1月の国会で決定するというのが通常のプロセスですが、野党の反対で決定がずれ込むこ

3 Tax Administration

Q: What kinds of taxes are levied?

Basically, taxes are levied on income, assets, and consumption. The taxes that individuals and enterprises pay can be divided into two categories: national taxes and local taxes. Income taxes accounts for approximately 51% of total taxes, assets about 15%, and consumption about 34%.

Income taxes for employees of large companies are withheld by the employer, and everyone else pays once a year. Taxes on assets related to income from real estate include property taxes, city planning taxes, and inheritance taxes. Under the name of consumption taxes comes taxes levied when products or services are rendered (8%), alcohol taxes, tobacco taxes, gasoline taxes, automobile weight taxes, and custom duties.

Among advanced countries, taxes in Japan are relatively high, with the highest applicable income rate being 45%, inheritance tax 55%, and the effective tax rate on corporations about 36%.

Q: How is the national budget decided?

The national budget is decided on the basis of the projected revenues and spending covering April 1 to March 31. A draft is prepared by the Ministry of Finance, finalized by the Cabinet, and presented to the Diet for passage. During this process the various government offices and individual politicians try to increase their share of the budget. In August, equitable appropriations are considered by the Finance Ministry and various other ministries and agencies. In December a draft is drawn up by the Finance Ministry,

ともあります。

予算が配分されると、各省庁は3カ月ごとに支払い計画書を財務省に提出し、承認されると日本銀行から支払われます。国家予算は単年度決算が原則のため、各省庁は3月31日までに予算の全てを消化しなければなりません。そのため無駄が多い、と指摘されています。決算書のチェックは会計検査院が行いますが、税金がどんな使われ方をしたのかを知る国民は多くありません。

Q: 国家予算の規模と中身は？

2015年度の予算規模は、およそ96兆円です。内訳は、社会保障費が約31.5兆円、公共事業費が約6兆円、文教科学費が約5.3兆円、地方自治体への交付分が約15.5兆円、防衛費が約5兆円、その他9.5兆円となっています。15年度は税収が54.5兆円と、1991年以来の高水準が見込まれますが、これは消費税アップ（5％から8％）と企業業績の改善による法人税の増収が背景にあります。

一方、超高齢化時代を迎えている日本での社会保障費が毎年1兆円ずつ増え続けていることで、予算の規模増大に拍車がかかっています。税収の不足分は国民からの借金という形の国債で補てんしてきましたが、低成長経済下の日本では国債発行にも限度があります。

and in January this draft is approved by the Diet. This is the normal process, though there may be delays owing to dissent from opposition parties.

Once the budget is decided, the various ministries and agencies present spending plans to the Treasury every three months, and the appropriate funds are dispersed by the Bank of Japan. Since accounts are settled on a yearly basis, all appropriations made to government offices must be used by March 31. This, it has been pointed out by some, leads to wasteful spending. Accounts are checked by the Board of Audit, but in fact most Japanese don't know how their tax money is being spent.

Q: What is the size of the national budget?

Expenditures for the national budget of 2015 amount to some ¥96 trillion. This can be broken down approximately as follows: ¥31.5 trillion for social security, ¥6 trillion for public works, ¥5.3 trillion for education and science, ¥15.5 trillion for local allocation tax grants, ¥5 trillion for national defense, and ¥9.5 trillion for others. Tax revenues for 2015 are expected to reach ¥54.5 trillion, the highest since 1991. This is based on a hike in the consumption taxes (from 5% to 8%) and to a growth in corporate taxes due to improved economic conditions.

On the other hand, due to the aging of the Japanese population, social security costs are increasing at a rate of ¥1 trillion a year, leading to the ballooning of the budget. The shortfall in tax revenues has been filled by borrowing in the form of issuing government bonds, but given the sluggish economy, there is a limit to borrowing of this type.

Q: 政府が発行する国債とは？

政府が発行する債券には目的に応じていくつかの種類がありますが、ここでは建設国債と赤字国債について述べます。

建設国債は、住宅や道路などの社会資本の事業資金調達のために発行する債券です。これを発行しても、なお歳入が不足すると見込まれる場合に、公共事業費以外の歳出にあてる資金調達を目的にした国債を発行することが特例として認められています。これが、いわゆる赤字国債です。建設国債も赤字国債も、発行には国会での議決が必要です。

赤字国債はインフレを誘発するおそれがあるため、発行には限度額が定められています。ちなみに2014年の国債発行額は181兆円で、そのうちの35兆円が赤字国債でした。なお、普通国債の発行残高は180兆円と巨額になっています。

世界のトップレベルを維持してきた日本の国債の格付けが今や上から4番目に下落しています。米国の格付け機関が、巨額の国債を償還するだけの経済成長が見込めないと判断した結果です。国債の格付けの低下は、海外の投資家の投資意欲を低減させます。

Q: 財政破綻は本当なの？

財務省の役人は財政難ということをよく口にし、政治家も財政改革の必要性を力説します。しかし本当はどうなのかについて、明確に答えられる人はいません。なぜなら、国家財政には

Q: What are government bonds?

Government bonds can be classified according to their purpose. Here we will take a look at construction bonds and "red-ink" bonds.

Construction bonds are bonds issued to finance housing, roads and other public infrastructure. When these bonds fail to produce sufficient revenue, then other bonds can be issued as a special measure to finance undertakings other than public works. These are called "red-ink bonds." A Diet resolution is required to issue either type.

Since red-ink bonds can induce inflation, a limit is set on the amount that can be issued. In 2014 issued bonds were valued at ¥181 trillion, of which ¥35 trillion were red-ink bonds. Further, the balance of ordinary government bonds was a prodigious ¥180 trillion.

Although the rating for Japanese bonds had long been kept at a high level, recently it has fallen to fourth place, the result of American rating agencies determining that the sluggish Japanese economy was incapable of redeeming its huge bonds. A drop in rating discourages foreign investors from investing in the Japanese market.

Q: Is financial collapse possible?

Treasury officials often speak of the possibility of financial collapse, and politicians are fond of speaking out on the need for financial reform. However, very few people are actually able to address these subjects with any certainty. The reason

複雑なしくみがあるからです。例えば、国の予算は一般会計として計上されますが、それ以外に特別会計という科目があります。

これは特定の収入・支出をもって一般会計とは別に設ける会計で、2015年度の歳出総額は約403兆円です。これには国債償還費約90兆円、社会保障給付費約62.6兆円などが含まれますが、主な収入源は国民が納付した年金税や健康保険税やその運用で得た利子収入などです。一般会計の4倍もの予算がある特別会計は財務省の"隠し金庫"とも呼ばれ、国家財政のあいまいさを助長しています。

Q: 消費税はまだ上がるの？

日本では1989年に3％、97年に5％、2014年に8％と消費税が増税されました。そして2015年に10％とさらに増税を予定していましたが、消費低迷などの理由で見送られ、2017年4月1日から10％になることが決定しています。しかし、今後増加し続ける一方の社会保障費をカバーするには20％程度にまで上げるべきという意見もあります。

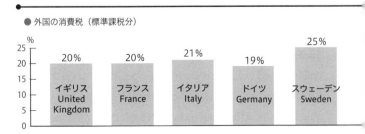

● 外国の消費税（標準課税分）

lies in the complexity of government finances. For example, the national budget is a general account, but the rest is handled under the heading of special accounting.

Special account budgets are designed for special government programs or institutions where close accounting of revenues and expenditures is essential. The annual special expenditures for 2015 were ¥403 trillion. This includes ¥90 trillion for the amortization of bonds and ¥62.6 trillion for social security costs. The principal source of revenue is the interest on pension and health insurance taxes. The special account budget is four times larger than the general account budget and is often referred to as the Treasury's "secret nest egg," further obfuscating the workings of national finance.

Q: Is the consumption tax going to be raised again?

A consumption tax was introduced in 1989 at 3%, raised to 5% in 1997, and to 8% in 2014. It was expected to be raised to 10% in 2015, but was postponed to April 1, 2017, due to low consumer activity. However, given the burgeoning costs of social security, some believe this tax should be raised as high as 20%.

Consumption Tax Abroad (Pro Forma Standard Taxation)

第4章 司法・治安
Law and Order

最高裁判所▶

1 司法

Q: 司法制度はどうなっているの?

日本の司法制度は、立法と行政から独立した「三権」の一つに位置付けられています。裁判官のトップの最高裁判所長官は総理大臣と同様に天皇が親任する特別職で、ここにも司法の独立が象徴されています。

裁判官と検察官は国家公務員ですが、弁護士は民間人という身分です。なお、検察官は行政職という立場になります。

Q: どんな裁判所があるの?

裁判は、一つの事件について三回まで裁判を求めることができる「三審制」を採用しています。裁判所はその制度に対応して設置されていて、全国に約430カ所ある簡易裁判所、同じく50カ所ある家庭裁判所と地方裁判所、高等裁判所（8カ所）、最高裁判所（1カ所）の5種があります。簡易裁判所が第一審になる民事事件以外の全ての第三審を担当するのが最高裁判所で、その判決は「法の番人」が下す最終決定になります。

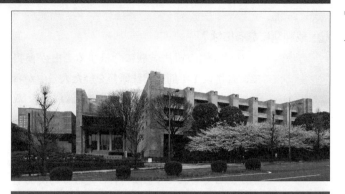

1 The Law

Q: What is the legal system?

The judiciary branch of government is one of three independent branches along with the executive and legislative. The chief justice of the Supreme Court is appointed by the prime minister and attested by the emperor.

Judges and prosecutors are civil servants, but attorneys at law are civilians. Public prosecutors are members of the executive branch.

Q: What kind of courts does Japan have?

In the adjudication of a single incident, three appeals are permitted. There are a number of courts around the country that make this possible: summary courts in 430 locations, family courts and district courts in 50 locations, high courts in 8 locations, and the Supreme Court in 1 location. Except in cases where a summary court is the court of first instance, the Supreme Court serves as the court of last appeal, the "guardian of the law."

Q: 裁判官になるには？

国家試験の司法試験に合格することが前提で、合格後1年間の司法研修を経た人の中から選ばれます。判事補10年の任期を務めた後、裁判官としてのキャリア・システムに基づき各種の裁判所で判事（裁判官）として仕事に携わります。検察官や弁護士から就任する例もありますが、ごくまれです。裁判官の定数は約3700名（2013年）です。

Q: 検察官の役割は？

検察官には、国家を代表して刑事事件の犯罪者を裁判にかける「公訴権」と犯罪の「捜査権」という強い権限が与えられています。検察庁は行政官庁として法務大臣の監督下にありますが、法務大臣は検察官トップの検事総長に対して指揮権を発動することは禁じ手とされています。検察官の起訴について、国民がチェックする「検察審査会制度」もあります。

Q: 弁護士の仕事は？

さまざまなトラブルに関しての法律事務を行うのが仕事です。民事では法律相談、和解や示談交渉、訴訟、不服申立てなど、刑事事件では被疑者や被告人の弁護活動を行います。弁護士は原則として司法試験に合格後1年間の司法研修を経た後に開業できますが、身分は自営業です。弁護士は約3万5000名で、そのうち女性は6000名です（2015年）。

Q: How does one become a judge?

The first condition for becoming a judge is to successfully pass the national bar exam. After clearing this hurdle, candidates must spend one year at the Legal Training and Research Institute. Judges are chosen from this group. After serving 10 years as an assistant judge (called the career system), the candidate becomes a judge at the various courts mentioned above. Judges are also chosen from among public prosecutors and practicing attorneys, but only rarely. As of 2013, the number of judges was some 3,700.

Q: What is the function of a public prosecutor?

Representing the government, the public prosecutor has the power to bring criminal cases to court and to investigate crimes. As part of the executive branch, the Public Prosecutors Office is under the Ministry of Justice, but it is generally considered unacceptable for the Justice Minister to exercise his authority over the Public Prosecutor General. The public can assess the work of the public prosecutor by means of the Committees for the Inquest of Prosecution.

Q: What is the function of a lawyer?

Lawyers deal with the legal aspects of contentious issues. In civil cases, they act as legal consultants, negotiate compromises or out-of-court settlements, institute legal proceedings, file appeals, and so forth. In criminal cases, they defend the suspect or accused. Lawyers can set up a private practice after passing the bar examination and completing one year of training. The number of lawyers in Japan at present is some 35,000, of which 6,000 are women (as of 2015).

司法研修所

> ▶司法試験
>
> 受験資格は法科大学院課程を修了するか予備試験合格者のいずれかです。予備試験は資格制限がなく、2段階の筆記試験に合格後、口述試験に合格(5年間で)しなければなりません。

Q: 裁判の種類は?

大別すると、民事裁判と刑事裁判の二つになります。民事裁判では訴えた側を「原告」、訴えられた側を「被告」と呼びますが、刑事裁判は訴えるのは検察官で、事件の容疑者は「被告人」と呼ばれます。

ごく軽い事件は簡易裁判所、家庭問題や未成年者の事件は家庭裁判所、それ以外の事件は地方裁判所が第一審を担当します。また、国や自治体などの公権力の行使の適法性を争う行政訴訟もあります。

Q: 裁判員制度って、なに?

刑事裁判で国民の代表が裁判員として関わる制度で、2009年5月から実施されています。裁判員候補は選挙の有権者名簿から無作為に抽出され、裁判官が認める以外の理由で辞退することはできず、候補になったことも含めて守秘義務が課されます。

> ▶ **The Bar Examination**
> In order to take the bar exam, examinees must have completed graduate studies at a law school or have passed the preliminary bar exam. The preliminary exam, for which there are no qualifications, consists of two stages: a written exam (within five years' time) and an oral test.

Q: What kinds of trials are there?

Broadly speaking, there are two types, those involving civil cases and those involving criminal cases. In civil cases, the party that brings the case to court is called the plaintiff (*genkoku*) and the party who is sued or accused, the defendant (*hikoku*). In criminal cases, the suing or accusing party is the public prosecutor (*kensatsu-kan*) and the suspect the defendant (*hikoku-nin*).

Minor cases are handled by summary courts, and cases involving family matters and minors by family courts. District courts are the court of the first instance in all other matters. Other than this, there is administrative litigation, which deals with lawsuits involving the appropriateness of laws concerning local or central government.

Q: What is the lay judge system?

The lay judge system is a kind of jury trial in which ordinary citizens are selected to take part in criminal cases as judges. It went into effect in May 2009. Lay judges are chosen at random from voter registrations, and they are mandated to meet this obligation except for reasons countenanced by a judge. They are sworn to strict confidentiality, even concerning the fact that they have been chosen as lay judges.

一つの刑事裁判で、6名の裁判員が裁判官と共に審理・判決に加わります。

Q: どんな罰則があるの？

刑罰には、軽い順に①拘留、②禁錮、③有期懲役、④無期懲役、⑤死刑のほか、財産刑として①没収、②科料、③罰金があります。

禁錮刑は原則1カ月以上20年以下、有期懲役刑は原則1カ月以上30年以下の期間が指定されます。懲役刑は刑務所内で所定の作業をさせる刑罰で、禁錮刑は所定の作業を行わずに自由を奪われる刑罰です。

3年以下の懲役または禁錮、50万円以下の罰金刑については刑の執行を1年〜5年以下に限って猶予する制度があり、執行猶予期間中に罪を重ねなかった場合には刑の執行を免れることができます。

無期懲役とは本人が死亡することで刑の満期となる刑罰で、「刑法」では10年以上服役すれば仮釈放できるとしていますが、実際には有期懲役者とのバランスをとる上から許可されるケースは多くありません。

罰金は、国家が個人または法人から強制的に金銭を取り立てる刑罰で1万円以上と定められています。1万円未満の場合は科料となります。

In a single criminal case, six lay judges take part with a judge to examine evidence and reach a decision.

Q: What kinds of punishment are carried out?

Punishment of convicted criminals consists of the following (in ascending order of severity): 1) custody, 2) detention, 3) limited imprisonment with penal labor, 4) life imprisonment with penal labor, and 5) capital punishment. Financial penalties include 1) confiscation, 2) light fines, and 3) heavy financial penalties.

As a rule, detention consists of more than one month and less than 20 years. Limited imprisonment consists of more than one month and less than 30 years. Limited and life imprisonment with penal labor refers to incarceration in which labor is carried out within the prison, and detention means the loss of freedom without penal labor.

In limited imprisonment with labor or detention of three years or less, and a penalty of ¥500,000, probation is possible with terms of one to five years, but if another crime is committed during probation, punishment cannot be evaded.

In life imprisonment with penal labor, the term of imprisonment reaches completion with the death of the prisoner. According to the law, parole is possible for such prisoners, but in order to maintain a balance with prisoners serving limited imprisonment, it is not often granted.

Financial penalties, which essentially refer to the government forcibly extracting money from individuals or corporations, involve sums of ¥10,000 or more. Lesser sums are considered fines.

Q: 死刑は行われているの?

先進国の中で日本は、米国と共に死刑存置国です。死刑囚は、刑務所でなく処刑場を備えた拘置所に収容されます。そこで刑の執行をされる日を待つことになるのですが、いつなのかは知らされません。処刑日は法務大臣が執行命令書にサインをしてから5日以内とされています。中にはサインを拒む法務大臣もいて、在任中に死刑執行がゼロというケースもあります。確定死刑囚は129名(2013年)で、執行されるのは年間5名前後です。

2 警 察

Q: 警察機構はどうなっているの?

日本には約26万人の警察官がいて、国内の治安を守っています。警察官のほとんどは都道府県の地方公務員という立場ですが、キャリアと呼ばれる一部の警察官僚は警察庁採用の国家公務員です。毎年、女性警察官は約1600名採用されています。

警察庁は国家公安委員会の、警視庁は東京都、道府県の警察本部は道府県の公安委員会の監督下にあります。全国には1169の警察署があり、その下に交番・駐在所が設置されています(2014年4月)。

Q: Is the death penalty imposed?

Among advanced countries, only Japan and the United States impose the death penalty. Death row inmates are incarcerated not in prisons but in a detention center equipped with an execution chamber. Death row inmates await the day of their execution within these centers, but they are not informed of the day when it will be carried out. Execution is administered within five days after the Justice Minister signs an order of execution. Some Ministers are reluctant to sign such orders, and consequently no executions are administered during their term in office. As of 2013, 129 prisoners are awaiting execution. Some five inmates are executed every year.

2 The Police

Q: How is the police organized?

There are about 260,000 police officers in charge of domestic law enforcement. Although most of them are civil servants in the employ of local administrative units, there are some career officers who are national civil servants under the National Police Agency. Approximately 1,600 female officers are hired every year.

The National Police Agency is under the National Public Safety Commission; the Metropolitan Police Department under the Tokyo Metropolis; and prefectural Police Headquarters under the Public Safety Commission. Nationwide there are 1,169 police stations (as of 2014), under which are situated police boxes (*koban*) and residential police boxes (*chuzaisho*).

Q: 警察官の階級は？

巡査から警視総監まで10階級（正式には9階級）があり、警部補以上は「司法警察員」、それ以下は「司法巡査」という区分がされています。警察庁採用のキャリアは、入庁時に警部補の階級からスタートし、30代前半で警察署長クラスの警視正へとスピード昇進をします。

Q: 逮捕されるとどうなるの？

刑事事件では、現行犯以外は裁判官が発令する逮捕状が必要になります。被疑者には黙秘権と弁護士を選ぶ権利があり、逮捕に際してはこの二つの権利があることを告げなければなりません。

逮捕された被疑者は、警察署の留置所などに拘束され取調べを受けます。警察の調書や証拠資料をもとに検察官は逮捕後48時間以内に裁判所に対して勾留請求をし、10日間の身柄拘束（最長25日間）期間内で起訴・不起訴・釈放の判断をします。

Q: 受刑者はどこに収容されるの？

裁判で刑が決定した犯罪者は、刑事施設に収容されます。刑事施設には、成人受刑者用の刑務所（男女別）、少年刑務所があり、女性の場合は未成年者も成人と同じ施設に収容されます。

施設内では受刑態度によって待遇を評価するランク付け（一般的に5段階）があり、それに

Q: What are the ranks of police officers?

From patrol officer to chief of the National Police Agency, there are 10 ranks (9 officially). Lieutenants and above are referred to as judicial police officers, and those below as judicial patrol officers. Those hired by the National Police Agency as career officers start out as lieutenants and are fast-tracked to chief of a large police station by their early thirties.

Q: What happens if you are arrested?

In criminal matters, with the exception of cases where the perpetrator has been caught in the act, a warrant from a judge is necessary for an arrest to be made. The suspect has the right to silence and a lawyer, and he or she must be informed of these rights at the time of arrest.

The arrested suspect is held in detention at a police station and is questioned there. Based on the report and evidentiary material provided by the police, within 48 hours a public prosecutor must receive permission from a judge to keep the suspect in custody pending trial. Within the following 10 days of detention, a decision must be made whether to indict or acquit.

Q: Where are convicted criminals incarcerated?

Individuals convicted of a crime are confined to penal institutions. Penal institutions are distinguished by whether they are for adults (separate for male and female prisoners) or for juveniles. Female adult prisoners and female juvenile prisoners are housed together.

Inmates are evaluated and ranked according to their behavior (usually five ranks), which affects the number of

よって面会の回数や差入れ内容が変わってくるそうです。

Q: どんな犯罪が多いの?

2013年のデータによると、刑法犯の認知件数はおよそ131.4万件で、そのうち警察が事件として取り扱った検挙件数は39.4万件。

近年、急増して大きな社会問題になっているのが、高齢者を対象にした電話による詐欺事件(振り込め詐欺)、薬物乱用(脱法ドラッグ)です。振り込め詐欺では判明しているだけでも被害額が年間489.5億円、薬物乱用は約1.3万件にのぼっています。

また、来日外国人による犯罪件数も増えていて、1.5万件を突破しました。

3 防衛

Q: 自衛隊は軍隊ではないの?

憲法第9条に「陸海空軍その他の戦力は、これを保持しない。国の交戦権は、これを認めない」と明記されている以上、日本は軍隊を持つことが許されていません。

とはいえ、他国から攻められた場合に限って防衛のための手段として対抗する武力を持つという解釈が、自衛隊の存在理由なのです。

visitors permitted and the nature of care packages receivable.

Q: What are the most common crimes?

According to data for 2013, there were 1.314 million violations of the Penal Code, of which 394,000 involved the police and resulted in arrests.

Crimes that have recently become social issues include fraudulent telephone calls targeting the elderly (asking for bank deposits under false pretences) and drug misuse (particularly of difficult to control substances). The known damages incurred annually by fraudulent telephone calls is estimated to be ¥48.95 billion. Cases involving misuse of drugs is said to be some 13,000.

The number of crimes committed by foreigners in Japan is also on the rise, exceeding 15,000 incidents.

3 Defense

Q: Is not the so-called Self-Defense Force in fact an army?

According to the Japanese constitution, "… land, sea, and air forces, as well as other war potential, will never be maintained. The right of belligerency of the state will not be recognized." This means that Japan is not permitted to maintain a military establishment, that is, an army.

The rationale for the existence of the Self-Defense Force (SDF) is that it provides the sole means of self-defense in case Japan is attacked by a foreign power.

しかし、年間予算5兆円の防衛費と約25万人の自衛官という規模、加えて装備や規律などからすると、外国に軍隊と認知されても不思議はありません。自民党の中には、自衛隊を国防軍と改称すべきという声も高まっています。

Q: シビリアンコントロールとは？

民主国家では、政治が武力集団である軍を統制するシステムの「シビリアンコントロール（文民統制）」が採用されています。日本もこれにならって自衛隊の最高指揮権は、内閣総理大臣が議長を務める安全保障会議にあると定めています。

Q: 自衛隊の組織はどうなっているの？

防衛省の下に陸上自衛隊（陸上総隊）、海上自衛隊（自衛艦隊）、航空自衛隊（航空総隊）があります。それぞれのトップは幕僚長と呼ばれ、3名の幕僚長が持ち回りで制服組の最高指揮者の統合幕僚長を務めます。自衛官の階級は幕僚長まで18あり、この点でも外国の軍隊同様のランク付けがされています。なお、約25万人の自衛官の他に、志願制の予備自衛官が約6万人（2014年）います。

陸上自衛隊は約16万人の隊員がいて、5つの方面隊、ヘリコプター団、水陸機動団、機動師団・旅団があります。方面隊の下には5師団、2旅

However, given that the annual budget of the SDF is ¥5 trillion, and that it has personnel of some 250,000 men and women, in addition to the equipment possessed and discipline displayed by the SDF, it should come as no surprise if foreign countries view the SDF as a military establishment. Within the Liberal Democratic Party, there is an increasing number of people who argue that the SDF should be renamed the National Defense Force.

Q: Is the Self-Defense Force under civilian control?

In democratic countries, the military is placed under civilian political leadership. In Japan, ultimate responsibility for the SDF lies in the hands of the Security Council of Japan, which is headed by the prime minister.

Q: What is the structure of the Self-Defense Force?

Under the Ministry of Defense there are three military branches: the Ground Self-Defense Force, the Maritime Self-Defense Force, and the Air Self-Defense Force. Each branch is headed by a chief of staff, and these three take turns serving as chief of staff of the joint chiefs of staff, the highest ranking military position. From chief of staff downward, there are 18 ranks, much like ranking in other countries. As of 2014 there are approximately 250,000 active personnel and some 60,000 reserve personnel.

The Ground Self-Defense Force has 160,000 personnel and encompasses 5 regional armies as well as helicopter, amphibious rapid deployment, and rapid deployment

団があります。海上自衛隊は、艦隊と5つの地方隊で編成されています。航空自衛隊には、総隊と3つの集団、補給本部があります。

Q: 自衛官には女性もいるの？

女性自衛官は1.2万人で、全体の5％ほどです。そのうち将校は約2000人、中には階級の上位3番目に当る将補に昇進した人もいます。

一般募集のケースでは、競争率が20〜50倍といわれるほど人気が高いのが女性自衛官で、艦長やパイロットとして男性顔負けの活躍をする先輩の姿に憧れて入隊してくる人も多いようです。

Q: 自衛隊の主な装備はどうなっているの？

陸上自衛隊には戦車が約900両、装甲車が約950両、野戦砲が約660門、航空機約500機などが配備されています。

海上自衛隊には、護衛艦53隻、潜水艦16隻、航空機およそ310機などです。

航空自衛隊には、航空機が約500機あり、そのうち戦闘機が370機ほどを占めています。

brigades and divisions. The regional armies have 5 divisions and 2 brigades. The Maritime Self-Defense Force is comprised of the fleet and 5 district forces. The Air Self-Defense Force includes the Air Defense Command, 5 district forces, and an Air Support Command.

Q: Do women serve in the Self-Defense Force?

At present there are some 12,000 female personnel in the Self-Defense Force, approximately 5% of the total. Of that number about 2,000 are commissioned officers, including those who have risen to the third highest rank of major general or rear admiral.

In general, the acceptance rate for female applicants is from 20 to 50 times the number of applications, with many hoping to emulate female officers who are already serving as navy captains or pilots.

Q: How is the Self-Defense Force equipped?

The Ground Self-Defense Force has approximately 900 tanks, 950 armored vehicles, 660 field guns, and 500 airplanes.

The Maritime Self-Defense Force has 53 escort ships, 16 submarines, and about 310 airplanes.

The Air Self-Defense Force has approximately 500 airplanes, of which some 370 are fighters.

第4章 司法・治安

Q: 海上自衛官と海上保安官の違いは？

　島国の日本の領海（海岸線から約22.2km）を守るのは海上自衛官の役目ですが、その役割を分担しているのが、海上保安官。こちらは国土交通省の外局の海上保安庁の職員です。

　海上の警察・消防の両面を担当する特殊任務のため、海上保安官には海上保安大学校または海上保安学校の卒業者しかなれません。この点で、一般募集での入隊が可能な自衛官とは大きく違います。外国船舶の不法行為や密猟の取締り、海難救助などの危険業務が多い中、海上保安官として活躍しているのは約1万2000名。

Q: What is the difference between the Maritime Self-Defense Force and the Japan Coast Guard?

It is the duty of the Maritime Self-Defense Force to protect the territorial waters of Japan (22.2 km from the coastline). This duty is shared by the Coast Guard, which is a government agency operating under the oversight of the Ministry of Land, Infrastructure, Transport and Tourism.

Since the Coast Guard is responsible for such specialized duties as firefighting and patrolling, its members must be graduates of the Japan Coast Guard Academy or the Japan Coast Guard School. This is a major difference between the Coast Guard and the Self-Defense Force, which accepts applications from the general public. There are approximately 12,000 members engaged in the control of illegal activities by foreign vessels, sea rescues, and other dangerous duties.

第5章 社会保障・医療
Social Security and Healthcare

医療用ロボット ダヴィンチ ▶

1 社会保障

Q: 社会保障制度はどうなっているの?

　日本国憲法は、国は国民の生活を生涯にわたって支えることを明記しています。これに基づき、社会保障制度が整備され、①社会保険、②社会福祉、③公的扶助、④保健医療・公衆衛生に大別されます。

　このうち社会保険は、医療、介護、年金の分野で国民から集めた保険料をもとに運営されています。しかし、少子高齢化時代に入ってしまったため、保険料収入と給付のバランスがとれなくなってきています。象徴的なのは、毎年、1兆円も増え続ける社会保障給付費です。

　2012年度の給付費は医療に35.1兆円、年金に53.8兆円、介護他に20.6兆円の計109.5兆円でしたが、40.3兆円は国が財政負担分として支出しました。国民の3人に1人が65歳以上の高齢者になる2025年度には、給付費が約150兆円必要になると見込まれています。

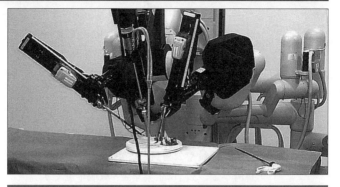

1 Social Security

Q: How is social security organized?

According to the constitution, the state has the duty to support the life of the people. The social security system is based on this principle and can be classified into four areas: 1) social insurance, 2) social welfare, 3) public assistance, and 4) healthcare and public hygiene.

Social security is supported by the premiums collected from the public in the areas of healthcare, welfare for the elderly, and pensions. However, with the aging of the population and low birthrate, an imbalance has been created between income and expenditure. The most outstanding example of this is the fact that social security outlays continue to increase at a rate of ¥1 trillion a year.

In 2012 expenditures amounted to ¥109.5 trillion, with healthcare accounting for ¥35.1 trillion, pensions for ¥53.8 trillion, and elderly welfare for ¥20.6 trillion, but of this amount ¥40.3 trillion was paid out by the government. By 2025, when one-third of the population will be age 65 or older, government expenditures are expected to reach ¥150 trillion.

消費税の増税分は、社会保障の充実と安定化のための財源という理由付けがされています。

Q: 年金保険のしくみは?

年金制度は3階建ての建物にたとえられます。1階は基礎年金ともいわれる国民年金、2階は会社員や公務員などが加入する厚生年金・共済年金、3階は企業年金・職域年金です。

国民年金は20歳になると加入が義務付けられ、60歳まで保険料を支払い、65歳から受給できます。一時、5000万件もの加入者記録が「消えた」ことで大きな社会問題になりました。また、保険料の未納が多く、赤字体質になっています。2階、3階の年金加入者は国民年金に上積みされた給付を受けることができます。

Q: 年金はいくらもらえるの?

2013年度のデータでは、国民年金の平均受給月額は5.45万円で、1万円未満〜7万円以上までと、ばらつきがあります。これは、年金を納めた期間に比例して受給額が決まるからです。

一方、厚生年金の平均受給額は、男性が16.64万円、女性が10.2万円で、国民年金の約2.7倍です。さらに企業年金分を加えると、月額25万円前後になる人もいます。そのぶん掛け金を多く

The reason given for raising the consumer tax is that it will help stabilize and enhance the social security system.

Q: How does the pension system work?

The Japanese pension system has been likened to a three-story building. The first story provides a basic pension and is called the National Pension Fund. The second story consists of Employees Pension Insurance and Mutual Aid Pensions for company employees and civil servants. The third story comprises corporate pension plans and occupational pension schemes.

All citizens must take part in the National Pension Fund upon reaching the age of twenty, continue to pay premiums until the age of 60, and begin receiving benefits at 65. At one point, the records of 50,000,000 people paying social security premiums simply disappeared, causing a huge social uproar. Moreover, there are many cases of failure to pay, and the result is a system drenched in red ink. For those taking part in the second and third levels of the pension system, benefits are accrued in addition to those of the National Pension Fund.

Q: How much can one receive from pension funds?

According to 2013 statistics on the National Pension Fund, the average person can expect to receive ¥54,500 per month, from a low of less than ¥10,000 to a high of ¥70,000. The amount depends on the number of years that premiums were paid.

In contrast, the average monthly benefit of the Employees Pension Insurance is 2.7 times that of the National Pension Fund (¥166,400 for men and ¥102,000 for women). With the addition of corporate pension plans, there are some people

払ってきたわけですが、いずれにしても、国民年金だけでは老後の暮らしは楽でないことだけはたしかです。

Q: 日本人の平均寿命は？

日本の平均寿命は年々延びていて、男性が80.21歳、女性が86.61歳（2014年）。女性は世界一で、男性は世界4位です。敗戦直後の国民の平均寿命は50歳ほどだったので、70年足らずで30歳も寿命が延びたことになります。

日本人を長寿にしたのは、何よりも戦争とは無縁な平和社会が続いたこと、栄養価の高い食事、そして医療の進歩です。しかし長寿社会になったのと引き換えに、介護や孤独死など老いをめぐる諸問題が起きています。

Q: 日本一の長寿県はどこ？

長野県です。2010年の国勢調査で、男女共に平均寿命がトップになりました。長野県には地域の健康を守る住民組織があり、日常的に健康教育や栄養指導を行っていて、その地道な活動が実を結んだといえます。また、標高が高くコメ作りに不向きだったことから野菜や果樹栽培が発達し、中でも特産のリンゴ・ブドウの皮には長寿遺伝子を活性化するポリフェノールが含まれるため、これが長野県民の長寿を支えているのではないかとの説もあります。

who receive a monthly average of around ¥250,000; the insurance premiums they paid were, of course, that much larger. In any event, it is safe to say that a national pension is not enough to ease the latter years of one's life.

Q: What is the average life expectancy of a Japanese?

The average life expectancy is growing year by year, with the average for men now being 80.21 and that for women 86.61 (as of 2014). That places women first in the world, men fourth. In the immediate postwar period, the average life span was 50, meaning that there has been a growth of 30 years in a short 70-year period.

This achievement was made possible by the peaceful years that followed the war, a more nutritious diet, and advances made in healthcare. On the other hand, this increase in life expectancy has ushered in other problems, such as care of the elderly and the forlorn deaths of elderly people living on their own.

Q: What prefecture has the longest life expectancy?

That would be Nagano prefecture. According to the 2010 national consensus, Nagano had the highest expected average lifespan for both men and women. The prefecture has community organizations devoted to protecting the health of the area's inhabitants by providing daily healthcare education and dietary guidance. It was such unheralded efforts that resulted in the good health of the prefecture. Another factor has been the fact that the elevation of the prefecture is too high for the effective production of rice, resulting instead in the cultivation of vegetables and fruit. One of the substances

Q: 介護保険とは？

老齢で介護が必要になった時などに、公的サービスを受けるための保険です。40歳になったら加入が義務付けられ、受給資格は①65歳以上、②40歳〜64歳の2種があります。保険料は市区町村ごとに決められますが、おおむね月額5000円前後です。

受給するには、市区町村の審査を経て「要介護認定」がされなければならず、これには必要度の高い順に5段階のランク付けがあります。サービスは内容ごとに単価が決められ、利用額の1割と支給限度額を超えた分は自己負担です。受給資格者3000万人のうち約550万人が介護サービスを利用しています（2013年）。

Q: どんな介護施設があるの？

一般的には「老人ホーム」と呼ばれ、公的施設と民間施設に大別されます。公的施設には、介護の必要度に応じて特別養護老人ホーム、介護保健施設、介護療養施設があります。利用料が安いことから希望者が多いのですが、特別養護老人ホームは待機者が40万人超といわれる狭き門です。

found in Nagano apples and grapes, polyphenol, is known to stimulate genes connected with long livelihood, and this is offered as one of the reasons for the prefecture's long life expectancy.

Q: What is nursing care insurance?

Nursing care insurance is insurance to provide public care services for the elderly in need of nursing. Participation in the program is mandatory for those of 40 years of age and above, and eligibility for benefits comes in two types: 1) for those 65 and above and 2) for those between 40 and 64. Premiums are determined at the local administrative level, but about ¥5,000 a month is the norm.

In order to receive insurance benefits, the applicants must be screened by the local administrative units and obtain a care requirement certification. The need for care is divided into five categories, with the service costs for each category being individually fixed. Costs exceeding the determined amount plus 10% are borne by the individual. Of the 30 million persons now eligible for benefits, 5.5 million are making use of available services (as of 2013).

Q: What kinds of nursing care facilities exist?

Nursing homes can be divided into two categories, the public and the private. The public facilities encompass homes for elderly people requiring special care, homes for the elderly with public elderly care insurance, and elderly nursing homes, depending on the extent of the care needed. The less expensive facilities are much in demand, and the homes for elderly people requiring special care are said to have a

その点、民間施設は入所しやすいのですが"お金次第"で、グレードが高くなると数千万円の権利金、月額数十万の経費がかかるケースもあります。

2 医療

Q: 医療制度の特徴は？

日本の医療制度の特徴は「国民皆保険」といって、誰もがいつでもどこでも、公平に医療を受けられる点にあります。外国人の場合も、外国人登録後1年以上滞在していると認められる場合は、受給資格があります。

医療保険は職種によっていくつかの種類があり、利用する場合は同一条件となりますが、70歳以上は年齢・所得によって自己負担割合が変わってきます。75歳以上は、都道府県を単位とする広域連合が運営する後期高齢者医療保険に加入することが義務付けられています。

Q: 混合診療とは？

日本では保険による医療が原則のため、保険が適用されない医療を受ける場合、その全額を実費で負担しなければなりません。例えば歯科治療では、治療費は保険が適用されても、高額な材質の義歯などを作った場合、その分は自己

lengthy waiting list of over 400,000 people.

In that respect, private facilities are easier to get into, but the higher levels can be extremely costly, with "moving-in" fees often amounting to several tens of thousands of yen and monthly fees of several hundreds of thousands of yen.

2 Healthcare

Q: What are the principal features of the healthcare system?

Universal healthcare is the principal feature of Japanese healthcare, meaning that anyone can receive healthcare coverage at any time. Foreigners are eligible to receive medical treatment the same as anyone else if their foreign registration card shows that they have been in the country for at least one year.

There are several types of health insurance depending on the occupation one is engaged in, although the conditions for using the system are the same. Also, the premiums paid by those over 70 vary according to age and income. For those over 75, joining a regional late-geriatric association run by local governments is mandatory.

Q: What is mixed treatment?

While as a rule all medical costs are covered by insurance, there are exceptional cases where the full costs must be borne by the insuree. For example, when dentures are made with expensive materials, the insuree must bear the cost of the material. This is called mixed treatment. However, in

負担になります。これを混合診療といいますが、現在、歯科以外の医療では原則的に認められていません。その理由は、混合診療を認めるとお金持ちが優遇されるおそれがあり、保険診療の公平さが失われるからです。

Q: 窓口負担とは?

医療機関で受診をする際、保険証を提示しなければなりません。継続して受診する場合でも、月1回提示する義務があります。受診後、一定の金額を請求され、その場で支払いますが、これを窓口負担といいます。

この負担分は、小学校入学前の子どもは2割、小学生～69歳が3割、70歳～74歳が2割(一定以上の所得者は3割)、75歳以上が1割(一定以上の所得者は3割)と、年齢・所得によって変わります。

Q: 病院はなぜ待ち時間が長いの?

医療機関は、入院用のベッド数によって病院と診療所に大別されます。しかし、多くの診療所は開業医といわれる医師が経営しています。そこで患者は、高度な検査機器を備え、医師がたくさんいる病院に集中します。その結果、病院は混雑し、「3時間待って、3分間診療」という状況になってしまうのです。これを改善するために、病院を受診する場合は初診料を高くしたり、開業医の紹介状が必要といった方式が採

general, mixed treatment is not allowed outside the field of dental care since doing so would give an unfair advantage to the wealthier classes.

Q: What does "pay on the spot" mean?

When receiving treatment at a medical institution, you must show your health insurance card. Even over a period of consecutive visits, you must show the card at least once every month. After receiving treatment, you must pay the applicable amount "on the spot" at the cashier's window.

The fee to be paid by the insuree amounts to 20% of the total costs for pre-elementary school students, 30% for those of elementary school age up to the age of 69, 20% for those aged 70 to 74 (30% for those with an income over a certain amount), and 10% for those 75 and older (30% for those with an income over a certain amount), with the insuree's proportion varying according to age and income.

Q: Why is waiting time at hospitals so long?

Medical institutions are classified as hospitals or clinics according to the number of beds available for hospitalization. Most clinics are run by general practitioners, and many patients prefer to go to a hospital that has the latest in medical equipment and a good number of attending physicians. This results in congestion at hospitals, giving rise to the phrase "a three hour wait for a three minute consultation." In an attempt to rectify this situation, hospitals charge higher first-time consultation fees or require letters of introduction from

用されています。

Q: 薬の値段はどのように決めているの?

薬価は中央社会保険医療協議会で検討され、厚生労働省が告知する薬価基準に基づいて決められます。

日本には昔から「薬九層倍」という言葉があり、薬が儲けが大きいことを意味しています。しかし、現代では薬は開発費が高く、競争も激しいことから大きな利益が見込めなくなってきているのです。それでも年間の医療費40兆円のうち薬剤費が7兆円を占めるほど、薬の需要は高まっています(2014年)。

Q: 大衆薬とは?

医師が処方する医薬品以外の薬を、一般用医薬品(大衆薬)といいます。とはいえ薬である以上、副作用の危険性があるため、薬剤師という国家資格を持った人しか販売できないことになっていましたが、2009年6月から規制が緩和されました。

風邪薬や頭痛薬など比較的副作用が少ないものに限って、登録販売者の資格があれば扱ってもよいことになったのです。そこでコンビニなどにも大衆薬が置かれることになり、便利になりました。登録販売資格で扱える大衆薬は、第2類医薬品と第3類医薬品の2種で、約230種あります。このうち第2類はやや副作用が強い薬で、販売者は購入者に対して情報提供するこ

clinical doctors.

Q: How is the price of medicine decided?

Upon advice from the Central Social Insurance Medical Council, the price of medicine is determined by the Ministry of Health, Labour and Welfare and announced in its official medical price standard.

From olden times, medicine has been known for its low production costs and high retail prices. Today, however, development costs have skyrocketed and price competition is fierce, lowering the expectations for huge profits. Even so, medicine accounts for ¥3 trillion of the total ¥40 trillion in annual medical costs (as of 2014), showing that demand is still growing.

Q: What is "medicine for the masses"?

Medicine that can be sold directly to the customer without a prescription is called *taishu-yaku* or "medicine for the masses"—that is, over-the-counter medicine. Since even such non-prescription drugs can have side effects, they could only be sold by a licensed pharmacist until June 2009 when regulations were loosened.

Subsequently it became possible for registered retailers to sell drugs with relatively mild side effects, such as medicine for colds and headaches. This opened the door for sale at convenience stores and similar outlets, making medicine much more accessible. The medicine that registered retailers can sell are called type 2 drugs and type 3 drugs, of which there are some 230 different varieties. Type 2 drugs have somewhat strongers side effects, and a pharmacist must be available at

とが義務付けられています。

Q: 日本人に多い病気は？

医療機関を受診した患者数では、高血圧、虫歯・歯周病、白内障がトップ3を占めます。高血圧は塩分の多い和食にも原因があるとされます。虫歯・歯周病が多いのは予防に対する意識が低いことが理由の一つにあげられています。白内障は老化に伴う目の病気で、超高齢化社会では必然的に増えるものです。

病気による死亡率では、がん、心疾患、脳血管疾患がトップ3です。がんは、今や国民の3人に1人がかかる病気とされますが、日本人に多いのが胃がんで、死亡者数が多いのは肺がん、食生活の欧米化に伴って増えているとされるのが大腸がんです。また、女性の乳がん、子宮がんも増加傾向にあります。

Q: 生活習慣病とは？

食事、睡眠、運動など日常の生活習慣が原因で起きる病気の総称です。この予防には、子どもの頃からの正しい生活習慣が必要とされます。

病気になりやすい悪い生活習慣とは、運動不足、間食や夜食のとり過ぎ、甘いもの・脂っこいものの食べ過ぎなどです。また、喫煙や飲酒、ストレスなども生活習慣病の誘発原因とされています。中でもタバコは、生活習慣病のみならず

the point of sale to provide information and advice.

Q: What kind of illnesses are Japanese susceptible to?

The three most common illnesses of people seeking medical care are high-blood pressure, dental caries and periodontal diseases, and cataracts. High-blood pressure is attributed to the abundance of salt in the traditional Japanese diet. Caries and periodontal diseases are a result of the low awareness of dental care. Cataracts are an accompaniment of the aging process and an inevitable phenomenon in a society with a superabundance of elderly citizens.

The three most frequent causes of death are cancer, heart disease, and cerebrovascular disease. One-third of Japanese now come down with cancer. The most common form is stomach cancer, but cancer of the lungs is the most fatal. With the spread of Western dietary habits, cancer of the colon has shown a conspicuous increase. Among women, the incidence of breast and uterine cancer is also growing.

Q: What are lifestyle-related diseases?

Lifestyle-related diseases is a collective term referring to diseases that occur due to unhealthy habits in daily life, especially those concerning sleep, exercise, and diet. The best way to prevent these diseases from happening is to inculcate good habits in children from an early stage in life.

The habits most likely to lead to illness are lack of exercise, eating between meals and partaking in late-night snacks, and indulging in fatty foods and sweets. Smoking, alcohol, and stress are also thought to induce lifestyle-related diseases. Smoking not only contributes to lifestyle diseases but also

肺がんの発症リスクも高いことから、最も有害とされています。

Q: メタボ健診とは？

2008年から40歳～74歳の人を対象に、年1回、自治体が無料で行っている健康診査です。検査メニューは身体測定、医師の診察、尿検査で、これをもとにメタボリックシンドローム（内臓脂肪症候群）の該当者かどうかを判定します。

身体測定では、腹囲をメジャーで測って男性は85cm、女性は90cm以上ならメタボのおそれありとされ、尿検査データとあわせて判断されます。メタボの該当者や予備群にあたる人は、保健指導などによって生活習慣の改善を指示されます。

Q: 在宅医療とは？

医療費削減のため、日本の医療行政は病院で長く治療を続ける患者を減らし、なるべく自宅で療養生活を送ってもらおうという方針を打ち出しています。

その是非はともかく「畳の上で死にたい」という言葉があるように、人生の終章を病院で過ごすことを嫌がる感覚は、日本人には根強く残っています。病院では得られない精神の安らぎが自宅にはあり、それが治療に大きな効果をもたらすという側面があることも無視できないのです。

increases the risk of lung cancer, and is thus to be doubly avoided.

Q: What is metabolic screening?

Metabolic screening is an annual health check-up that has been carried out since 2008 by local governments for those in the 40 to 74 age bracket. The examinations conducted are physical measurements, consultation with a doctor, and a urine test, and on this basis it is determined whether the examinee has metabolic syndrome (a cluster of biochemical and physiological abnormalities associated with the development of cardiovascular disease and type 2 diabetes).

In the physical measurements examination, men with a waist of over 85 centimeters and women of over 90 centimeters are considered likely victims of metabolic syndrome; a final judgment is made based on the results of the urine test. Those thought to have the syndrome, or likely to develop it, are given instructions on how to improve their lifestyle.

Q: What is home healthcare?

In order to cut healthcare costs, Japanese healthcare administrators have adopted the policy of providing home healthcare rather than having patients spend lengthy periods of time in the hospital.

Regardless of the merits of this policy, it is true that many people would prefer to spend their last hours at home rather than in a hospital. It is also undeniably true that the spiritual peace and repose provided by the home contributes substantially to the patient's well-being.

Q: 終末期医療とは?

末期がんなどにかかって回復の見込みがない患者の精神的苦痛を軽減することを主眼にし、医療的措置は苦痛を和らげる目的で行う、医療行為(ターミナルケア)です。

安楽死という形での患者の死が認められていない日本では、終末期の患者の場合に限って、延命措置を拒否することができます。原則的には本人の意思表示が必要ですが、医師と家族の話し合いで延命措置は不要とする場合も多いようです。

Q: 脳死判定とは?

呼吸はしているが、脳の機能がすべて失われた状態では「死んだも同然」というのが脳死です。人の死を何を基準に判定するのかは、国際的にも諸説があります。しかし脳死判定が問題視されるのは、それが臓器移植に関わるからです。脳死者の心臓、腎臓、膵臓、肝臓、角膜は、必要とする患者に移植されることで機能を続けます。家族の中には、そのことで脳死者が命を得たと解釈する場合もあります。日本では新たな脳死基準に基づいた「臓器移植法」が2010年7月から施行されましたが、脳死者の臓器移植例は多いとはいえません。

Q: What is the state of end-of-life care?

End-of-life care is care which attempts to soften the spiritual distress of terminally ill cancer patients and others, as well as to reduce physical pain through medical means.

Euthanasia is not recognized in Japan, but in certain cases involving terminal patients, the use of life support systems can be declined. As a general rule, the consent of the patient is necessary, but in many cases the non-use of life support is decided by the attending physician and the patient's family.

Q: What determines brain death?

Brain death refers to the condition when a person is still breathing but all brain functions have been lost. Internationally, there are many definitions of what determines death, and one reason this issue is important has to do with organ transplant. When the heart, kidneys, pancreas, liver, and corneas are transplanted to another person, they continue to function. Some families consider this as equivalent to a new life for their beloved one. In July 2010 an Organ Transplant Law went into effect in Japan based on a new standard for brain death, but in actual fact there are still relatively few cases of organ transplants from brain dead individuals.

第6章 経済・労働
Economy and Labor Force

日本銀行▶

1 経済

Q: 戦後の日本が経済復興できた理由は？

日本は、資源のない国です。米国と戦争を始めたきっかけのひとつが、石油の輸入を止められたからとも言われています。その日本が敗戦後に急速な経済力をもつことができたのは、東西冷戦の中で先進諸国が軍備に予算を取られている間に、平和憲法の下で経済のみに集中できたからです。また、輸入原料を加工し付加価値を付けて輸出する技術力の高さ、低賃金でも勤勉な労働力に恵まれたことも大きな理由としてあげられます。

その結果、米国は軍事面で守ってきた日本が、対米貿易で巨額の黒字を生み出していることを批判し続けました。1970年代は繊維製品、カラーテレビ、工業機械、80年代は自動車、半導体、VTR、鉄鋼などで日本が優位でした。日本の貿易依存度は55年が10％でしたが、70年には20％を超え、85年以降は22〜23％を維持していま

1 The Economy

Q: How did the postwar economy recover so quickly?

Japan is a country with few natural resources. It is even said that one of the reasons for the Pacific War was Western sanctioning of oil exports to Japan. Following the war, the Japanese economy was able to make a remarkable recovery due to the fact that while Western advanced countries were spending exorbitantly on munitions during the Cold War, Japan was able to concentrate its efforts on the economy under its postwar "peace constitution." Other reasons are the technological expertise that enabled Japan to convert raw materials into finished products for export, the low wages of its workers and their diligence and work ethic.

Thus, while on the one hand Japan was under the umbrella of American military might, economically it produced a huge trade surplus with the United States, for which it was continually criticized. In the 1970s Japan led the world in textile products, color televisions, and industrial machinery, and in the 1980s in automobiles, semiconductors, VTRs, steel, and others. In 1955 exports accounted for 10% of the

した。このような伸びは日本だけで、強力な工業生産力と輸出力は世界に脅威を与えました。

Q: 日本銀行の役割は？

日本経済の金融面での要としての日本銀行は、「日本銀行法」という法律に基づいて設立され、政府から独立した機関として機能しています。日本の中央銀行としての役割の一つが、一般の金融機関にお金を貸し出すことで、安い金利で借りたお金を金融機関は企業や個人にまた貸しをして利ざやを稼ぐのです。また、金融機関が持っている国債などを売買することで、市場に流れるお金を調整しています。

中央銀行の役割のもう一つが紙幣の発行で、正式には「日本銀行券」と言います。一方、貨幣（硬貨）の発行元は日本政府です。紙幣・貨幣という通貨の発行は毎年、日本銀行の在庫をチェックし、必要量を財務大臣が閣議を経て決定します。

● 日本の通貨
Japanese Currency

一万円券 10,000 yen note

五千円券 5,000 yen note

二千円券 2,000 yen note

千円券 1,000 yen note

GNP; in 1970 the number went over 20%; and following 1985 it maintained a steady 22-23%. Japan was the only country to post such numbers, and its industrial strength and export prowess were viewed with apprehension by the rest of the world.

Q: What is the role of the Bank of Japan?

The Bank of Japan was established under the Bank of Japan Law as an independent entity and the key player in establishing financial economic policy. As the central bank of Japan, one of its functions is to lend money to financial institutions at low rates, which institutions then lend to individuals and corporations and make a profit from the margin. Further, by buying and selling government bonds held by financial institutions, the Bank of Japan regulates the amount of money available on the market.

In another of its roles as the central bank of Japan, the Bank of Japan issues currency called Bank of Japan notes. Officially, the issuer of these notes is the government of Japan. Every year the Bank of Japan's stock of notes and coins is checked, and the Finance Minister gives the order for the production of the appropriate amount with the approval of the cabinet.

五百円硬貨
500 yen coin

百円硬貨
100 yen coin

五十円硬貨
50 yen coin

十円硬貨
10 yen coin

五円硬貨
5 yen coin

一円硬貨
1 yen coin

Q: 金融機関の種類は？

日本銀行以外の金融機関は、政府系と民間に大別されます。民間の金融機関には、都市銀行、地方銀行、ゆうちょ銀行、JAバンク、信用金庫、信託銀行、信用協同組合、外国銀行、ネットバンクなどがあります。

都市銀行の中で特に巨大な金融資産を持つ3大グループをメガバンクと呼びます。国営から民営に移行中のゆうちょ銀行と農協系のJAバンクも、金融資産の大きさから動向が注目されています。

Q: 景気は何を基準に判断するの？

景気を判断する指標としてあげられるのが、①国内総生産（GDP）とその成長率、②鋼工業生産指数、③第3次産業（サービス業）活動指数、④景気動向指数などです。

また、日本銀行が3カ月ごとに公表する「日銀短観」は、民間企業に対するアンケート調査に基づくため、実態を反映しているとして大事な景気指標とされています。

株価も景気を判断する上での重大な指標とされますが、近年は株価が上がっても景気が上向いたという実感が伴わないことが多いことから、あてにならないという声も大きくなっています。

Q: How many different types of financial institutions are there?

Aside from the Bank of Japan, other financial institutions can be classified as either private or government managed. Private institutions include city banks, regional banks, Japan Post Banks, JA Banks, credit banks, trust banks, credit unions, foreign banks, and online banks.

Among city banks, the three possessing the most formidable financial resources are called megabanks. Japan Post Bank and the agriculture-affiliated JA Bank, which are in the process of transforming themselves from public to private institutions, are also closely watched because of their huge holdings.

Q: What are the criteria for judging economic conditions?

The criteria for judging the health of the economy are 1) the rate of growth of the GNP (gross national product), 2) the steel industry production index, 3) the tertiary industry activity index, and 4) the diffusion index.

In addition, the Bank of Japan's Tankan (Short-Term Economic Survey of Enterprises in Japan), based on a quarterly questionnaire survey of private enterprises, is thought to present a realistic view of economic conditions and is thus highly valued.

Generally speaking, stock prices are also considered a good indicator of economic conditions, but recently, given that there seems to be no real sense of higher stock prices being accompanied by improved economic conditions, many now feel that stock is unreliable as an economic indicator.

第6章 経済・労働

東京証券取引所

> **▶ 証券取引所**
> 資本主義経済の中心的役割を担ってきた証券取引所は近年、廃止・統合が進み、日本経済の停滞を物語るように、9カ所あった取引所は東京・名古屋の二大取引所と札幌・福岡の計4カ所になってしまいました。

Q: 日本経済の伸びは期待できるの？

1991年、日本経済は株価と地価の急落と共に、いわゆるバブルがはじけて深刻な景気後退に見舞われ始めました。95年には1ドル80円という円高を記録したり、世界中からコメを含む農産物などの輸入規制の撤廃を求められたりして、国際的な競争力を失う事態に発展したのです。97年には経済成長率がマイナスになり、倒産企業やリストラによる失業者があふれました。

2000年に入って、前年2月の「ゼロ金利政策」が効を奏し最悪の事態を免れたものの、デフレ経済の進行で消費が冷え込みました。政府はデフレ脱却のための経済施策を打ち出していますが、今後は高い成長率は期待できないという意見が大勢を占めています。

Q: どんなものを輸出しているの？

2013年の輸出総額は、約69.8兆円でした。これは1980年（約30兆円）と比較すると2倍強に

> **▶ Stock Markets**
> Stock markets have long been considered an essential part of a capitalistic economy, but recently in deflationary Japan many of them have shut down or merged, leaving only four markets (the two largest in Tokyo and Nagoya, and two smaller in Sapporo and Fukuoka), whereas there used to be nine.

Q: Can further growth be expected from the Japanese economy?

In 1991, with a sudden plunge in stock and real estate prices, the Japanese economic bubble burst and the economy was irreparably damaged. In 1995 the yen hit a record high of ¥80 per dollar, a disaster for exporting firms. Internationally, voices called for the removal of regulations on rice imports and other products, and Japanese global competitiveness was crippled. In 1997 the economy recorded minus growth, and bankruptcy and restructuring produced droves of unemployed.

In 2000 the zero-interest rate policy of February of the previous year began to take effect and the worst scenario was avoided, but on the other hand, with the spread of deflation, consumer spending cooled down. The government is now adopting new policies to pull the country out of deflation, but the majority opinion is that these policies won't produce a high economic growth rate.

Q: What are the principal exports?

In 2013 total exports were valued at about ¥69.8 trillion. This is more than twice the figure for 1980 (about ¥30 trillion).

伸びました。以下に主要品目と割合を列記します。

① 自動車	14.9%
② 鉄鋼	5.4%
③ 導体等電子部品	5.1%
④ 自動車部品	5.0%
⑤ 有機化合物	3.6%
⑥ 原動機	3.6%
⑦ プラスチック	3.2%
⑧ 光学機器	3.2%
⑨ 電気回路等の機器	2.5%
⑩ 船舶	2.1%

ちなみに、自動車と部品および原動機（エンジン）は米国、鉄鋼は韓国、半導体等電子部品およびプラスチックは中国が最大の輸出先。

Q: どんなものを輸入しているの？

2013年の輸入総額は、約81.3兆円。以下に主要品目と割合を列記します。

① 原油および粗油	17.5%
② LNG	8.7%
③ 衣類と付属品	4.0%
④ 石油製品	3.3%
⑤ 通信機	3.3%
⑥ 半導体等電子部品	3.0%
⑦ 石炭	2.8%
⑧ 医薬品	2.6%
⑨ 電算機と周辺機器	2.4%
⑩ 鉄鉱石	2.1%

Below are listed the principal exports and their percentage of the whole.

① Vehicles	(14.9%)
② Steel and iron	(5.4%)
③ Semiconductors and electronic components	(5.1%)
④ Automotive parts	(5.0%)
⑤ Organic compounds	(3.6%)
⑥ Engines	(3.6%)
⑦ Plastics	(3.2%)
⑧ Optical instruments	(3.2%)
⑨ Electric circuits and similar equipment	(2.5%)
⑩ Ships and boats	(2.1%)

The top export destinations for these products are the United States (vehicles, automotive parts, and engines), South Korea (iron and steel), and China (semiconductors, electronic components, and plastics).

Q: What are the principal imports?

In 2013 total imports were valued at about ¥81.3 trillion. Below are listed the principal imported items and their percentage of the whole.

① Petroleum and crude oil	(17.5%)
② Liquefied natural gas	(8.7%)
③ Clothing and accessories	(4.0%)
④ Petroleum products	(3.3%)
⑤ Communication equipment	(3.3%)
⑥ Semiconductors and electronic components	(3.0%)
⑦ Coal	(2.8%)
⑧ Pharmaceutical products	(2.6%)
⑨ Computers and peripherals	(2.4%)
⑩ Iron ore	(2.1%)

エネルギー原料の分野での最大の輸入先は、石油がサウジアラビア、LNG（液化天然ガス）がカタール、石炭がオーストラリアです。

Q: 貿易収支はどうなっているの？

貿易収支は、輸入総額と輸出総額の差を示すもので、国力の指標の一つとされます。1980年代から黒字を続けてきた日本の貿易収支は2011年に赤字を記録し、以来、赤字が続いています（2014年）。

この原因の一つに、東日本大震災に伴って稼働停止した原子力発電の代替となった火力発電の燃料用の石油・LNG・石炭の輸入量が増えたことがあげられています。また近年、外交関係が悪化している中国向けの輸出が大幅に減っていることも、赤字要因とされます。

2 産　業

Q: 日本の産業構造の特徴は？

産業は通常、次のように分類されます。

① 第1次産業…農業、林業、漁業
② 第2次産業…鉱業、建設業、製造業
③ 第3次産業…上記以外のサービスを提供するもの

経済の発展に伴い、国の産業の比重は第1次

In the field of energy raw materials, the top import origins are Saudi Arabia for petroleum, Qatar for liquefied natural gas, and Australia for coal.

Q: What is the state of the balance of trade?

The balance of trade, that is, the difference between the total value of imports and the total value of exports, is considered an important indicator of a country's economic strength. Since the 1980s Japan had recorded a steady trade surplus, but in 2010 it registered a deficit that has continued to the present day (2014).

One reason given for this situation is the shutdown of nuclear reactors following the Great East Japan Earthquake and Tsunami of 2011 and the increased imports of petroleum, liquefied natural gas, and coal for thermal power plants to make up the difference. Aside from this, recent diplomatic contretemps with China have also led to an extensive diminution of Chinese exports.

2 Industry

Q: How is Japanese industry structured?

In general, industry is classified into the following sectors (or industries).

① Primary sector (agriculture, forestry, fishing)
② Secondary sector (mining, construction, manufacturing)
③ Tertiary sector (services)

In the historical development of an economy, the relative

から第2次、さらに第3次へと移行するとされますが、日本の場合は第1次から第2次への比重の移行は1960年代、第2次から第3次への比重の移行は70年代以降です。

2000年代には、就業人口の6割強を第3次産業が占め、残り4割弱の大半が第2次産業という構成です。

Q: 主要産業は？

労働生産性という点から見ると、製造業、サービス業が今の日本の主要産業です。これは、手先が器用で細やかな気配りができる日本人の特質に合った産業と言えますが、近年、少子化時代を反映して就業人口数は横這い状態です。一方、高齢化が進む日本では老人福祉・介護・医療関連の就業者数が増加しています。なかでも需要が増大している介護職は待遇改善が求められています。

Q: 産業の空洞化はなぜ起きたの？

産業の空洞化とは、主に製造業の海外工場移転によって国内工場が減少することをさす言葉です。原料を輸入したり加工製品を輸出する製造業は、為替相場に大きく左右されます。ドルに対して円が高くなると、人件費が安い海外に工場を移転し現地生産へと転換します。1980年代後半と90年代中頃の円高で、国内工場を移転

importance of these sectors starts with the first sector, shifts to the second and then to the third. In the case of Japan, the shift from the first sector to the second occurred in the 1960s, and from the second to the third in the 1970s and thereafter.

By the 2000s a little more than 60% of the working population was employed in the third sector, with the remainder, somewhat less than 40%, working in the second sector.

Q: What are the principal industries?

From the viewpoint of labor productivity, the two principal industries are the manufacturing and service industries. These sectors can be said to be compatible with two Japanese national characteristics, dexterity with the hands and attention to detail. On the debit side, with lower birth rates, the size of the working population has recently leveled off. On the positive side, with the aging of society, there has been an increase in the number of people engaged in welfare for the aging, nursing care, and healthcare in general. The need for nursing care is particularly on the rise, as is the need for an improvement in the working conditions of caregivers.

Q: How did the hollowing out of industry take place?

The hollowing out of industry mainly refers to the loss of domestic manufacturing plants due to their being moved abroad. Importing raw materials and exporting finished products as it does, the manufacturing sector is also under the sway of the exchange rate. When the yen appreciates against the dollar, more plants move overseas to take advantage of the cheaper labor. From near the end of the 1980s until the middle

した企業は大企業はもとより中小企業にまで及びました。2000年代は、もっぱらコスト削減のために東南アジアの新興国へ工場移転する企業が増えています。

Q: 自給率4割って、本当なの?

人口の割に国土が狭い日本は、少資源国です。日本人が自給自足の生活をしたのは江戸時代までで、西洋文明を取り入れた明治時代以降は輸入品に依存しなければならなくなりました。

なかでも食糧は、自給率4割以下という状況が続いて大きな問題になっています。ただし、これはカロリーベース換算で、生産ベースでは7割前後との見方もあります。とはいえ飼料・燃料・鉱物などの資源輸入が、ほぼ8〜10割ということを考えあわせると、全体的な自給率は2割程度が実態と言うべきかもしれません。

Q: 農業はどんな問題を抱えているの?

日本の農業は、稲作を中心に発展してきました。お米が日本で普及したのは、①気候風土が適していた、②水が豊富、③狭い土地でも生産性が高い、④栄養価が高く美味しいといった理由からです。

古代以来の基幹産業だった稲作に変化が起きたのは、1960年代に始まった経済成長でした。農地は工場や商業地に変わり、農家の子ども達は町に出て、安定した収入が見込める工場など

of the 1990s, the strong yen forced not only large corporations to move abroad but smaller ones as well. In the 2000s there has been an increasing number of companies relocating their plants to Southeast Asia in an effort to cut costs.

Q: The food self-sufficiency ratio is only 40%?

Japan is not only a small country in size relative to its population, but it is also poor in terms of natural resources. Self-sufficiency came to an end with the conclusion of the 200 odd years of the Tokugawa period. With the beginning of the Meiji period in 1868 and the rush to industrialization and Westernization, the reliance on imports commenced.

Food self-sufficiency in particular remains below 40% and is considered a critical issue. This number is calorie-based, and some say that a production-based figure would be more like 70%. However, considering that fodder, fuel, and mineral resources are from 80% to 100% imports, the overall self-sufficiency ratio might realistically be only 20%.

Q: What are the problems facing agriculture?

Agriculture in Japan developed based on rice cultivation. There are several reasons for this: 1) the climate was suitable; 2) water was readily available; 3) productivity was high even in small plots; 4) rice was highly nutritious and agreeable to the palate.

Rice cultivation continued from ancient times to be a time-honored occupation until the rapid economic growth of the 1960s. Agricultural land was then displaced by factories and commercial districts, and the children of

に勤め始め、農業は後継者難になりました。また、政府は60年代末からコメの在庫をなくすための"減反"を農家に割当てたため、二度と稲作ができない休耕地がたくさん生まれました。減反は、2018年の廃止が決定していますが、農地の減少、高齢化、後継者難で日本の農業の未来は明るいとは言えません。

Q: 漁業はどんな問題を抱えているの？

四方が海の日本は古代から漁業が盛んでしたが、農業と同様に後継者難と高齢化が問題になっています。水産物の需要が国際的に高まる一方で、海洋資源の減少が問題視されています。加えて、2011年3月に起きた東日本大震災で東北の主要7漁港が被災し、需給が停滞しました。原発事故による放射能汚染のおそれがあると、各国が輸入規制をしたことも痛手となっています。

Q: 捕鯨はいつから始まったの？

日本の捕鯨の歴史は長く、約5000年ほど前の縄文時代の遺跡から骨がみつかっています。江戸時代までは主に沿岸にやってきた鯨を捕獲していましたが、明治時代以降になると遠洋での

farmers moved to the cities for steady work in factories, leaving no one to look after the farm. Then, from the end of the 1960s, the government initiated measures to reduce the acreage devoted to rice in an attempt to cut back on surplus production. The result was a great deal of untended farmland that would never again be cultivated. This "reduction" policy is scheduled to come to an end in 2018, but still the future of agriculture cannot be called bright, what with loss of cultivatable land, the aging of the farming population, and the difficulty of securing successors.

Q: What kind of challenges is the fishing industry facing?

Being an island nation, from ancient times Japan has had a prosperous fishing industry, but that industry is now facing the same problems as agriculture: the aging of the fishing population and the issue of successors. While it is true that global demand for seafood is growing, the concern over marine resources is also on the rise. In addition, the earthquake and tsunami of March 2011 brought irreparable damage to seven principal fishing ports in the Tohoku region and disrupted supply and demand. With the accompanying nuclear incident at Fukushima, many countries placed sanctions on marine imports from that area due to the fear of contamination.

Q: When did whaling start?

Whaling has a long history in Japan. Whale bones have been found at Jomon-period sites dating back to about 5,000 years ago. In the Edo period (1603-1868) whaling was mostly carried out along the coastline, and it was only after the beginning of

捕鯨が始まり、やがて輸出用の鯨油をとるために南極海へ進出するようになったのです。鯨肉は安いため、日本人が好んで食べました。

鯨の捕獲に関しては国際捕鯨委員会（IWC）の規制があり、日本は1988年に商業捕鯨から撤退をよぎなくされ、調査捕鯨という名目での捕獲を続けてきました。しかし、2010年にオーストラリアが日本の調査捕鯨は国際条約違反として国際司法裁判所に提訴。2014年3月、日本の捕鯨は調査捕鯨として認められないとの判決が下りました。

Q: サービス業はどんな問題を抱えているの？

第3次産業としてのサービス業は1980年代までは職種が比較的はっきりしていたのですが、90年代以降は限定的な区分が難しくなっています。その原因の一つは、派遣労働者の増加です。受け入れる企業側の都合で雇用できる派遣労働者は今では、あらゆる職種に進出しています。不安定な雇用条件は、労働者の仕事に対するモチベーションの低下や早期離職に結びついています。

Q: エネルギー問題はどうなるの？

地球温暖化防止のため二酸化炭素排出を規制する国際合意の下、日本はクリーンなエネルギー源としての原子力発電や、太陽光などの再生可能エネルギーへの移行を進めてきました。しかし、2011年3月の福島の事故を機に稼働を停止した原子力発電の代替として火力発電が行

the Meiji period (1868-1912) that ships went further out to sea and eventually to the Antarctic for whale oil for export. Whale meat then was inexpensive and much eaten.

Following the restrictions of the International Whaling Commission, Japan withdrew from commercial whaling in 1988, allowing continued whaling only for scientific purposes. However, in 2010 Australia argued before the UN International Court of Justice that Japanese scientific whaling contravened international treaties. In March 2014, the Court ruled that Japan should cease scientific whaling in the Antarctic.

Q: What problems is the service industry facing?

The types of work comprising the tertiary service industry were fairly clear-cut into the 1980s, but from the 1990s onward definitive definition became more difficult. One reason for this lay in the increase of temporary workers dispatched from agencies. The types of temporary work undertaken at the convenience of employers expanded dramatically. Given the often less than favorable working conditions, motivation has come to be adversely affected and turnover high.

Q: What energy problems does Japan face?

As part of the international consensus that carbon dioxide emissions should be cut back to combat global warming, Japan has pursued a policy of clean energy in the form of sustainable nuclear and solar power, among others. However, with the Fukushima incident of 2011, nuclear power had to be replaced by thermal power, with an inevitable increase

われ、その燃料の石油・LNG・石炭が二酸化炭素排出という問題を復活させています。再生可能エネルギーの主役と期待されている太陽光発電は天候に左右されるため、安定的なベース電源にはなり得ず、設備費を含めるとコスト高になることが指摘されています。

Q: 原子力発電所はどうなるの？

福島の事故後、原子力規制委員会によって原子力発電所の新たな規制基準が策定され、法制化されました。そして政府は、新基準をクリアした原子力発電所は再稼働してよいとしたのです。2015年内には一部の再稼働が始まります。

一方、事故を起こした原子炉の廃止を含め、稼働を始めてから40年以上経った原子炉の廃止も検討されています。国内には、事故を起こした6基を含めて54基の軽水炉がありますが、うち11基の廃炉が決定しています。ちなみに、政府は2030年までの原子力発電の割合目標を20％程度としています（15年3月時点）。

Q: 核廃棄物はどうするの？

原子力発電には事故以外に、核廃棄物の処理・処分という大問題があります。原子炉で燃やした核燃料の残りの使用済み核燃料は、国内に1万7000トンもたまっていて、この処理をどうするか決まっていません。また、高レベル核廃棄物の最終処分場も未定です。

in carbon dioxide due to the problematic use of petroleum, liquefied gas, and coal. Solar power, in which high expectations were placed, is not only affected by the weather and therefore an unstable source of energy, but also costly in terms of new infrastructure.

Q: What is the future of nuclear power?

After the Fukushima incident, new safety rules for nuclear reactors were drawn up by the Nuclear Regulation Authority and made law. The government decided that any reactors that met these new standards could be restarted. Some reactors will go back online in 2015.

On the other hand, not only the complete shutdown of the reactors that caused the disaster but also any reactors that have been in operation for more than 40 years is being considered. There are 54 light-water reactors in Japan, including the 6 involved in the Fukushima incident, and 11 of these are scheduled to be decommissioned. Regardless, by 2030 the government estimates that nuclear power will account for 20% of Japan's electricity (as of March 2015).

Q: How is nuclear waste being handled?

Aside from the problem of nuclear accidents, there is also the issue of the disposal or reprocessing of nuclear waste. The spent fuel left over from reactors now amounts to 17,000 tons within Japan. It has yet to be decided how to dispose of this waste. Candidate sites for the final disposal of high level radioactive waste have yet to be determined.

第6章 経済・労働

3 労働

Q: 企業の雇用形態は?

日本の企業は、「終身雇用」を伝統としてきました。定年まで勤めるのを前提に採用し、昇格や昇給は「年功序列型」が常態でした。しかし、いわゆるバブル経済の崩壊で1991年以降、業績が悪化した企業は社員の中途退職を奨励したり、過剰な人員の配置転換を進めるなどのリストラを積極的に行うようになりました。その結果、短期の雇用契約によるパートやアルバイト、派遣社員が増加しています。

一方、若い世代には一つの企業で定年まで勤めるというライフスタイルを嫌い、自ら起業をしたり、実力本位の「年俸制」を採用している企業への就職を望む人が増えてきています。

Q: 失業率は?

総務省が毎月末に発表する労働力調査では、調査期間内の完全失業者数を労働力人口で割った「完全失業率」が示されますが、実はこの完全失業者とは公共職業安定所に求職の届け出をしている失業者のことで、それ以外の失業者は含まれていません。

ちなみに1980年代～94年は2％台だったの

3　The Work Force

Q: How is corporate employment structured?

Traditionally Japanese corporations have embraced a system of "lifetime employment." People were hired with the understanding that they would work until retirement, and advancement and pay raises would be carried out according to seniority. This was the norm. However, after the burst of the economic bubble in 1991, struggling enterprises began calling for early retirement and reassigning excessive employees to new positions, that is, proactive restructuring. As a result, there was a ballooning of employees on short-term contracts, such as moonlighters, part-timers, and temp staff.

On the other hand, there was also an increase in the number of young people who looked askance at lifetime employment, and who preferred to start their own business or work for a company where income was based on ability.

Q: What is the unemployment rate?

At the end of each month the Ministry of Internal Affairs and Communications publishes the results of its labor force survey for that month, in which the number of unemployed who are actively seeking employment is divided by the number of people in the labor force, producing the unemployment rate. However, the number of completely unemployed here refers only to the number who have applied to Public Employment Security Offices for work, and does not include other jobless people.

From the 1980s to 1994 the unemployment rate was in

が、95年以降3％台、98年以降は4～5％台を続け、2014年に3.6％に下がりました。したがって景気が回復しつつあると言うのは速断で、データ外の潜在的失業者を加えると失業率はもっと高くなるのです。

Q: 労働時間は？

「労働基準法」では、使用者に対して原則的に1日8時間、1週間で40時間を超えて働かせてはならないと定めています。さらに、労働時間が6時間を超える場合は45分以上、8時間を超える場合は1時間以上の休憩を与えることを義務付けています。

日本人はかつて、外国からワーカーホリック（仕事中毒）と揶揄されたほど長時間働き、しかも低賃金に耐えてきました。現在、法律が定める年間労働時間は最大2085.6時間で、欧米の先進諸国に近付いてきています。

Q: 休日は？

これも法律で、使用者は少なくとも毎週1日の休日か、4週間を通じて4日以上の休日を与えなければならないことが義務付けられています。週休2日制を採用する企業が一般的になったとはいえ、週1回の休日を与えるので精一杯という企業もまだ多いのが実情です。

一定の勤続年月・出勤率で年間10～20日まで有給休暇を与える制度もあり、これを加えると日本の労働者の年間休日数は120日超となり、1年の3分の1に当ります。しかし、フラン

the 2% range, in 1995 and thereafter 3%, and following 1998 4-5%, falling to 3.6% in 2014. While some may say that this decline can be attributed to improving economic conditions, that would be a little hasty, for if the statistically hidden unemployed are included, the rate would be much higher.

Q: What are the working hours?

According to the Labor Standards Law, as a rule employers cannot ask employees to work more than 8 hour a day or more than 40 hours a week. Further, it is stipulated that a 45-minute break is mandatory after 6 hours of work, and 1 hour after 8 hours.

In the past the Japanese were often called workaholics by foreign observers, working as they did long hours at low pay. At present, however, the law sets a limit on working hours at 2,085.6 hours a year, bringing Japan close to Western standards.

Q: What about paid vacation?

According to law, employers must give employees at least one paid vacation a week, or 4 or more paid vacation days a month. While there are many enterprises that have two days off a week, it is a fact that many can only manage one day.

If we add to this the fact that some corporations offer 10 to 20 days paid leave for employees who have served a certain length of time, the number of paid vacation days reaches more than 120 annually, one-third of the days in

スやドイツの労働者のように年間休日数が150日あって、夏は１カ月ものバカンスを楽しむといった状況ではありません。

Q: 賃金は？

使用者が支払う労働賃金は①通貨で、②全額を、③直接、④月１回以上、⑤一定期日を定めて支払わなければならないという原則があります。時間外労働、深夜労働（原則として午後10時～午前５時）または休日労働をさせる場合は割増賃金を支払う必要があります。賃金は下限が定められ、都道府県ごとの地域別最低賃金、特定の産業や職業に適用される特定最低賃金の２種があり、これ以下の賃金で働かせると罰せられます。

Q: 労働者の年収は？

国税庁の調査によると、給与所得者は約4646万人です。うち女性は1892万人ですが、65.5％が年収300万円以下で、しかも100万円台が26％を占めています。男性では年収300～400万円台が多く、約1000万人います。ちなみに、年収1000万円以上は、男性が約169万人で女性は約17万人（2014年）。

Q: 定年は何歳？

日本の企業の定年は1970年代が55歳、80年代以降が60歳と推移してきました。そして、2013年から65歳定年制の導入が義務化され、原則的

a year. Of course, this is in no way comparable to France and Germany, where workers get 150 vacation days a year, including a month's summer vacation.

Q: How are wages paid?

As a rule, wages must be paid 1) in currency, 2) in total, 3) directly, 4) at least once a month, and 5) on a fixed date. Extra pay is required for overtime work, late-night work (normally from 10 PM to 5 AM), and work on holidays or days off. There are two types of minimum wage: one is a minimum wage set by prefectures, the other applies to certain industries and occupations. The infraction of either is punishable by law.

Q: How much is average annual income?

According to the National Tax Administration Agency, there are 46,460,000 wage earners in Japan. 18,920,000 of these are women, of which 65% are earning less than ¥3,000,000 annually, and 26% around ¥1,000,000. There are around 10,000,000 male workers, the majority of whom are earning ¥3,000,000 to ¥4,000,000 annually. Males with an annual income of over ¥10,000,000 number about 1,690,000 and women about 170,000 (as of 2014).

Q: What is the age of retirement?

In the 1970s the age of retirement was 55, and in the 1980s and thereafter 60. In 2013 a new system was introduced mandating retirement at 65 and taking as its object all workers wishing to

に希望者全員を継続雇用制度の対象者としなければならなくなりました。この背景には、平均寿命が伸びたことが挙げられますが、継続雇用は、年功序列とそれに伴う賃金制度を採用してきた企業にとって人事システムの見直しを意味しています。

Q: 男女機会均等法とは?

男性は外で働き、女性は子育てをしながら家庭を守るというのが、日本人の伝統的な考え方でした。これを不平等とする女性側の声が高まり、職場での女性の待遇改善を定めた「男女機会均等法」が1986年に施行され、99年の法改正を経て雇用の機会の上でも、実際の仕事の上でも原則的に平等になりました。

しかし、現実は法律に追いついていません。例えば昇進について、7割以上の企業が女性管理職は1割未満と答えています(2014年)。その原因の一つに、92年以降の不況で企業が4年制大学の女子卒業生の採用を控えたことが指摘されています。女性管理職を増やしたくとも、育てるべき人材がいないのです。

Q: 女性が多い職場は?

働く女性は1975年の1160万人と比較すると、732万人増えています。女性が携わっている仕事は、サービス業、小売業、金融保険業、介護、事

take part in such extended employment. Behind this initiative was the rise in life expectancy, and those companies adhering to the seniority system of wage raises were forced to reconsider their personnel management system.

Q: What is the Equal Employment Opportunity Law?

The traditional Japanese way of thinking was that men should work out in society and women should stay home and take care of the children. Many women raised their voices against the unfairness of this notion, and consequently the Equal Employment Opportunity Law was adopted in 1986 to improve women's working conditions. With a major revision of the law in 1999, both employment opportunity and working conditions have become equal in principle.

However, reality has not always kept pace with the law. In the matter of advancement, for example, more than 70% of Japanese enterprises employ less than 10% of women in managerial positions (as of 2014). One reason for this is said to be the low hiring rate of female graduates of four-year colleges following the economic slump of 1992. Even though some corporations may wish to increase the number of female managers, they don't have the personnel to work with.

Q: In what occupations are women most prevalent?

In comparison to the 11,600,000 working women in 1975, the number has now increased by 7,320,000. The principal occupations women are engaged in include the service

務などが主ですが、中でもサービス業は3分の2が女性です。

労働形態はパートタイムが圧倒的に多く、年収100万円台以下の826万人の大半を占めているとみられています。パートタイムが多いのは、少しでも家計の足しになればという経済的理由と、結婚をして家庭に入った女性を積極的に採用する企業が少ないといった理由からです。

Q: 単身赴任が多いのは、なぜ？

外国人をしばしば驚かせるのが、家族と離れ ばなれで働いている単身赴任者の存在です。そこまでして働かなければならないなんて信じられない、というわけです。

しかし、日本で単身赴任が多いのは、家庭のためでもあるのです。その最大の理由が、子どもの教育問題です。有名校に進学させたいと願う親にとって、わが子を転勤に付き合わせ転校させるのは受験に不利になります。特に都会の進学校に通っている場合はなおさらです。

そこで父親は、週末に家族の元に帰って、月曜の朝早くに赴任地に向かう生活を良しとするのです。

industry, retailing, securities and insurance, nursing care, and clerical work, with the service industry workers being two-thirds of the total.

Part-time is by far the most prevalent type of work, with most of the total female work force of 8,260,000 earning less than around ¥1,000,000 a year. The reasons for the prevalence of part-time work is economic—the desire to add if only a little to the family income—and the fact that few employers are eager to hire women who have once left the work force to marry and take up household duties.

Q: Why are so many business people assigned to branch offices unaccompanied by their families?

One phenomenon that often comes as a surprise to foreign observers is the number of people who are assigned to branch offices unaccompanied by their families. It is hard for them to believe that anyone would go so far even for the sake of business.

Contrary to appearances, however, this is done partly for the sake of the family. The primary reason is the children's education. If every time the family breadwinner is reassigned, the children must transfer to a new school, they will be put at a disadvantage when taking entrance exams, especially at the more prestigious urban schools leading to acceptance at a renowned university.

It is this fact that makes it acceptable for the family breadwinner to return to home and family on the weekends and return to his or her post early Monday morning.

Q: 外国人が働くために必要なことは？

外国人が日本で働く上で、在留資格とそれに応じた在留期間の定めがあります。在留中の活動に制限がない人は①永住者（特別永住者を除く）、②日本人の配偶者・実子・特別養子、③永住者・特別永住者の配偶者または永住者の子として日本で生まれた在留者、④定住者（日系3世等）です。

その他の場合は、日本の法律が定める在留資格と在留期間内での活動と報酬を得ることができます。なお2015年3月から在留資格に「介護職」が加えられました。

Q: 企業が社員を解雇できるのは、どんな時？

解雇には①普通解雇、②整理解雇、③懲戒解雇があります。普通解雇と懲戒解雇は社員に問題がある場合で、整理解雇は会社都合です。

企業が社員を解雇する場合は、少なくとも30日以上前の予告が法律で義務付けられています。ただし、客観的、合理的な理由のない解雇は認められません。予告なしで解雇する場合は、懲戒解雇以外は少なくとも30日分以上の平均賃金を解雇予告手当として支払わなければなりません。

Q: What is needed for a foreigner to work in Japan?

For a foreigner to work in Japan, he or she must possess a residence status that permits work and a permissible period of stay that would allow that work. Foreign residents with no restrictions on the work they may do are 1) permanent residents (excluding special permanent residents), 2) spouses, biological children, and special adoptions of Japanese citizens, 3) spouses of permanent residents or special permanent residents, or those born and living in Japan as the children of permanent residents, and 4) long-term residents (such as third-generation Japanese).

In cases beyond these, Japanese law otherwise prescribes the residence status and periods of stay under which remuneration may be legally gained. Further, in March 2015 nursing care was added as a permissible residence status.

Q: When can an employee be fired?

There are three types of dismissal: 1) normal dismissal, 2) dismissal for economic reasons, and 3) disciplinary dismissal. Normal dismissal and disciplinary dismissal take place when there is an issue with the employee's conduct; economic dismissal takes place at the employer's convenience.

Law mandates that at least 30 days notice must be given prior to dismissal. However, dismissals without objective or rational foundation are not permitted in any case. If notice is not given (except in the case of disciplinary dismissal), a fee equal to at least 30 days of average wages must be paid.

Q: ブラック企業とは？

若者を大量に採用し、使い捨てるように扱う企業が社会問題化しています。このようなブラック企業は、企業への隷属を強いる日本型雇用の延長線上で生まれたもので、被害者はパートやアルバイトのみならず正社員にまで及んでいる点に問題があります。

政府は、こうした「ブラック企業」名を公表すると共に、悪質企業を排除することで若者の就職や雇用継続を支援する法整備を進めています。2016年4月からは、非正規社員を正社員採用につなげるため、サービス分野の検定制度がスタートする予定です。

Q: 過労死って、なに？

働き過ぎが原因で、労働者が病気による突然死や自殺をすることです。これが日本特有なのは"KAROSHI"が外国の辞書に掲載されていることでも分かります。

過労死は労働基準監督署が認定することになっていますが、厚生労働省は2002年に認定基準マニュアルを発表しました。過労による自殺者（未遂者も含む）は2013年が196人で、過去10年ほどの間に10倍に増えているそうです。その大半は男性で、近年は働き盛りの40〜50代だけでなく、20代の若者にも広がっています

Q: What is a "black company"?

Companies that employ large numbers of young people to be used as expendable pawns has recently become a social issue. These so-called black companies are an extension of the corporate loyalty traditionally required of employees, and the victims are not just moonlighters and part-timers but full-time employees as well.

The government is now taking legal measures to eradicate such corrupt companies by publicizing their names and supporting young people in other ways in their search for meaningful and long-term employment. In April 2016 a new system for certifying workers in the service sector will go into effect, easing the transition from non-regular to regular employee status.

Q: What does "death from overwork" mean?

This phrase refers to sudden death or suicide caused by overwork. That this is a particular Japanese phenomenon is attested to by the fact the Japanese word *karoshi* appears as a loanword in foreign dictionaries.

Karoshi comes under the purview of the Labor Standards Inspection Office, an agency of the Ministry of Health, Labour and Welfare, and in 2002 the Ministry issued a manual of standards for ascertaining *karoshi*. In 2013 the number of suicides and attempted suicides due to overwork stood at 196, nearly 10 times the figure for the previous ten years. The majority are men, which includes not only the hardest working forty and fifty year olds, but also young men in their twenties.

Q: 名刺はどんな時に必要なの？

日本では初対面の人と会う時、名刺交換をする習慣が定着しています。特にビジネスでは名刺が不可欠で、部署が変わったり昇進するたびに名刺をつくり直します。また、年初には業界や団体などの「賀詞交換会」が恒例行事になっています。

日本人の名前は、音が同じでも文字が異なる場合がよくあります。例えば、一郎には「いちろう」「かずお」「かずろう」などがあって、正確な読み方を相手に伝えるためにも名刺が必要なのです。

ゲーテの名刺

▶名刺
印刷した名刺は、明治時代に西洋から伝えられました。それ以前は、和紙に名前を手書きしたものを相手に渡していました。

Q: 印鑑はどんな時に必要なの？

契約などで承認したことを示す時、欧米ではサインをしますが、日本では印鑑（ハンコ）を押すのが慣例です。印鑑は①実印、②認め印に大別されます。実印は、居住地の市区町村に登録しておき、重要な契約の際には登録証明書を発行してもらう必要があります。認め印は苗字だけのものが多く、職場の書類や家庭の届け出など日常的によく使われます。

実印
legal seal

認め印
private seal

Q: How are business cards used?

Traditionally, business cards are exchanged on first meeting someone. This is particularly true in business contexts, and new cards must be made whenever there is a change in one's title or division. It is also common practice to exchange business cards at New Year's gatherings held by a particular industry or organization.

Business cards are also useful in notifying others of how to pronounce one's name. Japanese generally use Chinese characters (*kanji*) to write their names, and since *kanji* can have more than one pronunciation, business cards are useful in providing the correct one.

> ▶ **Business cards**
> Business cards were introduced from the West during the Meiji period (1868-1912). Before that, it was the custom to write one's name on a piece of Japanese paper (*washi*) and present that to the other party.

Q: When are seals necessary?

While in the West the authorization of a contract or other such document is made by signing it, in Japan this is customarily done with a seal. There are basically two types of seals: the *jitsu-in* or legal seal, and the *mitome-in* or private seal. The legal seal must be registered with the local administrative region in which one resides and a certificate of registration obtained when authorizing important documents. Private seals, generally engraved only with one's surname, are widely used on workaday company papers and routine notifications such as deliveries from the post office.

国にも「国璽」と呼ばれる印鑑があり、外交文書などに用いられます。英国などの場合は蠟に刻印する方式ですが、日本では朱肉をつけて書面に押します。

日本の国璽

On the national level, there is the seal of state, which is impressed on diplomatic documents. In the United Kingdom, the seal is impressed on wax, while in Japan it is pressed on a pad of cinnabar ink and then applied to the paper.

第7章 外交
Diplomacy

国際連合本部 ▶

1 国際関係

Q: 外交関係がある国は、いくつ?

195か国です。国連加盟国は193か国ですが、このうち北朝鮮だけは未承認のため正式な外交関係はありません。国連非加盟国で日本が承認しているのは、バチカン市国、コソボ共和国、クック諸島で、中華民国(台湾)、パレスチナなど正式な外交関係がない国がいくつかあります。正式な外交関係がある国同士は、外交官を相手国に駐在させます。日本の在外公館数は200を超えます(2014年)。

Q: 国連に加盟したのは、いつ?

国際連合(国連)は1945年10月、第二次世界大戦の戦勝国を中心にした51か国が加盟してスタートしました。本部がニューヨークに置かれているのは、米国が誘致に積極的だったからです。

1 International Relations

Q: How many countries does Japan have diplomatic relations with?

Japan has diplomatic relations with 195 countries. This includes all of the 193 UN member states, excepting North Korea, which Japan does not recognize as a sovereign state. Non-UN members that Japan recognizes are the Vatican City, Republic of Kosovo, and the Cook Islands. There are a number of countries with which Japan has no diplomatic relations, such as the Republic of China (Taiwan) and Palestine. When two countries establish diplomatic relations, they post a diplomat to the other country. At present Japan has over 200 foreign missions (2014).

Q: When did Japan join the United Nations?

The United Nations was established in October 1945 by 51 nations, chiefly the victorious nations in World War II. The headquarters was situated in New York owing to American enthusiasm for the project.

日本は敗戦6年後に加盟申請をしましたが、常任理事国のソビエト連邦（当時）が拒否権を発動したため否決されました。加盟できたのは、日ソ国交正常化後の1956年12月です。

Q: 国連の分担金は、いくら？

国連の活動を維持するために、加盟国は国力に応じた割合のお金（分担金）を負担しています。2014年（2012 - 14年）の上位6か国は、次の通りです。① 米国6.21億、② 日本2.76億、③ ドイツ1.82億、④ フランス1.42億、⑤ 英国1.32億、⑥中国1.31億（金額：米ドル）。

Q: 常任理事国になれないのは、なぜ？

国連では、安全保障理事会が強大な権限を持っています。なかでも米国、英国、フランス、ロシア、中国の5か国は常任理事国として、重要問題の決定に対する拒否権が与えられています。つまり、5か国のうち1か国でも反対すれば国連決議ができない状況なのです。

米国に次ぐ国連分担金を負担している日本が、常任理事国になっても不思議ではありません。なれないのは、国連憲章の「敵国条項」（第二次世界大戦での連合国の敵国として日本、ドイツ、イタリアが認定）がネックになっていると言われています。

Japan applied for membership six years later, but owing to the opposition of the Soviet Union, a permanent member the Security Council, it was rejected. It was only in December 1956 that Japan was accepted, following the normalization of Japanese-Soviet relations.

Q: How is UN funding shared?

The operating costs of the UN are shared by member states according to economic strength. The top six contributing countries for the 2012-2014 period are as follows: 1) United States ($621 million), 2) Japan ($276 million), 3) Germany ($182 million), 4) France ($142 million), 5) United Kingdom ($132 million), and 6) China ($131 million).

Q: Why can't Japan become a permanent member of the UN Security Council?

In the UN, the Security Council possesses immense power. Five members of the Security Council have permanent status and have veto power over all resolutions. In other words, if one permanent member opposes a resolution, it cannot be passed.

Considering the fact that Japan's contribution to UN funding is second only to that of the United States, it wouldn't be surprising if it were to become a permanent member of the Security Council. It is commonly said that one roadblock to this happening is the enemy-nation clause in the UN charter that approves the use of force against the losing nations in World War II—Japan, Germany and Italy.

第7章 外交

Q: ODAとは、なに？

開発途上国や国際機関に供与する「政府開発援助」です。飢えや貧困に苦しみ、教育や医療を満足に受けられない人々がいる国、環境問題や情報技術格差などを抱える国などを対象にODAを通じて発展を手助けし、地球全体の問題解決を図るのが目的です。

日本は経済成長期にODAに力をそそぎ、1990年代は世界一の拠出国となりました。拠出額は97年の約1.17兆円をピークに減少し、2014年は約0.55兆円と半減しています。これは日本が迫られている行財政改革が原因です。

アジアの新興国の発展は、日本のODAで経済インフラ整備が進んだためと評価されています。

Q: 日本もPKOに参加しているの？

国連平和維持活動（PKO）は、国際紛争や国内紛争の平和的解決に向けた国連の活動の一つです。

日本は1991年の湾岸戦争を機に積極的な国際協力を求められ、「PKO協力法」を成立（92年）させてペルシャ湾に自衛隊を派遣しました。以来、8つの紛争地でのPKO活動に参加してきました。2015年1月現在で派遣継続中のPKOは「国連南スーダン共和国ミッション（UNMISS）」（2011年7月～）です。

Q: What is Japan's contribution to ODA?

ODA (official development aid) refers to government aid to international institutions and developing nations. The aim is to assist countries suffering from famine and poverty, those where education and healthcare is not fully developed, and countries afflicted with environmental problems and gaps in information technology, thereby making an overall contribution to international peace and stability.

When the Japanese economy was at its height, Japan contributed heavily to ODA, and in the 1990s was the world's foremost donor nation. Reaching a peak of some ¥1.17 trillion in 1997, it began to decline thereafter, falling to ¥0.55 trillion in 2014, a victim of administrative and financial reform.

The emergence of newly developing Asian countries is said to be partially due to Japan's contributions to economic infrastructure.

Q: Is Japan participating in UN Peacekeeping Operations?

Peacekeeping Operations (PKO) refers to activities by the UN aimed at peaceful resolution of international and civil conflicts.

In 1991, at the time of the Gulf War, Japan was asked to play an active role in PKO operations, and after the passage of the PKO Cooperation Law in 1992, it dispatched Self-Defense Forces to the Persian Gulf. Subsequently, Japan has participated in PKO operations in eight conflicted areas. As of January 2015 it is taking part in the United Nations Mission in South Sudan (UNMISS, ongoing since July 2011).

Q: 日本が加盟している国際経済機構は？

世界の自由貿易推進をめざして1995年に設立された国際貿易機関（WTO）、アジア地域の経済機構としての東南アジア諸国連合（ASEAN・10か国）、環太平洋地域の多国間経済協力を推進するための非公式なフォーラムであるアジア太平洋経済協力会議（APEC）などです。

ASEANには加盟10か国に日本・中国・韓国を加えたASEAN＋3と、さらにオーストラリア・ニュージーランド・インドを加えたASEAN＋6があります。

Q: TPPとは、なに？

太平洋に面した各国間で、貿易自由化のための関税撤廃と市場開放を進めるための環太平洋経済連携協定（TPP）の交渉が進んでいます。この協定は2005年にシンガポール、ブルネイ、ニュージーランド、チリの4か国が調印したP4協定を基に発展したもので、交渉参加国（8か国）を含め12か国の経済機構です。日本は2013年4月に参加しました。

この協定は24分野に及ぶ市場開放と関税撤廃をめざしているため、保護産業を抱えている国（例えば日本はコメ、牛肉などの農産物）は国内の反対もあって、交渉が難航しています。TPPは、世界の総生産の約4割、貿易額の3分の1を占めるとされています。

Q: What international economic organizations does Japan belong to?

With the aim of promoting world free trade, Japan is a member of the World Trade Organization (WTO, established in 1995), the Association of Southeast Asian Nations (ASEAN, comprising 10 Southeast Asian countries), and the Asia Pacific Economic Cooperation (APEC; a forum that promotes free trade throughout the Pacific-Rim region).

Japan participates in ASEAN+3, which consists of the 10 ASEAN countries plus Japan, China, and South Korea, and ASEAN+6, which consists of the further addition of Australia, New Zealand, and India.

Q: What is the Trans-Pacific Partnership?

The Trans-Pacific Partnership (TPP) is a proposed agreement among Pacific-Rim countries to create a customs-free, free-trade market among member nations. It is built on an agreement (called the P4) concluded in 2005 by Singapore, Brunei, New Zealand, and Chili. There are 12 participating countries (8 involved in the negotiations). Japan officially joined negotiations in April 2013.

TPP aims to create customs-free, free-market conditions in 24 categories, and since some of these categories include protected items (for example, rice, meat, and other agricultural products in Japan), the negotiations have met with domestic opposition and are experiencing difficulties. The TPP countries account for 40% of total world production and 30% of total trade.

2 外交課題

Q: 米国とは、どんな問題があるの？

　　日米関係を象徴するのが、安全保障条約です。この条約の特徴は、米国は日本を防衛する義務があるが、日本は米国を防衛する義務がない代わり米軍基地の土地を提供するなどの特権を与えるとされている点です。近年、日本政府が自衛の措置に関する新たな3要件を示し、従来より踏み込んだ集団的自衛権行使を閣議決定（2014年7月）しました。その背景には、米国の強い要請があったとも言われます。

　　日米安保条約との関連で、日米地位協定が結ばれています。この協定は終戦の時の日米関係（日本は敗戦による米国の占領国）を反映しているため、日本の裁判所は在日米軍の兵士や軍属を裁くことができないなど米国優位の内容になっています。国内の米軍基地の7割がある沖縄では、日米地位協定が生み出す問題を抱えています。

　　他の大きな問題としては、経済摩擦です。米国は対日貿易で巨大な赤字をこうむってきました。日本が戦後に経済発展できたのは核の傘で守ってきてあげたから、というのが米国の言い分です。米国は、日本をTPP交渉に参加させることで市場開放を迫り、経済的にも優位に立と

2 Diplomatic Issues

Q: What kinds of issues are there with the United States?

The most outstanding issue between Japan and the United States involves the Japan-US Security Treaty. A prominent feature of this treaty is that while the United States is obliged to defend Japan militarily, Japan is not obliged to defend American forces, but instead provides the United States with land for bases as well as other privileges within Japan. In July 2014 the cabinet approved three new conditions for the use of force by the Self-Defense Forces, expanding the interpretation of the right to self-defense beyond previous conventional thinking. It is said this was done at the strong insistence of the United States.

In the process of formulating the Japan-US Security Treaty, an agreement was also concluded on the status of forces. This agreement reflects the relationship of the two countries at that time (Japan as a defeated nation under US occupation), placing the United States in a position of superiority: for example, in the fact that American military personnel and attached civilians could not be judged in Japanese courts. In Okinawa, where 70% of American bases are located, this status of forces agreement is still a source of contention.

Another outstanding problem between the two countries is economic friction. The United States has long recorded a deficit in trade with Japan. The American argument is that Japanese postwar economic development was made possible by the fact that Japan was protected by the American "nuclear umbrella." Now, with American insistence that Japan take

うとしています。

Q: 中国とは、どんな問題があるの?

近年、日中関係が良好ではありません。原因は主に政治的対立にあり、その影響は貿易量の低減に表れています。一方、民間交流は活発で観光・商用などで日本を訪れた人は約240万人(2014年)で、円安も手伝って急増中です。

政治的対立点は、主に以下の2つです。①歴史認識の対立：日中戦争時の南京虐殺、靖国参拝問題など。②領土問題：東シナ海の尖閣諸島(中国名：釣魚島)の領有権をめぐる対立。

Q: ロシアとは、どんな問題があるの?

領土問題です。北海道の東端・根室岬の沖合に連なる国後島、択捉島、歯舞諸島、色丹島は1855年に江戸幕府とロシアの間で結ばれた条約で日本領と定められました。ところが90年後、ソ連邦軍が攻め入って占領し、翌年にソ連邦の領土と宣言して約1万7000人の日本人島民を追い出したのです。

その後、日ソ共同宣言(1956年)で歯舞島と色丹島の2島を日本に返還することになったのですが、ソ連邦も解体後のロシアも約束を守って

part in the TPP negotiations, the United States is hoping to make inroads into the Japanese market and achieve the same kind of superiority in economic terms.

Q: What kinds of problems exist with China?

Recent relations with China are not good. The principal reason lies in political disagreement, and the results are seen in the decline of trade between the two countries. Conversely, the number of Chinese people visiting Japan for tourism and on business has spiked, reaching some 2,400,000 in 2014, thanks in part to the depreciation of the yen.

The political contention between the two countries has two roots: 1) differences in historical perspective concerning the "Nanking Massacre" during the Second Sino-Japanese War, the Yasukuni Shrine issue, as well as other matters, and 2) a territorial dispute over the Senkaku Islands (Diaoyu in Chinese) in the East China Sea.

Q: What problems exist with Russia?

Mainly, territorial issues concerning the islands lying to the east of Hokkaido's Nemuro Peninsula: namely, Etorofu, Kunashiri, Shikotan, and Habomai. In 1855, in an agreement between Russia and the Tokugawa shogunate, these islands were declared Japanese territory. But 90 years later, near the end of the Pacific War, they were occupied by Soviet troops and the next year annexed by the Soviet Union, which proceeded to expel some 17,000 Japanese islanders.

According to the Japan-Soviet Joint Declaration of 1956, Habomai and Shikotan were to be returned to Japan, but that promise was never kept, even after the dissolution of the

いません。日本は4島一括返還を前提に交渉を進めようとしています。

Q: 韓国とは、どんな問題があるの?

日韓関係は近年、悪化しています。韓国と日本は、海を隔てた隣国同士で古くから人的、文化的交流が盛んに行われていました。現代の日本人の祖先は朝鮮民族という説もあるほど、顔立ちも似通っています。いわば身内の関係だけに、対立は根深くなります。

決定的な対立関係の原因は、1910年に帝政時代の日本が大韓帝国を植民地にし、日本名を名乗らせて日本語による教育を行い、労働者や兵士として日本に強制連行したことです。韓国が政治問題としている従軍慰安婦問題も、日本の併合時代のことです。日本による統治は、太平洋戦争での敗戦の年（1945年）の9月まで続きました。韓国では子ども達に併合時代の日本人がいかに悪かったかを教えていますが、日本では韓国がかつて日本の植民地だったことを認識している子どもは多くありません。

Q: 北朝鮮とは、どんな問題があるの?

韓国と北朝鮮は、もともと同じ民族です。日本が朝鮮半島を植民地にしていた時代、日本軍は北緯38度を南北に分けて支配していました。第二次世界大戦後、南を米国、北をソ連邦が占

Soviet Union. Japan is continuing negotiations with Russia on the premise that all four islands should be reverted to Japanese administration.

Q: What issues exist with South Korea?

Recent relations with South Korea have not been good. Japan and Korea are neighboring countries separated by a narrow sea and have long enjoyed people-to-people and cultural exchange. In physical appearance the two peoples are very similar, to the extent that some scholars believe that the Japanese originated in Korea. Being closely related, contention between the two tends to be deep and long-lasting, like family feuds.

The critical moment in the relations of the two countries occurred in 1910 when Imperial Japan annexed Korea, forcing Koreans to adopt Japanese names, mandating education in the Japanese language, and conscripting Koreans as laborers and soldiers in the Japanese army. The issue of "comfort women" now being taken up by the South Korean government is a legacy of this same period. The annexation of Korea continued until the end of the Pacific War in September 1945. In South Korea children are taught how terrible Japanese annexation was, but in Japan there are few children who realize that Korea was once a Japanese colony.

Q: What issues exist with North Korea?

North Koreans and South Koreans are, of course, genetically the same people, but when Japan occupied the Korean peninsula, it administratively divided the country into north and south along the 38th parallel. Following the end of the

領しました。そして1948年、南で大韓民国（韓国）が、北で朝鮮民主主義人民共和国（北朝鮮）が独立を果たしました。ところが50年、両国間で戦争（朝鮮戦争）が始まり、南を米国軍・国連軍が支援し、北をソ連軍・中国軍が支援しました。戦争は決着がつかず休戦となりましたが、53年以来休戦状態が今日まで続いています。

2002年9月、小泉総理が訪朝して金正日総書記と会談をした結果、70〜80年代に起きた日本人の拉致を公式に認めて謝罪、拉致被害者5名が帰国しました。国交正常化を進める平壌宣言を発表しましたが、その後、正常化交渉は中断したままで、拉致問題も進展していません。

北朝鮮は、日本の併合時代の賠償を強く求めています。拉致問題、核兵器開発疑惑、日本を射程に入れた中距離ミサイル開発など国際世論を無視した国家言動は、北朝鮮が今も戦時体制下にあることを背景にしているのですが、長く平和になじんできた日本人には理解が及びません。

Q: 中東諸国とは、どんな問題があるの？

第一に、石油問題です。日本はサウジアラビア、アラブ首長国連邦（UAE）など中東諸国か

Pacific War, the United States occupied the southern half, and the Soviet Union the northern. In 1948 the southern Republic of Korea and the northern Democratic People's Republic of Korea were established. In 1950 the Korean War broke out, with the United States and the UN supporting the south and the Soviet Union and China the north. With neither side achieving a definitive victory, an armistice was declared in 1953, which continues to the present day.

In September 2002 Japanese prime minister Junichiro Koizumi visited North Korea and met Supreme Leader Kim Jong-il. As a result, North Korea admitted the abduction of Japanese citizens in the 1970s and 1980s and apologized, with five abductees being allowed to return to Japan. Negotiations were announced for the normalization of relations, but they remain stalled at present, and no progress has been made regarding the abductions.

North Korea is demanding reparations for damage inflicted during the Japanese annexation of Korea, and is entangled in a number of other diplomatic problems, including abductions, the suspicion of developing nuclear weapons, the development of medium-range ballistic missiles that can reach Japan, and other behavior that ignores international opinion. The fact is that North Korea still considers itself to be in a state of war. For Japanese, who have enjoyed decades of peace, this is difficult to comprehend.

Q: What issues are there with Middle Eastern countries?

First and foremost is the problem of petroleum. Japan relies on roughly 87% of its petroleum imports from Saudi

ら原油を輸入していますが、輸入量のほぼ87％を依存しています。原油の生産量・価格は、中東などの12か国が加盟しているOPEC（石油輸出国機構）が決めています。かつて日本は、原油の価格高騰によって二度のオイルショック（1973年、79〜80年）を経験しています。

第二に、中東諸国の不安定な政治状況です。中東諸国の多くはイスラム教が浸透していて、キリスト教徒やユダヤ教徒との抗争、イスラム過激派のテロなどが多発しています。近年は、現地の抗争やテロに巻き込まれて犠牲になる日本人もいます。

日本の外務省は海外渡航者に対して、4段階の危険度で現地の情勢をリアルタイムで広報しています。

レベル1	十分注意してください。
レベル2	渡航の是非を検討してください。
レベル3	渡航の延期をお勧めします。
レベル4	退避を勧告します。渡航は延期してください。

Arabia, the United Arab Emirates, and other Middle Eastern countries. The price and production of petroleum is decided by the Organization of the Petroleum Exporting Countries (OPEC), which consists of 12 Middle Eastern countries. In the past Japan has experienced two crises ("oil shocks") due to skyrocketing oil prices (1973 and 1979-80).

Second is the unstable political situation in the Middle East. Middle Eastern countries are largely Islamic, giving rise to conflict with Christians and Jews and frequent acts of terrorism carried out by Islamic extremist groups. In recent years there have been cases where Japanese have fallen victim to these conflicts and acts of terrorism.

The Japan Foreign Ministry issues danger warnings at four levels to travelers going abroad, providing real-time information on local conditions.

Level 1	Exercise caution.
Level 2	Rethink your need to travel.
Level 3	Deferring of travel plans recommended.
Level 4	Leave area of warning and defer any plans to return.

第8章 暮らし
Chapter 8 Everyday Life

英虞湾（あごわん）▶

1 日本人の特質

Q: 日本人って、どんな民族なの？

世界の民族的な特徴は、狩猟民族と農耕民族に大別されます。狩猟民族は移動をして食料を得る必要があるため、狩りのテクニックや情報量がものを言います。一方、農耕民族は定住をして収穫の時を待つというタイプです。その意味で日本人は元来、農耕民族と言えます。

特に稲作が定着した3世紀頃には、人口が250万ほどに増大し、大規模集落が各地に形成されました。稲の栽培はとても手間がかかり、田植えや稲刈りでは多くの人手が必要です。そこで勤勉と協調性が日本人の基本的な労働観として形成されたのです。この労働観が、戦後日本の経済成長の原動力になりました。

世界は今、高度情報化時代。これを主導したのは米国に象徴される狩猟民族です。どこにどんな獲物がいるかという情報量が貧富を分ける

1 What Characterizes the Japanese People?

Q: What kind of people are the Japanese?

Peoples throughout the world can be basically divided into hunters and farmers. Hunters must be constantly on the move to gain sustenance, and they not only become adept at the techniques for stalking their prey but knowledgeable in the ways of their movements. Farmers, on the other hand, are sedentary and patient as they wait for harvest time. For the most part, Japanese belong to the farming or agricultural type.

By the 3rd century AD, when rice cultivation had become firmly established, the population had grown to about 2,500,000, and large-scale villages appeared throughout the country. The cultivation of rice was labor-intensive, with the planting and harvesting requiring the hands of many people. Cooperation and diligence were essential, and these characteristics became ingrained in the Japanese people. It was this work ethic that provided the driving force behind the rapid growth of the postwar Japanese economy.

The world now has entered an information-intensive age. It has been led by hunter societies such as the United States. Since it is all-important to know the whereabouts of

ため、情報に対する意識が高いのです。欧米型の暮らしになじんできたことで近年、日本人の労働観も変質しつつあります。

Q: イエス、ノーをはっきり言わないのは、なぜ？

日本人は、外国人に比べて自己主張をしないと言われます。国際会議などで、「顔が見えない日本人」と揶揄されることもあります。要するに個性的でなく、何を考えているのか分からないというわけです。イエス、ノーをはっきり言わないのは、対人関係を悪くしたくないという思いが強いからです。これは、農耕民族として協調性が重視されてきたことと無縁ではありません。

「出る杭は打たれる」という言葉があるように、集団生活を維持するには皆が同じレベルであることが必要で、そこからはみ出す人は異端とされます。島国で狭い土地に住む日本人にとって、所属する集団の中で生きてゆくには、自己主張をしない、目立とうとしないことが大事な処世術なのです。

Q: 日本人の特性とは？

日本を訪れた外国人が驚くのは、一般的に日本人が礼儀正しく、清潔好きで、細やかな気配りをしてくれることだそうです。こうしたことも、農耕民族としての集団生活を通して培われてきた特性と言えるでしょう。

日本は、外国と比べ四季の区別がはっきりし

the prey, these societies are immensely eager to accumulate information. As Japan has become more and more familiar with Western ways, its work ethic has begun to undergo a gradual change.

Q: Why can't Japanese give a clear yes or no answer?

It is often said that Japanese are less assertive than other people. At international conferences and other such forums, Japanese have been described as being faceless, that they don't stand out as individuals, and that it is hard to know what they are really thinking. Japanese often don't give a clear-cut yes or no answer for fear of antagonizing the other party. This characteristic undoubtedly has its roots in the cooperation and collaboration that is so essential to an agricultural society.

As expressed in the proverb "The protruding nail is driven down," it is necessary for everyone to be on the same plane in order to sustain life in a communal setting; anyone who sticks out from the crowd is treated as a heretic. For Japanese, living in tightly-knit communities on small confined islands, getting along amicably with others means not being self-assertive and not drawing attention.

Q: What are the outstanding Japanese cultural traits?

Foreign visitors to Japan often say they are surprised by how polite Japanese are, how cleanly, and how attentive to the smallest detail. These traits can be attributed to the communal life of an agricultural people.

Compared to many other countries, the four seasons

ています。そして、季節の移り変わりを感じながら生活をしてきました。農耕民族には、自然を畏れながらも共生する知恵があります。外国人、特に欧米人を驚かせるもう一つが、神様が多いことです。これは、自然を神として畏れ崇めてきたからに他なりません。

古来、日本は多神教の国です。一神教では神に見放されたら救いはないといった厳格性がありますが、多神教の日本では「捨てる神あれば、拾う神あり」ということわざが示すように、神と人間の関係はおおらかでゆるやかです。とかく、ものごとをあいまいにしがちな日本人の特性は、多神教の民族だったことも影響しているのです。

2 衣

Q: 洋服はいつから着るようになったの？

日本人が洋服を着るようになったのは江戸時代末期からで、明治政府が近代化の象徴として軍人や役人に着用を義務付けたことをきっかけに、一般人にも普及し出しました。ただし女性は、上流階級の社交上の礼装として着用される程度で、一般的に着るようになったのは大正時代以降です。

of the year are very distinctive in Japan. The Japanese have long lived with these seasonal changes, observing and feeling them in their daily lives. Over time, Japanese developed the practical intelligence to live in coexistence with nature while at the same time fearing it. Another thing noted by foreign visitors, Westerners in particular, is the plethora of gods in Japan. This too is attributable to a long history of both fearing and revering nature.

Japan has been a polytheistic country from ancient times. In monotheistic countries, God is very strict, and once you have lost his favor, it is lost forever. But in polytheistic Japan, the relationship between the gods and man is much more flexible and forgiving, as indicated by the proverb "If one god disowns you, there is always another to save you." The Japanese tendency to leave things up in the air may have its origins here.

2 Clothing

Q: When did Western clothing become common?

Western clothing came to be worn near the end of the Tokugawa period (1603-1868), and then when the new Meiji government required it of soldiers and civil servants as a sign of the movement toward Westernization and industrialization. From there, Western garb began to spread among the masses. However, women wore Western dress only on high-society formal occasions, and it was only in the Taisho period (1912-26) that Western clothes became more widely worn.

Q: 和服はどんな時に着るの？

年配者や仕事上で着る必要がある人以外、日常的に和服を着る人はほとんどいなくなりました。年の初めに気分を改めるために和服で正月を迎えたり、仕事初めに女性が着物で出勤するといった風習がまだ見られますが、あとは伝統行事や結婚式などの祝い事で和服姿が見られる程度です。

着物の一種の浴衣は、和風旅館に宿泊するとおなじみですが、略式なので公式の場には出られません。近頃、夏の花火大会で浴衣を着て見物する若者が増えているのは、ファッションの一種のようです。

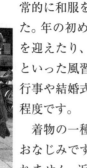
浴衣

Q: 男性の和服の正装は？

男性の場合の正装は、黒紋服です。これを着るのは生涯一度、結婚式の新郎になった時だけという人も少なくありません。しかも黒でなく、きらびやかな色紋服が流行しているので、本来の正装である黒紋服の出番は少なくなる一方です。

紋服とは、家系を表す紋章を入れた和服のことですが、自分の家紋を知らない人もたくさんいます。

Q: 女性の和服の正装は？

女性の場合の正装は、既婚者は留袖、未婚者は振袖とされます。留袖は黒地に家紋を入れ、

Q: When is Japanese clothing worn?

Except for older people and those whose work requires it, Japanese clothing has virtually disappeared from daily life. Sometimes you see women wearing kimonos on the first working day of the New Year or on New Year's Day to mark a fresh start in the coming year. Otherwise, the principal occasions are traditional events, weddings and other celebrations.

The light cotton kimono called a *yukata* is a familiar sight at Japanese inns, but it is strictly informal and not to be worn out in public. However, young people can be seen wearing *yukata* at summer fireworks as a sort of fashion statement.

Q: What does formal Japanese wear for men consist of?

Formal attire for men consists of black wear emblazoned with the family crest (*kuromon-puku*). For many men, the only occasion on which they wear such formal attire is on their wedding day. Recently more colorful formal wear with the family crest has become popular, and so the need for black formal attire is gradually diminishing.

While it is true that formal men's garb requires the family crest, many people these days don't know what their family crest is.

Q: What does formal attire for women consist of?

Formal wear for women is divided into two types: *tomesode* for married women and *furisode* for unmarried. *Tomesode* is

膝下には華やかな模様が描かれています。振袖は色地にあでやかな模様が描かれ、袖丈が足元近くまである大振袖、それよりも短い中振袖、小振袖があります。

外出用の略式の和服として訪問着があり、既婚・未婚を問いません。女性の和服には時と場所による決まりごとがあります。

3 食

Q: 和食の特徴は

日本人の食生活は、パンや肉類を多く食べる欧米型になってきています。2014年12月、ユネスコが「和食」を無形文化遺産に登録しました。その特長の一つに挙げられたのが栄養バランスに優れた食生活です。

和食の基本はコメを主にした一汁三菜で、ご飯に汁もの、おかず三種（主菜一品、副菜二品）で構成されたメニューです。動物性油脂が少ないことから肥満防止に役立ち、ご飯は栄養価が高いだけでなく腹もちが良いので、間食を避けることができます。しかし、日本ではコメ離れが進み、肉や菓子類など高カロリー食物を好む傾向が強くなり、肥満が社会問題化しています。ユネスコに申請する際の和食の定義は、「三世代前の日本人が家庭で常食としていたもの」だったそうです。和食は日本人にとって、過去の遺

a black kimono with a family crest and a colorful design on the area below the knees. The *furisode* has a colorful design on a colored background and sleeves of three different lengths (long, medium, and short), with the longest reaching the floor.

There are also semiformal kimonos for women, worn when going out and paying visits, in which there is no difference between married and unmarried women. According to time and occasion, there are numerous rules governing women's wear.

3 Food

Q: What is Japanese cuisine (*washoku*)?

While on the one hand Japanese are eating more Western food like meat and bread these days, on the other hand Japanese cuisine was named an Intangible Cultural Heritage by UNESCO in December 2014. One of the features of *washoku* was said to be its superlative nutritional balance.

The traditional menu is described as *ichiju-sansai*, which means "one soup and three dishes." Basically, this indicates a meal composed of rice, a soup, one main dish, and two supplementary dishes. It is low in animal fat and thus a guard against obesity, and the rice is not only high in nutritive value but filling, warding off the desire to eat between meals. Of late, however, there is a strong tendency toward high-calorie foods such as meat and confectionaries, allowing obesity to raise its ugly head. When *washoku* was submitted to UNESCO for consideration, it was described as the customary meal in Japanese households three generations ago. For the Japanese people, it seems that *washoku*

産的存在になりつつあります。

Q: 日本人の一般的な食事習慣は？

一日三食で、家族全員が揃って食べる家庭は少なくなりつつあります。朝食はパンや牛乳といった欧米型の食事が増え、昼食は昔は家庭で作った弁当を食べるのが一般的でしたが、今は学校給食や外食ですませてしまう人が大半です。サラリーマンや生徒達には朝食抜きが増えていることが指摘されています。夕食は比較的、家族全員が揃って食べることが多いようですが、それでも週に二、三日程度と言われます。

家庭の食事は、子供達の好みを反映するためハンバーグやカレーライスなどになりがちで、昔からの和食が敬遠される理由もここにあります。

Q: よく食べる魚料理にはどんなものがあるの？

外国人にもよく知られているのが、寿司、天ぷらです。寿司ネタは魚介類の肉を薄く切ったものですが、寿司づくりは習練が必要なため専門店で食べるのが一般的です。

家庭でよく食べるのは魚介類の刺身で、ワサビやショウガと醤油をつけます。刺身の定番は、マグロです。

天ぷらにすると美味しいのがエビ、イカ、白身の魚などです。揚げたてを食べるのが、天ぷらの最も美味しい食べ方です。その他、手軽な調理法として、魚に塩をちょっと振りかけて焼

is slowly becoming a thing of the past.

Q: What is the usual meal like?

The number of families that eat three meals a day together is becoming rather rare. Breakfast consists simply of bread or toast and milk. Lunch, formerly a homemade box lunch, is now mostly a school cafeteria lunch or eaten out. Salaried workers and students often skip breakfast entirely. Dinner is when the family is most likely to come together, but even then it is often only two or three times a week.

Even when the family sits down at the table together, the meal is most likely to consist of what the children favor, hamburger or curry rice. Traditional Japanese food is given a wide berth.

Q: How is fish most often eaten?

Abroad, the most widely known Japanese ways of eating fish are sushi and tempura. Sushi makes use of thinly sliced fish or other seafoods, and since the slicing is a rather delicate task, sushi is most often eaten out at a sushi restaurant.

At home, seafood fare consists mostly of fish (*sashimi*) and other seafood that has been sliced into eatable portions, dipped in ginger, *wasabi* mustard, or soy sauce. The standard for *sashimi* is tuna.

The seafoods most often used in tempura are shrimp, squid, and light meat fish. Tempura tastes best when it is still hot. Other simple ways of eating fish include grilling after lightly salting (*shioyaki*), grilling after applying a soy-based

く塩焼き、醤油をベースにしたタレを付けて焼く照り焼き、醤油の中に入れて煮込む煮付けなどがあります。

Q: 醤油・味噌はいつから使うようになったの？

食材を微生物の働きで発酵させる方法は、人類が太古の昔に発見しました。日本では縄文時代の遺跡から、発酵食品をつくっていたことが確認されています。

醤油も味噌も、その原型とされるものは8世紀頃からあったようですが、庶民の間で普及するようになったのは16世紀中頃と言われます。いずれも大豆を発酵させた調味料ですが、醤油は今や世界100か国で流通する日本を代表するブランド名になっています。

大豆の発酵食品として、豆腐や納豆があります。豆腐は奈良時代に中国から日本に伝わったとされます。大豆は「畑の肉」と呼ばれるように、植物性たんぱく質が豊富で、肉や牛乳などのタンパク質に比べて脂肪分が少ないため、低カロリー食材として日本人が好んで食べます。しかし、原料の大豆の90％ほどを輸入に頼っています。

その他の発酵食品には日本酒、茶、鰹節、漬物、寿司などがあります。

Q: うどん、そばの違いは？

歴史的には、うどんは中国から伝わった製法をもとにした麺、そばは日本独自の麺という違

sauce (*teriyaki*), and stewing in soy sauce (*nitsuke*).

Q: When did soy sauce and miso come to be used?

Early humankind soon discovered how to prepare food by fermentation using microorganisms. In Japan, evidence of fermented foods has been discovered in sites from the Jomon period (about 12,000 to 300 BC).

Evidence of what might be called the prototypes of miso and soy sauce have been found from the 8th century, but it was only in the mid 16th century that they became widely used among the common people. Both are made from fermented soy beans and are now used as a representative Japanese seasoning in more than 100 countries around the world.

Natto and tofu are also made from fermenting soy beans. *Natto* is said to have been brought to Japan from China in the Nara period (710-784). Soy beans are so rich in vegetable proteins that they have been called the "meat of the fields." They are also low in fat compared to meat and milk, and have long been a favorite low-calorie food among Japanese. The beans themselves are mostly imported, accounting for nearly 90% of Japanese consumption.

Other fermented Japanese foods include saké, tea, *katsuobushi* (dried, fermented, and smoked skipjack tuna), pickled vegetables, and sushi.

Q: What is the difference between udon and soba?

Historically, udon are a type of noodles made according to a process that originated in China, while soba are noodles made

いがあります。材料の違いは、うどんが小麦粉、そばがそば粉を使うことです。ただし、そばもつなぎ(接着材)に小麦粉を使っています。つなぎの小麦粉の割合や、卵や芋をつなぎとして使うことで、そばにはいくつかの種類があります。

また、醤油をベースにしたつゆの中に麺を入れ温めて食べる「かけそば」、冷たいつゆにつけて食べる「もりそば」など、食べ方もさまざまです。日本そばは、寿司・天ぷらと並ぶ代表的な日本料理とされます。

Q: すきやきって、なに?

薄くスライスした牛肉や野菜などを、底の浅い鉄鍋で焼いたり煮たりする日本独特の料理です。味付けは醤油と砂糖が基本で、溶いた生卵にからめて食べます。

すきやきは、明治時代になって流行した牛鍋から発展したもので、それまでの日本人は牛肉を食べる習慣がありませんでした。現在、牛肉は和牛4種とそれ以外の国産牛、輸入牛に大別され、15段階の格付けがされています。最上級がA5等級で、和牛と呼ばれる品種です。

牛肉を、すきやきの場合よりもさらに薄くし、熱湯にくぐらせて食べるのが、しゃぶしゃぶです。

Q: 寿司はいつから食べるようになったの?

寿司の語源は「酸し」で、すっぱいことを意味していたというのが有力な説です。奈良時代頃

in a uniquely Japanese way. As far as ingredients are concerned, udon is made of wheat flour, and soba of buckwheat. Soba also uses wheat flour as a binding. According to the ratio of wheat, and whether egg or yam is also used as a binding, there are various varieties of soba.

There are also differences in how soba is eaten depending on whether it is dipped in a warm soy-based sauce (*kakesoba*) or a cold sauce (*morisoba*). Along with sushi and tempura, soba is one of Japan's most typical foods.

Q: What is sukiyaki?

Sukiyaki is a unique Japanese cuisine prepared by cooking or simmering thinly sliced meat and vegetables in a shallow pot. Its basic seasonings are soy sauce and sugar, and it is usually eaten after dipping it in a raw beaten egg.

Sukiyaki developed from beef hot pots in the Meiji period (1868-1912). Until then, Japanese were not accustomed to eating beef. At present, beef is divided basically into four breeds of Japanese cattle (*wagyu*) and other domestic breeds as well as imported beef. There are 15 ranks in all. The top rank, A5, consists mostly of the breed known as Japanese Black.

Shabu-shabu can be considered a type of sukiyaki, where the meat is sliced even more thinly and submerged in boiling water before eating.

Q: When did sushi come into being?

The etymological origin of "sushi" is probably the word meaning "sour" (*su*). Vinegared rice has been eaten since

から食べられていたようで、握り寿司などで使う酢飯(すめし)に、そのなごりがあります。

昔は魚介類を飯と塩で乳酸発酵した「なれずし」が主流で、保存食として重宝されました。今も日本各地に、特有のなれずしが伝わっています。江戸時代になって、酢飯の上に魚介ネタを乗せて握って客に出す「早ずし」が流行し、これが現在の握り寿司(江戸前寿司)に受け継がれています。

江戸前寿司

▶ 江戸前寿司
　江戸前とは、江戸の町の前に広がる海(現在の東京湾)にちなんだ言葉です。海では魚介類がたくさん獲れ、それを新鮮なうちに客にたべさせようと"早ずし"が工夫されました。

Q: うなぎはいつから食べるようになったの？

日本人の好物のうなぎは、古代人も食べていたようです。奈良時代にはむなぎと呼んでいたことが『万葉集』に記されています。栄養価が高く、体力増強にも役立つということで、日本では夏バテ防止のために土用(どよう)の丑(うし)の日に食べると良いと言われていますが、これは江戸時代からの風習です。

うなぎの調理法は、関東と関西で大きく異なります。関東では背中から切り分けるのですが、

the Nara period (710-784), and the origin of the word has survived in the "sour" vinegared rice (*sumeshi*) used in *nigirizushi* (hand-pressed sushi).

In the distant past, the principal type of sushi was *narezushi*, which consisted of lacto-fermented seafoods and rice that was much valued as a way of preserving food. Even now local varieties of *narezushi* have come down to us. In the Edo period (1703-1868) a type of "quick" sushi became popular that featured seafood placed on vinegared rice and pressed conveniently together by hand. The present-day version of this is the familiar *nigirizushi* (or *Edomae-zushi*) that is so common today.

▶ Edomae-zushi

Edomae originally referred to the bay that was in "front of the town of Edo" (now Tokyo). The seafood caught in this bay (present Tokyo Bay) was delivered to customers while still fresh in the newly invented form of "quick sushi" or *Edomae-zushi*.

Q: When did grilled eel become a favorite food?

Eel was a favorite food of Japanese even in the distant past, and is mentioned in the Nara-period poetry anthology *Collection of Myriad Leaves* in the 8th century. High in nutritional value and said to be a fortifier against the summer doldrums, grilled eel has been especially recommended on the Midsummer Day of the Ox since the Edo period.

The preparation of eel differs greatly between the Kansai and Kanto regions. In Kansai, the eel is first sliced through the

関西では腹から切り分けます。武士が多かった江戸では切腹に通じるとして、うなぎの腹に包丁をあてるのを嫌ったためと言われています。

2014年、ニホンウナギがIUCNレッドリストに絶滅危惧種として選定されました。日本人が食べるうなぎはほとんどが養殖もので、輸入うなぎも増えています。

Q: 改まった席で出される料理とは?

結婚披露宴や料亭・旅館などで出される日本料理は、会席膳とも言います。この献立は一汁三菜(吸い物・刺身・焼き物・煮物)を基本としています。

料理は①先付(前菜)、②椀物(吸い物)、③向付(刺身)、④鉢肴(焼き物)、⑤強肴(煮物)、⑥止め肴(酢の物またはあえ物)、⑦食事(ご飯・味噌汁・漬物)、⑧水菓子(果物)の順に出されます。

同じ呼びかたの懐石は、禅宗の修行僧の食事に由来し、ルーツは同じなのですが、会席のほうは酒席で出される料理という大きな違いがあります。

Q: 食器の正しい置き方は?

食事内容が欧米型になったと言っても、日本人が伝統的に行なってきた食事作法は、まだ受

belly, but in Kanto this is done through the back. Since Kanto and Edo were the home of the samurai, they associated any reference to cutting the belly with ritual disembowelment (*hara-kiri* or *seppuku*), a subject they preferred not to contemplate. Or so the story goes.

In 2014 the Japanese eel was placed on the International Union for the Conservation of Nature and Natural Resources' list of threatened species. The eel eaten by Japanese today is mostly of the cultured variety, with imports increasing.

Q: What is the most formal Japanese cuisine?

The cuisine served at weddings, high-class Japanese restaurants, and inns is called *kaiseki*, or simply put, dinner cuisine. It consists of the "one soup and three dishes" mentioned above (basically, soup, *sashimi*, something grilled, and something stewed).

The order in which dishes are served is as follows: 1) an appetizer, 2) clear soup, 3) *sashimi*, 4) grilled fish, 5) a dressed or vinegared dish, 6) something stewed, 7) the main course (rice, miso soup, and pickled vegetables), and 8) fruit.

There is another type of cuisine called *kaiseki* (though written with different Chinese characters), which originated in the food eaten by Zen ascetics. Though the two types of *kaiseki* have the same roots, the one mentioned in the previous paragraph is distinguished by the fact that it is served at banquets.

Q: Is there a fixed order to the placement of tableware?

Even while it is true that Japanese eating habits have become Westernized, traditional etiquette is still generally followed.

け継がれています。箸は頭を右にして手前に置く、ご飯茶碗は左、味噌汁は右に置くのが基本とされます。

箸の持ち方、使い方の作法もあり、正しい持ち方（下図）を子供の頃からしつける家庭も多く、料理を突き刺したり、皿の上であれこれと選ぶしぐさなどは禁じられています。

Q: 日本酒の種類は？

日本酒は「清酒」とも呼ばれます。原料は米、米麹、水です。米を精米して洗い、糠を取り除き、適当な分量の水を吸収させた後、水をきって蒸し、麹と水を加えて20日間ほど発酵させ、圧搾機にかけて酒と酒粕に分離します。分離した酒の滓を取り除いたものが、清酒です。

精米とは、米粒を磨いて内部のたんぱく質や脂肪を削り取ることですが、削り取る割合を「精米歩合」と言い、これが50％以下が大吟醸酒、60％以下が吟醸酒、70％以下が本醸造酒といった区別がされています。

● 箸の正しい持ち方　The right way to hold chopsticks

① 箸の一本を、親指の腹と薬指の先で固定させる。

One chopstick is secured between the ball of the thumb and the tip of the ring finger.

② もう一本を、親指の先と中指の先で挟むようにして、上から人差し指を添える。

The other is held between the tip of the thumb and tip of the middle finger, and steadied by the index finger above.

③ 食べ物をつまむ時は、人指し指と中指を上下させる

Move the middle and index fingers up and down to pick up food.

The rule is for chopsticks to be placed in the forefront with the pointed end facing left, and the rice bowl on the left and soup bowl on the right.

The usage of chopsticks is also subject to various rules, with the right way to hold them taught to children in most households from an early age. Stabbing food or playing with it while deciding what to eat next is a definite no-no.

Q: How many different kinds of saké are there?

Japanese saké is also called *Nihon-shu*, or more accurately *seishu*. The ingredients are rice, yeast (*koji*), and water. The rice is polished and washed, the bran removed, the rice soaked in water, the water removed and the rice steamed, water and yeast (*koji*) added and fermented for 20 days, then placed in a compressor and the bran and saké separated. The lees are then removed, the result being *seishu*.

By polishing the rice, the protein and fats in the rice grains can be removed, and the percentage of weight remaining after polishing is called the rice polishing ratio. Types of saké are classified according to this ratio. If it is below 50%, the resulting saké is called *daiginjo-shu*; if below 60%, *ginjo-shu*;

● お椀の開け方　The correct placement of bowls

蓋が付いているお椀は、蓋が開けにくい場合が多いが、開けかたにはちょっとしたコツがある。

Some bowls have lids, and these can be difficult to remove. However, there is a knack to it.

お椀の口を指で内側に軽く押さえ付けながら、蓋の上部をつまんで回すと簡単に開く。

Press down lightly on the rim of the bowl with your fingers, then hold the top of the lid and twist. It will open easily.

また、原酒は製成後にアルコール１％以上の加水調整をしていないもの、生酒は製成後に加熱処理をしていないものなどの分類もあります。

清酒は毎年７月から翌年６月を製造年度として、この間に出荷されたものを新酒、製成後１年以上貯蔵されたものを古酒、３年以上貯蔵されたものを長期貯蔵酒と呼んでいます。

Q: 日本酒の飲み方は？

大きく分けると、温めて飲むのと、冷えた状態で飲む２つの方法があります。冷やというのは、冷蔵庫で冷やしたものではなく、本来は常温のお酒のことです。

温める場合は、温度によって表現が変わります。30度前後はひなた燗、37度前後は人肌燗、40度前後はぬる燗、45度前後は上燗、50度前後は熱燗、55度前後はとびきり燗などと言います。

こうした言葉の中に、繊細な日本人の感性と表現力の豊かさを読み取ることができます。お酒を注文する時、「人肌燗で」などと言えば、通人です。

and if below 70%, *honjozo-shu*.

There are other ways of classifying saké. *Genshu* has not been diluted more than 1% ADV. *Namazake* has not been pasteurized.

Seishu refers to saké produced each year from July to June of the following year. Saké shipped during this period is called *shinshu* (new saké), and that aged for over a year is called *koshu* (old saké). Saké aged for over three years is called *choki chozo-shu* (long-term storage saké).

Q: Is there a particular way to drink saké?

Basically, there are two ways to drink saké, either hot or cold. "Cold" means at room temperature, not refrigerated.

Different terms apply when drinking saké hot, according to the temperature. Around 30 degrees is called *hinatakan* (sun-warmed), about 37 degrees *hitohadakan* (skin warm), about 40 degrees *nurukan* (lukewarm), about 45 degrees *jokan* (prime warmth), about 50 degrees *atsukan* (hot), and about 55 degrees *tobikirikan* (over-the-top hot).

Even in the names given to the temperatures of saké, one can gain an appreciation of Japanese sensitivity to the minutest matters. When ordering saké, if you casually say, "Make it *hitohadakan*," you will surely be considered a connoisseur.

4 住

Q: 日本の住宅の特徴は?

日本の住宅は古来、木造でした。一方、西洋の住宅は伝統的に石造りです。ここに、日本人と西洋人の自然の捉え方の違いを見ることができます。石造りの住宅は堅牢で外界に対して閉鎖的ですが、木造住宅は開放的で、例えば中庭のように自然を積極的に取り込むといった工夫がされています。また、建材も天然素材を用いるのが和風建築の大きな特徴です。

しかし、1970年代以降、住宅の工業化が進むにつれて国産材の供給難や伝統工法を身に付けた職人の減少などで和風建築は衰退しつつあります。

Q: 土地や建物の値段はどのように決めるの?

土地・建物の面積は、日本独特の坪という単位で示します。一坪は、約3.3平方mです。土地の値段は法律で基準が決められ、それに基づいた実勢価格で取引されています。東京の都心部では、一坪数千万円という土地もあります。建物の値段は、使う材料のグレード次第ですが、坪単価50万円前後が一般的です。

例えば東京郊外で、都心まで1時間ほどの場所に約30坪(約100平方m)の一戸建て住宅を買

4 Japanese Housing

Q: What distinguishes Japanese housing?

From the ancient past Japanese houses have consisted of wood. Western houses, on the other hand, have traditionally been made of stone. This difference allows a glimpse into how the two traditions view nature. Western housing is very solid and sturdy, creating a world of its own that holds nature at arm's length. Japanese housing, conversely, is open to nature and tries to incorporate natural elements into the house itself, such as seen in the creation of enclosed gardens that can be viewed from the interior. Another significant feature of Japanese housing is its use of architectural materials in their natural form.

However, in the 1970s the industrialization of housing construction began, domestic lumber was hard to come by, and experienced craftsmen became few and far between. The traditional wooden home went into a decline.

Q: How is the price of land and houses decided?

The area of land and houses (and buildings in general) is calculated in a unique Japanese measurement called a *tsubo*. One *tsubo* is the equivalent of 3.3 square meters. The price of land is decided on the basis of this legal standard. In central Tokyo one *tsubo* may cost as much as several tens of thousands of yen. The *tsubo* price of a building will be somewhere around ¥500,000, depending on the grade of the construction material.

If you want to buy a 30-*tsubo* (about 100 square meter) residence in the suburbs about an hour from downtown

おうとすると、3000～5000万円ほど必要になります。

Q: 賃貸住宅の契約時にいくら必要？

契約に際しては、①敷金(保証金)、②礼金、③仲介手数料、④1カ月分の家賃(入居日によって日割り計算)が必要です。敷金(通例は家賃の2カ月分)と礼金(同1カ月分)は家主が、仲介手数料(同1カ月分)は不動産業者が受け取ります。賃貸契約は一般的に2年契約で、続行する場合は更新料が必要になります。敷金は転居する際に返金されますが、室内を破損した場合などの修理費用は差し引かれます(東京の場合)。

Q: しゃがんでするトイレがあるって、本当？

腰掛け式の、いわゆる洋式便器が普及している日本ですが、公衆トイレや地方の住宅では、しゃがんでする和式便器が多く見られます。洋式便器の普及は、お年寄りにとって体の負担が少ない、掃除がしやすいなどの理由からです。

和式便所

▶ **和式便器**

昔から使用されてきた木製の和式大便器を、ホーロー製の水洗式にしたもの。男性の場合は別に小便器があるが、一般家庭では大小兼用として使われることが多い。

Tokyo, you could expect to pay ¥30-50 million.

Q: What is the initial cost of renting a house or apartment?

The initial costs upon signing a contract are 1) *shikikin* (security deposit), 2) *reikin* (key money), 3) *chukai tesuryo* (brokerage fee), and 4) the equivalent of one month's rent (paid pro rata depending on when occupancy takes place). The security deposit (usually equivalent to two-months rent) and the key money (also two months) are paid to the landlord; the brokerage fee is paid to the real estate agent. Contracts are generally for two years, and a renewal fee is required upon extension. The security deposit is returned when the renter moves out, but any fees paid for damage to the property are deducted, at least in the case of Tokyo.

Q: Are squat toilets still used?

While so-called Western toilets, where one sits on the bowl rather than squatting over it, are now wide-spread, there are still a good many squat types to be seen in public places and rural residences. The spread of Western toilets is due to the fact that sitting is less taxing for older people than squatting, and cleaning and maintenance is much easier.

▶ The squat-type toilet

The traditional wooden squat-type toilet was converted into a porcelain water-flushed bowl. There is often a separate bowl for men to urinate, but in most cases the one bowl serves for both defecation and urination.

Q: 寝具の特徴は?

日本伝統の寝具はふとんで、体を横たえるための敷きぶとん、体の上にかぶせる掛けぶとんがあります。布の袋の中に綿が入っていますが、高級品には羊毛(敷きぶとん)や羽毛(掛けぶとん)を入れます。

ふとんには汚れ防止のカバーを掛けたり、シーツを敷き、これらを取り換えて使います。寝汗がしみ込んだふとんは、洗濯せずに天日で乾かします。ふとんは、使わない時は押入れなどに収納しておきます。

Q: なぜ、玄関で靴を脱ぐの?

外国人をしばしば戸惑わせるのが、家の玄関で靴を脱がなければならないことです。外観が洋風の家でも、玄関で靴を脱ぎスリッパにはき替えなければなりません。こうした習慣は、室内が畳の部屋だった時代のなごりが受け継がれていることによるものです。玄関から先は土足禁止…これが日本の流儀なのです。

Q: 畳は、なにでできているの?

近頃は板張りの洋間が増えていますが、お年寄りほど畳敷きの和室を好む傾向があります。畳の表面は、イグサという植物を乾燥させて編み込んだ敷物でできています。板張りと違って柔らかく、独特の匂いがあり、心をなごませるのです。

畳のサイズには地域性があり、関東の江戸間

Q: What does Japanese bedding consist of?

Traditional Japanese bedding consists of the futon (or *shikibuton*) for lying on and the *kakebuton* for covering oneself. The futon is essentially a bag with cotton inside, though pricier items contain wool (*shikibuton*) or down (*kakebuton*).

To keep them clean, futon have a cover or sheet, which are periodically changed. Futons that have accumulated some sweat are not washed but hung out in the sun. When not in used, futon are stored in a closet or elsewhere.

Q: Why are shoes removed in the entryway?

One Japanese custom that sometimes confuses foreign visitors is the fact that shoes must be removed in the entryway. Even in homes that are Western in every other respect, shoes must be exchanged for slippers when entering the house. This custom is a legacy of the day when most of the rooms of the house were covered with easily soiled tatami matting. In any case, Japanese etiquette requires the shoes to be taken off before entering the house proper.

Q: What are tatami mats made of?

While Western-style rooms with wooden flooring are becoming ever more prevalent, older people still retain a liking for tatami-covered Japanese rooms. The surface of tatami consists of rush straw that has been dried and woven. Different from wooden flooring, tatami is soft and possesses a distinctive smell that is both restful and relaxing.

The size of one tatami mat varies somewhat according

（880mm×1760mm）、関西の京間（955mm×1910mm）、団地間（850mm×1700mm）などがあります。畳は5年おき程度で、表面を新しいものに張り替えるのが良いとされます。

Q: 床の間って、なに？

家の中心的な和室に一画に作られた空間で、掛軸や生け花などを飾ります。床の間を背にした位置が上座で、客をもてなす時にはこの位置に座ってもらいます。

ちなみに、ビジネスマナーでもどこが上座なのかが重要視され、例えば応接室では入口から一番遠い座席が上座とされます。

Q: 襖と障子の違いは？

襖と障子は、いずれも和室の仕切り用の建具です。襖は、木の骨組みの両面に和紙や布を貼り、引き手が付いています。唐紙とも呼ばれることから、中国渡来のものと推察されます。

襖を日本独自に発展させたのが障子で、扉や窓としての役割があります。その歴史は古く、平安時代からとされます。木の枠に和紙を貼った障子は、電灯やガラスがなかった時代は採光のための建具として重宝されました。

また、一部がガラスで障子の部分を開閉でき

to region, with the Kanto size being 880 by 1760 mm, the Kansai size 955 by 1910 mm, and the *danchi* (apartment complex) size 850 by 1700 mm. It is generally held that every five years or so the surface of the tatami should be rewoven.

Q: What is a *tokonoma*?

The *tokonoma* is a recessed area built into the wall of the main Japanese room, where a hanging scroll or a flower arrangement is displayed. The primary guest or person at a gathering of people sits with his or her back to the *tokonoma*, a position known as the *kamiza* (superior seat).

The *kamiza* retains its importance in other venues, such as business meetings, where, for example, the seat nearest to the door of a reception room is consider the *kamiza*.

Q: What is the difference between a *fusuma* and a *shoji*?

Fusuma and *shoji* are both used as partitions in a Japanese room. A *fusuma* has a wooden frame covered with opaque Japanese paper (*washi*) or cloth on both sides and has a finger catch for opening and closing. From the fact that it is also called a *karakami* (Tang paper), it is suspected to have come originally from China.

The *shoji* is a Japanese enhancement of the *fusuma* and serves as a door or window. Its history is fairly old, with its first appearance being made in the Heian period (794-1185). The wooden frame is covered with translucent *washi*, which had the invaluable role of introducing sunlight into interiors in an age without electric lighting or glass.

In some later *shoji* the lower half is made of glass, over

るものは「雪見障子」といって、部屋を閉めきったままで外の景色が見られます。このように風流を重視した点に、和風建築の特徴があるといっても過言ではありません。

5　冠婚葬祭

Q: 子どもが産まれてすぐしなければならないことは?

14日以内に、出生の届け出を市区町村役所にしなければなりません。「出生届書」は子どもの名前や両親についての必要事項を記載するほか、医師や助産師が記載する「出生証明書」が付いています。

したがって、子どもの名前は法律上、14日以内に決めなければならないのが原則です。子どもの名前を書いた「命名書き」を飾る習慣もあります。

また、生後100日目には、子どもの健康と成長を願って行う「お食い初め」という儀式も一般的に行なわれています。

Q: 七五三とは、どんな行事なの?

子どもの成長を願って、主に神社参拝をします。男の子は3歳と5歳、女の子は3歳と7歳になった年の11月15日に近所の神社に連れて行き、参拝後に「千歳飴」を食べる神事です。

which the papered upper half can be raised or lowered. This is called a *yukimi shoji* (snow-viewing *shoji*), allowing the garden outside to be seen from the inside while keeping out the cold air. It is this integration of interior and exterior that forms one of the distinctive characteristics of traditional Japanese architecture.

5 Weddings and Other Special Occasions

Q: What is required after the birth of a child?

Within 14 days of the birth of a child, notification must be made to the nearest local government office. This birth registration includes not only the name of the child but pertinent information concerning the parents, as well as a birth certificate signed by the doctor or midwife in attendance.

Thus the name of the child must be legally decided within 14 days. There is also the custom of displaying in the home the name of the child written on a piece of special paper.

On the 100th day after birth, another ritual is commonly held called *okuizome* (first meal), in which the future health and well-being of the child is prayed for.

Q: What does 7-5-3 mean?

This refers to a visit to a temple or, more commonly, a shrine to celebrate the growth and well-being of young children. This takes place on November 15 when boys are three and five years old and when girls are three and seven. In conclusion, the children are given *chitose-ame* (thousand-year candy) to eat.

江戸時代に始まったとされますが、地域によっては11月15日に限定していないケースもあります。

Q: 成人式とは、どんな儀式なの？

子どもから大人になることを意味し、日本では満20歳の男女（前年の4月2日〜翌年4月1日の間）を招いて、毎年1月15日（国民の祝日）に市区町村が主催して「成人式」が行われています。

元来、日本では奈良時代以降から11〜16歳の男児が成人したことを示す儀式が行われ、武士階級の「元服(げんぷく)」はよく知られています。成人を20歳としたのは明治時代からで、欧米にならったとされます。

「成人式」では成人代表や来賓のスピーチなどが主で、出席者は記念品をもらって帰ります。参加者の多くは友人たちと再会できる場ということで、おしゃれをして出かけるチャンスと考えているようです。なかには、目立とうと奇抜な言動をして周囲のひんしゅくを買う新成人もいて、警官隊が出動する会場もあります。

ちなみに、2015年の新成人人口はおよそ126万人（男性65万人、女性61万人）で、21年ぶりに増加しました。

This custom is said to have started in the Edo period (1603-1868). According to the region, the day is not necessarily restricted to November 15.

Q: What is the coming-of-age ceremony?

The coming-of-age ceremony is an annual rite of passage celebrating the transition from childhood to adulthood. Ceremonies are held by local administrative units for all twenty-year-olds (that is, those who have turned twenty between April 2 of the previous year and April 1 of the following year). It is a national holiday.

From the Nara period (710-784) onward, a coming-of-age ceremony was held for boys reaching adulthood between the ages 11 and 16. Among the samurai class, the rite of passage called *genpuku* is one example of this. In the Meiji period (1868-1912), twenty was designated as the age when adulthood is reached, supposedly following Western example.

The ceremony consists mainly of speeches by representatives of the new adults and the invited guests, after which the young participants receive commemorative gifts as the ceremony concludes. Most of the guests apparently look upon this occasion as an opportunity to meet old friends and dress up accordingly. Now and then, feeling their newly found independence, some of the new adults get a little out of hand, causing such fusses that the police is called for.

In 2015 the new adult population reached some 1,260,000 (650,000 men and 610,000 women), the largest number in 21 years.

Q: 日本人の一般的な結婚式とは？

日本で広く行われているのが、神前結婚式です。特に信仰心がなくとも、神様の前で結婚の誓いをすることを、現代の若者はごく当たり前のこととして受け入れているようです。これはキリスト教の教会での挙式に憧れる女性が多いことにも共通しています。

結婚式場やホテルでは、祭壇を常設して神主や牧師に出張してもらうといった方法を採用しています。近年は、宗教色をなくした人前結婚式も普及し始めています。

結婚式は身内だけが出席し、記念撮影をした後、招待客が待つ宴会場に移動して新郎新婦のお披露目(ひろめ)をします。

Q: 結婚式の費用はいくらかかるの？

招待客の数が、挙式費用の目安になります。結婚式場の場合は、一般的に招待客70名でおよそ350万円といったところが相場です。つまり、招待客一人当り5万円前後で予算を組む必要があります。そんなにお金がないという場合は、グレードを下げたり、招待客数を減らす、会場を変えるなどの工夫をしなければなりません。

結婚式は本人たちだけでなく、両家のプライドも関わってくるため、どうしても華美になりがちです。親に挙式費用の支援をしてもらった新婚夫婦は約7割とも言われます。一方で、たった一日のためにお金を使うのは嫌と、二人だけで記念写真を撮って終わりというケースも増え

Q: What is a typical Japanese wedding?

The most common type of wedding is a Shinto ceremony. Even though the happy couple may not be particularly religious, they have no qualms about pledging their troth before the Shinto gods. The same applies to marriages at Christian churches, which are especially fashionable among young women.

In wedding halls and large hotels, altars have often become permanent fixtures, and priests and ministers are invited to provide the services. In recent years civil services before family and friends are also on the increase.

The actual wedding ceremony takes place before close family only, followed by commemorative photographs. The bride and groom then repair to a spacious reception hall to greet relatives and friends assembled there.

Q: How much does a wedding cost?

The number of invited guests provides an indication of what the costs will be. The standard fee for 70 guests would be about ¥3,500,000, that is, about ¥50,000 per person. If this is prohibitive, then the overall quality of the ceremony must be ratcheted down a notch, the number of guests cut back, or a less expensive venue found.

Since it is not only the wishes of the bride and groom that are involved but the pride of the two families, weddings tend to be rather gorgeous. Weddings in which the families have chipped in to cover costs amount to some 70% of the whole. Still, some couples are reluctant to spend so much money on a single day of their lives, leading to the increasing incidence

Q: 結婚のお祝いの相場は、いくら？

披露宴に招待された場合、お祝い金をいくら包むべきか悩む場合が多いようです。お祝い金の額は時代によって変わってきていますが、友人や職場の同僚なら3万円、職場の上司や目上の親戚なら5万円、親族は5～10万円というのが今の相場とされます。

Q: 日本人の結婚年齢は、いくつ？

昔は結婚年齢が低く、女性は10代で嫁ぐのが当たり前とされた時代もありましたが、今は25～34歳が多くなっています。2013年の人口動態調査では、初婚の女性約46.2万人のうち、25～29歳が約19.4万人、30～34歳が約10.9万人で、合わせると6割強を占めています。男性もほぼ同様の傾向が見られます。

● お金を包む袋

Envelopes for monetary gifts

● 結婚以外の慶事用

Envelopes for auspicious occasions other than marriage

of weddings that end with the commemorative photograph.

Q: What is the going rate for a wedding gift?

At Japanese weddings it is customary to present the bride and groom with a monetary gift rather than a present. The amount involved is often the subject of considerable cogitation. While it is true that this type of thing changes with the times, the standard now seems to be ¥30,000 for friends and colleagues, ¥50,000 for higher-ups at the workplace and older relatives, and ¥50,000 to ¥100,000 for close family.

Q: What is the average marriage age?

The marriage age used to be much lower than now. There were times, in fact, when it was entirely acceptable for women to marry in their teens, though now between 25 and 34 is becoming more common. The demographic survey for 2013 shows that out of about 462,000 women marrying for the first time, 194,000 were between 25 and 29, and about 109,000 were between 30 and 34, accounting for more than 60% of the total. The same trend is evident for men as well.

● 葬儀では「御霊前」が宗派を問わず使える

● お見舞い用

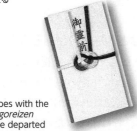

Envelopes with the words *goreizen* ("for the departed spirit") may be used regardless of religious affiliation.

Envelopes for use when visiting the ill

Q: 外国人との国際結婚は多いのですか？

国際的な交流が進んでいる近年、国際結婚は増加しています。2012年の人口動態調査では年間の婚姻件数約75.7万組のうち、日本人男性と外国人女性のカップルが約1.7万組、日本人女性と外国人男性のカップルが約6500組でした。これは正式に届けを出した数なので、内縁関係のカップルを含めるともっと多くなります。

外国人の妻で多いのが中国人（約42％）とフィリピン人（約20％）、夫で多いのが韓国・朝鮮人（約28％）と米国人（約18％）です。

Q: 毎年、離婚する人はどれくらいいるの？

2013年の人口動態調査では、1年間の離婚件数は約23.1万件でした。2分16秒ごとに1組の夫婦が離婚をしたことになります。正式な離婚に至らないまでも、同居していながら会話もない家庭内離婚も増加しています。日本の法律では、離婚後6カ月以上たたなければ再婚できないことになっています。

Q: 日本人が祝う記念日にはどんなものがあるの？

一般的なものとしては「長寿祝い」があります。元来は奈良時代に中国の風習を取り入れたもので、やがて日本独自のものに発展しました。年齢の数え方は、昔は生まれた年を1歳として新年を迎えるごとに1歳ずつ加えた数え年を用

Q: Are international marriages common?

With the modern-day increase in international exchange, the frequency of international marriages has also increased. According to the demographic survey for 2012, of the 757,000 marriages that took place, those between a Japanese man and a foreign woman amounted to about 17,000, and marriages between a Japanese woman and a foreign man to about 6,500. This counts only marriages that have been registered with the authorities; if common law marriages were included, the numbers would be much higher.

Cases where the wife is Chinese account for about 42%, and where Filipino, about 20%. Among marriages where the husband is a foreigner, North and South Koreans account for about 28%, and citizens of the United States for about 18%.

Q: How many divorces are there a year?

According to the 2013 demographic survey, the number of divorces reached 231,000 a year. That means there was a divorce every 2 minutes 16 seconds. The number of couples who are living together but otherwise have no communication is also on the increase. Incidentally, Japanese law states that a woman cannot remarry until six months after the date of divorce.

Q: What ages are objects of special commemoration?

The most common dates for celebration are those that have to do with reaching a certain venerable age. This custom was introduced from China in the Nara period (710-784) and gradually took on a unique Japanese form. Until the recent past the way ages were calculated was different from today. A

いていましたが、今は還暦以外は満年齢で祝う人が多いようです。

還暦（60歳）　古稀（70歳）　喜寿（77歳）
傘寿（80歳）　米寿（88歳）　卒寿（90歳）
白寿（99歳）　百寿・鶴寿（100歳）

　日本では、かつて100歳まで長生きする人は珍しかったのですが、今は5万人以上もいる長寿社会になっています。
　他には、結婚25年目を祝う銀婚式、50年目を祝う金婚式などがあります。

Q: 贈り物で注意しなければならないことは？

　病気のお見舞いなどでは、鉢植えの花は「根付く＝寝付く」という意味で縁起が悪いとされているので避けなければなりません。同様に4（＝死）、9（＝苦）という数も不吉とされがちなので、果物などを贈り物にする場合は、数に気を付ける必要があります。

Q: 日本の一般的な葬儀は？

　葬儀は宗教と関連が深いのですが、特定の信仰をしていない日本人の場合、仏式で葬儀をするのが一般的です。これは、江戸時代の国民す

new-born baby was considered one year old at birth and then gained another year with the coming of the New Year. This is called *kazoedoshi*. Now, except for *Kanreki* (celebrating the age of 60), most people count their age based on their birthday (this is called *mannenrei*). The principal days for celebrating old age are as follows:

Kanreiki (60)	*Koki* (70)	*Kiju* (77)
Sanju (80)	*Beiju* (88)	*Sotsuju* (90)
Hakuju (99)	*Hyakuju* or *Kakuju* (100)	

Formerly, the number of people who reached the age of 100 was rather few, but now there are over 50,000.

Other days calling for celebration are the 25th year of marriage (the silver anniversary) and the 50th year (the gold anniversary).

Q: Is caution required in presenting a gift?

When taking a gift to someone in the hospital, potted plants are to be avoided because "taking root" is a homonym for "taking to bed." Likewise anything that has to do with the numbers 4 and 9 is considered unlucky because they are homonymous with "death" and "agony." When giving someone fruit or anything that is countable, care must be taken with how many there are.

Q: What is the typical funeral like?

Funerals usually have strong religious associations, but except for special cases, Buddhist funerals are the norm for most Japanese. This is a legacy of the Edo-period system

べてが寺に所属するという檀家制度のなごりが現在にも続いていることによるものです。

日本人の大半は、仏教寺院の墓地に先祖代々のお墓があります。そのため、亡くなった人を埋葬する関係上、必然的に仏式で葬儀をすることになるのです。

Q: 仏式の葬儀はどのように行われるの？

亡くなると、まず通夜が行われます。本来は遺族や近親者が終夜、遺体を見守ることを意味していましたが、現在は葬儀場などに遺体を運び、多くの参列者を迎えてお別れをしてもらう儀式になっています。そして翌日、故人の成仏を祈る葬式に引き続いて最後の別れを行う告別式が行われます。告別式の後、遺体は遺族や近親者が付き添って火葬場に運ばれ、火葬にされます。

仏教では死者の霊は49日間、この世とあの世の中間にとどまっているとされるため、亡くなった日を含め7日ごとに霊をなぐさめる法要を行うのが正式とされますが、現代では簡略化され、最初の7日目の「初七日」は葬儀の際に行い、最後の7日目の「四十九日」の法要だけ行うのが一般的です。

なお、遺族や近親者のみで通夜、葬式を行う場合を「密葬」と言います。

Q: 葬儀の費用はいくらぐらいかかるの？

全国平均で約200万円というデータがあります（日本消費者協会調べ、2010年）。これには、

according to which all Japanese had to be registered at a Buddhist temple.

The majority of Japanese have a family tomb at a Buddhist temple where their ancestors have been laid to rest. Consequently, when a funeral takes place, it is of necessity conducted according to Buddhist convention.

Q: What does a Buddhist funeral consist of?

When someone passes from this life, the first rite to be held is a wake. This originally meant that blood relatives and close family would spend the entire night with the deceased. Now it generally means moving the body to a funeral home where large numbers of family and friends participate in a rite of final departure. The next day, after prayers are offered for the deceased's achieving Buddhahood, a ceremony of final farewell is held. The family and close relatives then accompany the deceased to a crematorium where the body is cremated.

According to Buddhist belief, since the spirit of the deceased is in a state of suspension between this world and the world to come for the first 49 days, every seven days a ceremony is held to console the departed spirit. In recent practice, this is generally abbreviated so that a service is held on the 7th day and then on the 49th.

Wakes and services attended by family alone are called *misso* (lit., cryptic services).

Q: How much does a funeral cost?

According to the Japan Consumers' Association (2010), the national average is ¥2,000,000. This includes funeral services

葬儀費用（平均約126万円）、寺院費用（平均約51万円）、飲食接待費用（平均約45万円）が含まれています。葬儀費用の最低額は20万円で、"密葬"の場合の費用のめやすになります。

Q: 埋葬はどのようにするの？

宗教に関係なく遺体はほとんどの場合、火葬にされます。日本では昔は遺体をそのまま地中に埋める土葬も多く見られましたが、土地不足や衛生上の問題から土葬が制限されるようになりました。一部ですが、土葬を認めている自治体もあります。

火葬後の遺骨は骨壺というケースに入れ、しばらくの間、自宅で家族が供養・保管した後、お墓に納めます（納骨）。

墓石

> ▶墓石
>
> お墓は石でつくられていて、下部に納骨スペースがあります。壺のまま入れるケースと専用袋に移し換えて納めるケースがあります。お墓がない場合は、納骨堂という施設を利用する方法があります。

Q: 死後の法要はいつまでするの？

仏式では、亡くなってから49日目を「忌明け」と言い、法要を行うと共に香典やお供え物を頂いた方に挨拶状を添えてお礼の品物を送る慣わし（香典返し）があります。その後は、亡くなった年を1年として数える「年忌法要」があ

(¥1,260,000), temple costs (¥510,000), and reception and refreshment fees (¥450,000). The minimum cost of funeral services is ¥200,000, which is the approximate cost of "cryptic" services.

Q: How are the deceased interred?

Regardless of religious persuasion, cremation is the general rule. In the not too distant past, burial in the earth was commonly practiced, but with the increasing lack of sufficient space and due to hygienic reasons, this tradition came under restriction. Some—though not many—local government bodies still allow burial in the earth without cremation.

After cremation, the ashes of the deceased are placed in an urn and kept in the family home where they can be offered daily prayers. After an appropriate period has elapsed, the urn is interred in the family tomb.

▶ Family Tombs

Family tombs are gravestones that have a recess in the bottom for the placement of the deceased's ashes. The cremation urn is sometimes placed as-is in this recess; sometimes the ashes are transferred to a special bag. In cases where the deceased does not possess a family tomb, communal ossuaries are available for use.

Q: How long do services for the dead continue?

According to Buddhist practice, on the 49th day after the deceased's passing, a special service is held and "a return gift" is sent to those who offered monetary or other offerings at the time of the funeral, along with a note expressing the family's appreciation. Thereafter, on the day the deceased

ります。一周忌（死後1年目）、三回忌（同2年目）、七回忌（同6年目）、十三回忌（同12年目）、十七回忌（同16年目）、二十三回忌（同22年目）、二十七回忌（同26年目）を経て、三十三回忌（同32年目）を「年忌止め」として終えるのが一般的ですが、五十回忌（同49年目）や百回忌（同99年目）を行うケースもまれにあります。

神式では十日祭、百日祭、一年祭……百年祭。キリスト教式の場合も、カトリック教会での追悼ミサ、プロテスタント教会の記念ミサなど、死者の霊をとむらう行事が折々に行われています。

6 行 事

Q: 国民の祝日は？

日本には1948年に制定された「国民の祝日に関する法律」があり、2014年6月の法改正で「山の日」（8月11日）が新たに加えられ、2016年から年間日数が16日となります。祝日が日曜日と重なるときは、翌日の月曜日は休みです。

元日（1月1日）
: 年の初めを祝う。2日、3日を加えた3日間は連休になるのが一般的。

成人の日（1月の第2月曜日）
: 20歳の人の祝い。

passed, memorial services are generally held. These take place on the 1st year since passing, the 2nd year, the 6th year, the 12th year, the 16th year, the 22nd year, and the 26th year, with the 32nd being the concluding year. Memorial services are also held on the 49th and 99th year, but only rarely.

In the Shinto religion, memorial services are held on the 10th day since passing, the 100th day, the 1st year, and so on until the 100th year. In Catholic churches in Japan, requiem masses are held for the repose of the souls of the dead, and similar services are conducted in Protestant churches.

6 Holidays and Special Occasions

Q: What are the national holidays?

The Public Holiday Law was established in 1948 and last amended in June of 2014, at which time Mountain Day (August 11) was added (to be first observed in 2016), bringing the total number of holidays to 16 for 2016. When a holiday overlaps with a Sunday, the following Monday becomes a holiday. The national holidays are as follows:

New Year's Day (January 1)
> To celebrate the beginning of the year. The 2nd and 3rd are traditionally added for a three-day holiday.

Coming of Age Day (second Monday in January)
> To celebrate reaching the age of 20. See also "coming-of-age ceremony."

建国記念の日（政令で定める日　2月）
　　　2月11日に行われていた紀元節にちなむ祝日。国を愛する心を養う日と意義付けられているが、反対論もある。

春分の日（3月20日または21日）
　　　太陽が春分点を通過する日で、自然をたたえ、生物をいつくしむ日と定義されている。

昭和の日（4月29日）
　　　昭和天皇の生前、天皇誕生日として祝っていたのを継続した。2006年まで、みどりの日と呼ばれていた。

憲法記念日（5月3日）
　　　1947年のこの日に新憲法が施行されたのを記念する日。

みどりの日（5月4日）
　　　3日と5日が祝日なので3連休にしようとの意味合いが強いのは、4月29日だったのをこの日に移動させたことからうかがえる。

こどもの日（5月5日）
　　　こどもの健康、幸福を願う日。昔の男児の成長を祝う「端午の節句」にちなむ。

海の日（7月の第3月曜日）
　　　1941年に制定された海の記念日を復活させた祝日で、本来の7月20日に戻そうという声も高まっている。

山の日（8月11日）
　　　海の日があるなら山の日もつくろう、ということでできた祝日。八という漢字が山の形を連想させるので8月になったとの説もある。

Foundation Day
: (a day in February to be established by government ordinance)
: To celebrate the foundation of the nation and love of country. It replaces a prewar holiday known as Kigensetsu (held on February 11) and has many detractors as a remnant of nationalism.

Vernal Equinox Day (March 20 or 21)
: To celebrate nature and living things on the day when the sun crosses the vernal equinox.

Showa Day (April 29)
: Originally to celebrate the birthday of Emperor Showa during his lifetime. Until 2006 it was known as Greenery Day.

Constitution Memorial Day (May 3)
: To celebrate the day in 1947 when the postwar constitution went into effect.

Greenery Day (May 4)
: To celebrate and commune with nature. By moving this day from April 29 to May 4, the intent was apparently to create three consecutive holidays in combination with May 3 and May 5.

Children's Day (May 5)
: To celebrate the health and happiness of children. It takes place on the day that traditionally marked the growing-up of male children (Tango no Sekku).

Marine Day (third Monday in July)
: To celebrate the blessings of the ocean. It represents a rebirth of Marine Memorial Day established in 1941. Some argue that it should be returned to July 20, where it was originally.

Mountain Day (August 11)
: The rationale for this day seems to have been, if there is a marine day there should also be a mountain day. According to some quarters, August was chosen because the shape of the Chinese character for 8 resembles a mountain (August is called the Eight Month in Japanese).

敬老の日（9月の第3月曜日）
　　　老人を敬い、長寿を祝う日。1966年に制定された。

秋分の日（9月22日または23日）
　　　太陽が秋分点を通過する日。亡くなった人をしのぶ日ともされる。

体育の日（10月の第2月曜日）
　　　1964年に開催されたオリンピック東京大会を記念して66年に制定。99年までは10月10日だった。

文化の日（11月3日）
　　　日本国憲法が公布された1946年11月3日を記念して制定された祝日。

勤労感謝の日（11月23日）
　　　天皇家の新嘗祭という神事にちなんだもので、敗戦直後にGHQによって収穫祭とされた時期を経て1948年に制定された。

天皇誕生日（12月23日）
　　　今上（現在の）天皇の誕生日を祝う日。

Q: お正月は、なにをするの？

　年の初めにあたる正月は、本来は収穫をつかさどる神や、祖先の霊を迎える行事です。玄関の門松やしめ飾りは神々を迎えるためのもので、丸い鏡餅を供えるのは神様に食べてもらうためです。

　正月は家族が集まってお屠蘇というお酒を飲んだり、汁の中に餅を入れたお雑煮やお節料理を食べ、その後に神社や寺に出掛けて1年を健康で無事に過ごせるように祈ります。1日〜3

Respect for the Aged Day (third Monday in September)
> To show respect for the elderly and celebrate long life. This day was established in 1966.

Autumnal Equinox Day (September 22 or 23)
> To celebrate the day on which the sun crosses the autumnal equinox. It is also a day on which to honor one's ancestors and remember the dead.

Health and Sports Day (second Monday of October)
> Originally established in 1966 to commemorate the opening of the Tokyo Olympics (1964). Until 1999 it was held on October 10.

Culture Day (November 3)
> This day was established to commemorate the promulgation of the postwar constitution on November 3, 1946.

Labor Thanksgiving Day (November 23)
> This day replaced an imperial Shinto rite called Niiname-sai and was established in 1948 after first being designated a harvest festival by the postwar occupation forces.

Emperor's Birthday (December 23)
> To celebrate the birthday of the present emperor.

Q: What do people do on New Year's Day?

In origin New Year's Day is a day on which the gods of the harvest and family ancestors are celebrated. The *kadomatsu* (lit., gate pines) and *shimenawa* (sacred straw cords) that decorate the front of houses are there to welcome the gods, and the *kagamimochi* (round rice cakes) set out are meant as a repast for the gods.

New Year's is a time for the family to come together and drink a special saké called *otoso*, eat a clear or white miso soup (*ozoni*) containing rice cakes, partake of a special meal of traditional New Year's food (*osechi-ryori*), and thereafter

日の間の初詣で参拝者が多いベスト3（2014年）は、明治神宮（約316万人・東京都渋谷区）、成田山新勝寺（約305万人・千葉県成田市）、川崎大師（約302万人・神奈川県川崎市）。

Q: 節分って、どんな行事なの？

立春（2月3日または4日）の前日に、それぞれの家で行う「邪気を払い、福を招く」行事です。「鬼は外、福は内」と声を出しながら豆をまきます。大阪では節分に恵方巻と呼ばれる太巻き寿司を食べると縁起が良い、とされています。

Q: お彼岸とは？

彼岸とは仏教用語で「あの世」を意味します。先祖や亡くなった方の供養のためにお墓参りなどをします。お彼岸の期間は年2回で、春彼岸（3月の春分の日とその前後3日間の計7日間）と秋彼岸（9月の秋分の日とその前後3日間の計7日間）です。

Q: お節句とは？

子どもの成長を願って行う行事で、女の子は3月3日の「桃の節句」、男の子は5月5日の「端午の節句」があります。それぞれ平安時代、

visit a temple or shrine to pray for health and happiness in the coming year. This "first visit" is called *hatsumode*. The three sites with the most visitors during the three-day New Year's period are 1) Meiji Shrine in Shibuya Ward, Tokyo (about 3,160,000), 2) Narita-san Shinsho-ji in Narita City, Chiba Prefecture (about 3,050,000), and 3) Kawasaki Daishi in Kawasaki City, Kanagawa Prefecture (about 3,020,000).

Q: What is *setsubun*?

Setsubun (lit., season division) is the last day of winter, which falls on February 3 or 4. It also refers to the "bean-scattering" ceremony that takes place on this day. In each household, beans are scattered as a way of purifying the house of bad fortune and attracting the good, while the words "Devils out, good fortune in" are shouted. In Osaka *futomaki-zushi* (thick sushi rolls) called *ehomaki* are eaten on this day to bring good luck.

Q: What is *higan*?

Literally meaning "the other shore," *higan* is a Buddhist term referring to the world of enlightenment. Visits are paid to the family tomb on this day to pray for one's ancestors and the recently deceased. *Higan* occurs twice a year, on the vernal and autumnal equinoxes, including the three days before and after.

Q: What are *osekku*?

Osekku (lit., seasonal festivity) refers to events carried out in the hope that one's children will grow up healthy and happy. The one for girls, Momo no Sekku (Peach Festival; also

奈良時代から主に貴族階級が行った祝事にちなみます。女の子の家では雛祭りをし、男の子の場合は鯉のぼりを室外に立てます。

雛飾り

▶ **雛祭り**
昔の衣装を着た雛人形を飾り、桃の花や白酒をそえて、女の子の成長を祝います。江戸時代から始まったとされます。

武者飾り

▶ **武者飾り**
男の子の節句では、強くたくましく育ってほしいとの願いを込め、武士が着用した武具のミニュチュアや武者人形を室内に飾ります。

Q: 七夕って、どんな日なの?

七夕は、7月7日の夜、天の川をはさんで離ればなれの牽牛星と織女星が年1度会うという中国の伝説に由来した行事です。

この日は、短冊に願い事を書いて、竹の枝に結びつける風習が伝えられてきました。

called Dolls' Day or Girls' Day), is held on March 3. The boys' festival, Tango no Sekku (Beginning Horse Festival; taken from the Chinese zodiac), is held on May 5. They trace their roots back to felicitous occasions in the Nara (710-784) and Heian (784-1185) periods. The girls' festival is highlighted by indoor displays of dolls dressed as Heian-period aristocrats, and the boy's by pennants in the shape of carp (*koi-nobori*) for flying outside.

▶ Dolls' Festival

These displays of dolls in period costumes, accompanied by peach blossoms and special white saké, are a means of invoking health and happiness. The present form is said to have originated in the Edo period (1603-1868).

▶ Armored Samurai

Another part of the Boys' Festival is the display of miniature armored samurai in the hope that the boys in the family will grow up strong and brave.

Q: What is Tanabata?

The Tanabata (lit., the evening of the seventh) festival has its origins in the Chinese legend about a cow herd and a weaver princess who, separated by the Milky Way, can meet only once a year. It is held on the seventh day of the seventh month.

One custom related to this day is that of writing a wish on a special piece of paper and tying the paper to a bamboo branch.

第8章 暮らし

Q: お盆とは?

お盆は、亡くなった親族や祖先の霊を供養する行事で、7月13日〜16日(地域によっては8月13日〜16日)の間に行われます。元来は仏教行事でしたが、宗教にかかわらず日本の伝統行事になっています。13日に迎え火をたいて霊を迎え入れ、16日に送り火をたいて霊をあの世に送り返します。

Q: お月見って、なに?

月を鑑賞する行事は、奈良時代以降に中国から伝えられたとされます。お月見の日は、だんご、もち、さといも、ススキを供えて月をながめます。1年で最も美しいとされる9月中旬の満月を、中秋の名月と言います。旧暦8月15日に当ることから十五夜とも呼ばれます。日本独自の行事として旧暦9月13日のお月見は十三夜と言い、だんごの他にクリや枝豆をお供えして鑑賞します。

Q: 大晦日には、なにをするの?

12月31日の大晦日は、1年の区切りをつける日です。家の大掃除、お正月の準備などで多忙な年末の最終日を家族揃って過ごし、除夜の鐘

Q: What is Obon?

Obon (from a Sanskrit word meaning "hanging upside down") refers to the custom of praying for ancestors and recently deceased from July 13 to 16, or (depending on the region) from August 13 to 16. Originally, Obon was a Buddhist practice but now it has become a pervasive part of Japanese culture. On the 13th fires are lit to welcome the returning spirits, and on the 16th fires are lit again to see them off to the other world.

Q: What does "moon viewing" mean?

The practice of viewing the moon as an object of aesthetic beauty is said to have been introduced to Japan from China in the Nara period (710-784). On that day various objects are put on display as offerings to the moon, such as rice dumplings (*dango*), rice cakes (*mochi*), eddoe (*satoimo*), and pampas grass (*susuki*). The moon is said to be most beautiful when full in mid September and is called the "wonderful moon of mid-autumn" (*chushu no meigetsu*). From the fact that it appears on August 15 on the old Japanese calendar, it is also called the "full-moon night of the 15th" (*jugoya*). In a particularly Japanese variation on this custom, September 13 on the old calendar is referred to as "the full-moon night of the 13th" (*jusanya*), when *dango*, chestnuts, and green soy beans (*edamame*) are displayed as offerings to the moon.

Q: What is *omisoka*?

Omisoka refers to December 31 or New Year's Eve and is an important date in marking the end of one year and the beginning of the next. The family comes together as a whole,

を聞き、元日の朝まで起きて新しい年神様を迎える年越しの行事が各地で行われます。

Q: 他に、どんな行事があるの？

春は、お花見です。古くには梅の花を観賞するのがお花見とされたようですが、日本のお花見といえば桜が定番になっています。桜の花は、パッと咲いてパッと散ることから、武士道のいさぎよさに通じるとして愛でられたのです。

桜は日本中で咲きますが、縦に長い列島ということで、南と北では時期が異なります。気象用語の桜前線は、北上する桜の開花日を示します。

夏は、花火大会です。花火は江戸時代に隅田川で打ち上げられたのが始まりで、現在は全国各地で大規模な花火大会が開催されています。冬の花火大会もあります。

秋は紅葉狩りといって、紅葉を鑑賞しに出掛ける人々がたくさんいます。日本人は、四季を楽しむためにさまざまな行事を生み出してきたのです。

the house undergoes a year-end cleaning, and the bells of nearby Buddhist temples ring out at midnight to signify the washing-away of the illusions and delusions of the past year. People stay up till early morning to greet the gods of the new year, and various events take place in local areas throughout the country.

Q: What other special events are there?

First of all is the appreciation of the beauty of flowers, called *hanami* (lit., flower viewing). In the distant past this referred to the plum blossom, but now it is associated exclusively with the cherry blossom. Cherry blossoms are quick to bloom, and quick to scatter, and thus are thought analogous to the spirit of the samurai, who faced death without the least hesitation.

Since the Japanese archipelago stretches from south to north, the blooming of the cherry tree varies from region to region. The weather bureau uses the term cherry-blossom front (*sakura zensen*) to indicate this movement.

Summer is distinguished by its fireworks displays. The first of these displays is said to have taken place along the Sumida River in the Edo period (1603-1868), but now large-scale events can be seen throughout the country. There are even some that take place in winter.

In autumn there is *momijigari* (lit., maple hunting), and many people make excursions to view the changing of the leaves. This is just one of the many customs that involve an appreciation of seasonal changes.

第9章 教育・宗教
Education and Religion

伊勢神宮 ▶

1 教育

Q: 日本の教育制度はいつできたの?

日本の近代学校制度は、明治5 (1872) 年に発布された「学制」という法令に基づき実施されました。国民すべてが教育を受けることができるというのが建て前でしたが、学業に必要な経費は生徒負担だったため、全員が就学できたわけではありませんでした。

現在の教育制度は、昭和22 (1947) 年に成立した「学校教育法」をベースにしています。小学校 (6年) と中学校 (3年) が義務制で、その上の高校や大学は義務制ではありません。

Q: どんな学校があるの?

設置者によって国立学校 (国)、公立学校 (地方自治体)、私立学校 (学校法人) に分類されます。

1 Education

Q: When did the present education system come into being?

A modern system of education was first established in 1872. This system was based on the principle that all citizens had the right to an education, but since the costs were borne by the students, not all were able to take advantage of this opportunity.

The education system in effect today is based on the Fundamental Law of Education established in 1947. Elementary (six years) and junior high school (three years) are mandatory, but not high school and university.

Q: What kinds of schools are there?

Schools can be classified according to who established the school (the state, local governments, or private individuals) and in many other ways.

幼児教育
  幼稚園（1～3年）　　　　　　　※3～5歳
初等教育
  小学校（6年間）　　　　　　　※6～12歳
中等教育
  中学校（3年間）　　　　　　　※13～15歳
  義務教育学校（9年間）※6～15歳
  中等教育学校（6年間）※13～18歳
高等教育
  高等学校（3年間）
  高等専門学校（5～5年6カ月）
  短期大学（2年間）
  大学（4年間）
  大学院（2年以上）
その他
  特殊教育学校 ※身体不自由な人が対象
  専修学校（1年以上）
  専門学校（1年以上）

Q: 在学者数は？

学校基本調査（2014年度）によると、以下の通りです。なお、小学校と中学校は過去最低を更新中。

幼稚園	155.7万人
小学校	660.0万人
中学校	350.4万人
高等学校	333.4万人
専門学校	58.9万人
大学	255.2万人
大学院	25.1万人

Preschool education
    Kindergartens (1 to 3 years).   * From ages 3 to 5.
Elementary education
    Elementary schools (6 years).   * From ages 6 to 12.
Secondary education
    Junior high schools (3 years).   * From ages 13 to 15.
    Compulsory education (9 years).   * From ages 6 to 15.
    Secondary education (6 years).   * From ages 13 to 18.
Upper-secondary education
    High schools (3 years)
    Technical colleges (5 or 5 1/2 years)
    Junior colleges (2 years)
    Universities (4 years)
    Postgraduate schools (more than 2 years)
Others
    Special needs schools (for children with physical disabilities)
    Vocational schools (more than 1 year)
    Professional training schools (more than 1 year)

Q: How many students are there in each type of school?

According to the School Basic Survey of 2014, the number of students is as follows. (The number of elementary and junior high students was the lowest on record.)

Kindergarten	1,557,000
Elementary school	6,600,000
Junior high school	3,504,000
High school	3,334,000
Vocational schools	589,000
Universities	2,552,000
Graduate schools	251,000

Q: 不登校者が増えているって、ほんとう？

義務教育の小学校、中学校の児童・生徒のうち年間30日以上の長期欠席者で不登校を理由にしているのは、小学校が2.4万人（前年度より3000人増）、中学校が9.5万人（同4000人増）でした（2014年度学校基本調査）。

不登校の原因としては、いじめが問題視されています。

Q: 学習塾や予備校が多いのは、なぜ？

学校の授業についていくのが大変なことと、それだけでは進学のための試験に合格するのが難しいからです。日本は就職などで「学歴」が重視されるため、一流企業に就職するには大学も一流でなければならないという風潮があります。また、公務員もキャリア組は東京大学をはじめとする有名国立大学や私立の有名大学出身者で占められています。

少子化が進んでいる日本では定員割れの大学も出始めていますが、一方、一流大学は競争が激しくなっています。学習塾や予備校も、独自のカリキュラムを武器に生き残りに必死です。

Q: 進学率は、どれくらい？

義務教育終了後、ほぼ全員が高校などへ進学します。高校から大学・短大に進学する人の割

Q: How many students have school phobia?

Students at compulsory elementary and junior high schools who don't attend school for more than 30 days in a year due to school phobia or "school refusal" is 24,000 students in elementary school (up 3,000 over the previous year) and 95,000 in junior high school (up 4,000 from the previous year), according to the 2014 School Basic Survey.

The principal cause of school refusal is bullying (*ijime*).

Q: Why are there so many cram and prep schools?

The reason for this phenomenon lies in the difficulty of keeping up with studies at school and in passing the exams for the next level of education. Japanese society stresses academic achievement in seeking employment, and in order to get into a first-rate company it is necessary to graduate from a first-rate university. Further, to become a civil servant or launch oneself on a career track, it is necessary to graduate from Tokyo University or one of the other prestigious national universities or famous private colleges.

With the recent low birthrate, many universities are failing to meet their admissions quota. On the other hand, competition for top universities is heating up. Cram and prep schools, armed with their own unique curriculums, are struggling mightily to survive.

Q: How many students go on to higher levels of education?

After finishing compulsory junior high school, nearly all students advance to high school. About 50% of these

合は約5割で、先進国（OECD：経済協力開発機構）平均が約6割なので高いとはいえません。ちなみに米国は7割強ですが、入学する以上に卒業するのが難しいという点では、入学してしまえばよほどのことがない限り卒業できる日本とは事情が異なります。

2 資格制度

Q: どんな資格があるの？

　国家資格、公的資格、民間資格に大別されます。国家資格は、法律に基づいて国や国から委託を受けた機関が実施する試験の合格者に与えられます。公的資格は国家資格に準じ、官庁や大臣が認定します。民間資格は業界団体や企業などが独自の審査基準を設け任意で認定するもので、なかには資格付与を口実にした悪徳商法も存在します。

　資格は就職する場合、学歴よりも重要視されることが多く、資格取得者でないとできない仕事もたくさんあります。

students go on to enter junior college or university. Given that in advanced industrialized countries, the ratio is about 60% (OECD), Japan cannot be considered as being at the head of the class. In the United States, about 70% move on to college, but since it is easier to get into an American college than to graduate, the situation is somewhat different from Japan, where, barring some catastrophe, graduation is virtually guaranteed.

2 Education through Certification

Q: What kinds of certificates are there?

Certificates can be broadly divided into the national, the public, and the private. National certificates are those awarded by the central government, or an organization commissioned by the central government, to examinees who have passed the relevant examination as stipulated by law. Public certificates are awarded by government agencies or ministries and are comparable to national certificates. Private certificates are awarded by industry-wide organizations or individual corporations based on their own criteria. Among the latter are fraudulent schemes that award specious certificates for a fee.

Since there are many jobs that cannot be undertaken without proper certification, certificates are often given precedence over academic achievement when seeking employment.

Q: 取得が難しい資格は？

国家資格では、司法試験、公認会計士、国家公務員総合職、弁理士、ITストラジストなどが超難関とされます。公的資格では国際公務員、民間資格ではアクチュアリー（保険数理士）などです。

Q: 職能資格とは、なに？

企業では、働く人の役割と職務遂行能力を格付けしています。6等級あって、1～3等級は一般職、4等級は監督職、5～6等級は管理職です。役職名は主任（3～4等級）、係長・課長代理（4等級）、課長・副部長（5等級）、部長（6等級）などです。

一方、公務員の場合は職務を10級に格付けし、主事（1～2級）、主任（3級）、主査（4級）、副主幹（5級）、主幹（6級）、課長（7～8級）、部長（9～10級）といった役職名が付きます。この職務の級と号給を職種ごとに一覧にした「給料表」に基づいて月給やボーナスの額が決まります。

Q: What kinds of certification are the most difficult to obtain?

Among the national certificates, by far the most difficult to obtain include those for the bar, certified public accountant, career national civil servant, patent attorney, and IT strategist. Among the public certifications is one for international public servants, and among private certificates is one for actuaries.

Q: What does "competence certification" mean?

Japanese companies have a system of ranking employees based on their function and ability to execute their duties. There are six rankings: the 1st to 3rd apply to general work, the 4th to supervision, and the 5th and 6th to management. The relevant titles are manager (3rd-4th ranks), subsection manager or acting section manager (4th rank), section manager or acting department director (5th rank), and department director (6th rank).

Civil servants are divided into 10 ranks according to their job description: superintendent (1st-2nd ranks), section chief (3rd rank), chief examiner (4th rank), deputy controller (5th rank), controller (6th rank), section manager (7th-8th ranks), and department director (9th-10th ranks). Wages and bonuses are paid out in accordance with a pay scale of ranks and job descriptions.

3 宗 教

Q: 日本人は無宗教の人が多いの？

国内の宗教法人（約18万）の報告による信者数は、以下の通りです（2013年文化庁データ）。

神道系	約1億77万人
仏教系	約8470万人
キリスト教系	約192万人
諸教	約949万人

合計で2億人弱になります。人口が1.3億人弱なので人口よりも信者数が多いというわけです。なぜ、このようなことが起きるかというと、各宗教団体の報告のまま集計しているからです。

ところで、日本人に「あなたが信じている宗教は何ですか？」と尋ねると、「ありません」と答える人が多いはずです。ところが「あなたの家の宗派は何ですか？」という質問には、「たしか、浄土宗だったような気がする」といった返答が多くなります。

たしかに無宗教を公言する人が多いのは事実ですが、先祖代々、何らかの宗教に関わってきたというのが日本人なのです。特に仏教系は江戸時代にはどこかの寺院に所属しなければならないとされ、神道系は明治時代以降の国家神道の定着で国民総信者となった歴史があります。上記のデータはそれを反映したもので、個人の信仰の対象としてでなく、先祖が所属していた

3 Religion

Q: Why do so many Japanese say they are not religious?

There are approximately 180,000 religious organizations in Japan, with their number of adherents as listed below (2013, Ministry of Culture).

Shinto linage	(about 100,770,000)
Buddhist lineage	(about 84,700,000)
Christian lineage	(about 1,920,000)
Others	(about 9,490,000)

The total comes out to a little less than 200,000,000, which is odd since the population of Japan is only around 130,000,000. The reason for this discrepancy is that the total has been calculated on figures provided by the religious organizations themselves.

The problem is that when asked if they believe in a particular religion, most Japanese answer in the negative, but when asked what religion their family has been traditionally associated with, they come up with the name of a sect.

Thus, while it is true that many Japanese profess no particular religious belief, it is also true that their ancestors have had some religious affiliation. In the Tokugawa period (1603-1868) the government required that all households be registered with a Buddhist temple, and in the Meiji period (1868-1912) Shinto was adopted as the state religion and all citizens considered its adherents. The statistics given above reflect this convoluted history, indicating not personal belief

なごりなのです。

Q: 神道は、日本の国教なの？

神道は日本固有の宗教ですが、明治維新後に天皇を神格化する国家神道になりました。太平洋戦争の敗戦で政教分離が行われ、その後は数多い宗教の一つになっています。敗戦直後、神を祀る神社は全国に約11万ありましたが、そのほとんどが宗教法人として現在に至っています。

Q: 靖国神社とは？

靖国(やすくに)神社が他の神社と大きく異なるのは、祀られているのが国のために戦って亡くなった人という点です。

この神社の前身は明治2（1869）年に明治天皇が建立した東京招魂社(しょうこんしゃ)で、明治維新に到る戦いで亡くなった人々の霊を祀ることを目的としていました。明治12（1879）年に靖国神社と改称され、以来、幕末（1853年）から太平洋戦争までの100年近くの間に戦没した246.6万人を神霊として祀っています。このなかに、いわゆる東京裁判で敗戦後にA級戦犯として処刑された人々が、のちに含まれたことに対する賛否両論があります。また、政府要人の靖国参拝を中国と韓国がしばしば批判しています。

but ancestral association.

Q: Is Shinto the state religion of Japan?

While Shinto is the native religion of Japan, it was only in the Meiji period (1868-1912) that it became a state religion and the emperor designated a living god. After the defeat in World War II and the separation of religion and state, Shinto was relegated to the status of one of many religions. In the immediate postwar period, there were some 110,000 Shinto shrines throughout the country, most of which have survived until today as religious corporations.

Q: What is the significance of Yasukuni Shrine?

What distinguishes Yasukuni from other shrines is the fact that it is dedicated to those who died in the service of the Empire of Japan.

It was established in 1869 as Tokyo Shokonsha by Emperor Meiji to honor those who had died in fighting on behalf of the new Meiji government. It was renamed Yasukuni Shrine in 1879 and later rededicated to the spirits of the 2,466,000 people who had fallen in the service of the country from 1853 to the end of World War II. It came to include those executed as A-class war criminals by the Tokyo War Crimes Tribunal, giving rise to considerable controversy. The fact that government ministers occasionally visit the shrine to pay their respects to the spirits of Japanese soldiers, among others, is often an object of Chinese and South Korean criticism.

Q: 神社はお寺とどこが違うの？

宗教上の違いは種々ありますが、最も大きな違いは神社ではお葬式を行わないという点です。その理由は、神道は遺体や遺骨を「ケ(穢れ)」として忌み嫌うためです。したがって、神社にはお寺のように敷地内に墓地がありません。

神道では「ケ」に対する言葉として「ハレ(晴れ)」を用います。「ハレ」は、神社の儀式やお祭りなどの非日常世界を意味しているのです。

Q: 神社参拝は、どのように行うの？

神社の入り口に当るのが鳥居です。中央は神様の通り道とされるので、なるべく左右の端を通るようにするのが作法です。まず、御手洗で手を洗い、口の中もすすぎます。これは「穢れ」を落として神様の前に出ることを意味する重要な儀式です。

拝殿前に立ったら、軽くおじぎをして、お賽銭を入れ、鈴を鳴らし、2回おじぎをした後、2回柏手を打ち、最後にもう1回おじぎをして退出となります。これを「二礼二拍一礼」と言います。出雲大社のように四拍する神社もあり、あらかじめ参拝の作法を確認して出掛ける必要があります。

Q: What makes a Shinto shrine different from a Buddhist temple?

There are many theological as well as practical differences, but the most telling is that shrines do not conduct funerals. The reason is that Shinto avoids contact with the body and the remains of the deceased as being impure. This also explains why there are no graveyards within the compounds of Shinto shrines.

In contrast to the notion of impurity, there is the notion of the "bright." This refers to the world of the extraordinary as seen in Shinto rituals and festivals.

Q: What is the proper procedure for praying at a Shinto shrine?

The large gate (*torii*) in front of a shrine represents the entrance to the sacred compound. The center of the gate is reserved for the passage of the gods, so it is customary to make use of the left or right sides. Inside the compound, wash your hands and rinse your mouth with the water provided. This is an important ritual in that it removes impurities and indicates that one is ready to appear before the gods.

Standing before the shrine building, bow once lightly, leave a donation in the box provided, and ring the bell. Then bow twice, clap the hands twice, bow once more, and then withdraw. This is called the "two bows, two claps, one bow" system. Some shrines, such as Izumo Shrine, employ four claps or some other variation.

Q: 仏教には、どんな宗派があるの?

仏教は、広くアジアで信仰されてきた宗教です。仏教発祥の地インドは今やヒンズー教徒が多数を占め、かつての仏教国・中国や韓国、北朝鮮は仏教と無縁の国になってしまっています。

仏教徒が多くいるのは東南アジア諸国で、「小乗仏教」と呼ばれる宗派が主流です。この宗派は、僧侶になって自身の悟りを得ることを目的としています。一方、日本の仏教の主流になっているのが「大乗仏教」で、広く大衆を救う教えを基にしています。

日本国内で活動している仏教の宗派は13とされていますが、信徒数が多いのは浄土宗、浄土真宗(本願寺派、大谷派)、真言宗、天台宗、日蓮宗、曹洞宗、臨済宗です。また、日蓮を宗祖とする創価学会は、形骸化した寺院から独立し、国内だけでなく海外192か国・地域に布教活動を展開している日本最大の信徒団体です。

Q: 禅とは、どんな教えなの?

12、13世紀にかけて中国から渡来した宗派で、国内には臨済宗、曹洞宗などがあります。心から迷いを無くして、真理に到達するために瞑想をする、というのが基本的な教えで、そのために座禅という修行を行います。ただし、迷いを無くすというのは至難のわざで、欲望だらけの世界で生きる俗人には縁遠く、だからこそ座禅にあこがれる人がいるのかも知れません。

Q: How many Buddhist sects are there?

Buddhism is a religion that spread widely throughout Asia. Today, its country of origin, India, is largely populated by adherents of Hinduism, and in countries where Buddhism formerly thrived, such as China, South Korea, and North Korea, it is now a minor player.

Most Buddhist followers are in Southeast Asia and belong to the Hinayana school. In the Hinayana school the goal is to become a monk and achieve enlightenment. The Buddhism that came to Japan was the Mahayana, the goal of which is to save as many people as possible.

There are said to be 13 Buddhist sects in Japan, the ones with the most adherents being the Jodo, Jodo Shinshu (Hongan-ji and Otani branches), Shingon, Tendai, Nichiren, Soto, and Rinzai sects. The Soka Gakkai, which takes Nichiren as its founding father, broke off from its moribund parent body to spread widely not only in Japan but to 192 countries and territories throughout the world. It has since become Japan's largest religious organization.

Q: What is Zen Buddhism?

Coming to Japan in the 12th and 13th centuries from China, Zen now has two domestic sects, the Soto and the Rinzai. Zen's basic goal is to rid oneself of delusion and achieve enlightenment through meditation (*zazen*). The appeal of *zazen* lies in the almost insuperable difficulty of living without illusion in our modern materialistic world.

第9章 教育・宗教

Q: 僧侶は、なぜ髪を剃っているの?

お寺の僧侶が髪を剃っているのは、俗世を離れた存在であることを示すためです。本来、仏教は悟りを得るための修行に出ることを「出家」といい、出家者は生涯独身を貫かねばなりませんでした。その覚悟を示すために髪を剃ったのです。ちなみに、カトリックの司祭などが頭のてっぺんの髪を丸く剃るのは、仏教の影響ともされます。

Q: お寺での参拝の作法は?

お寺の入り口が、山門です。この門を入る前に合掌して一礼します。本堂に向かう途中に手水場があるので、そこで手を洗い、口をすすぎ清めます。本堂前にお線香をたく香炉があれば、その煙を体に招いて身を清めます。本堂では鐘がつるしてあればそれを鳴らし、お賽銭を入れ、音を立てないように合掌し、頭を下げます。この時、願いごとを念じます。

おみくじ

▶ おみくじ

吉凶を書いた紙片のことで、神社や寺などで箱から直接引く。吉凶を占う「おみくじ」は大吉以下、凶まで6種類が一般的。吉札は持ち帰ってよいが、凶札は木の枝などに結び付けて帰る。

Q: Why do Buddhist monks shave their heads?

Monks shave their heads as a sign that they have left the mundane world. Originally, monks had to leave their homes and families to embark on an unmarried journey of ascetic practice, and shaving their heads was a sign of their determination. It is said that the Catholic custom of priests' shaving the top of their heads is a Buddhist influence.

Q: What is the proper procedure for praying at a Buddhist temple?

The *sanmon* ("mountain gate") is the imposing entrance to a Buddhist temple, and before passing through it one places the hands together in prayer and bows lightly. Going toward the main hall, there will be a washbasin where the hands are washed and the mouth rinsed in an act of purification. Before the hall there may be a censer where incense is being burned; waft some of the incense toward your body to purify it. If there is a bell in front of the hall, ring it and place a donation in the box provided there. Then place one's hands soundlessly together in prayer and lower the head, while making a wish.

▶ What are *omikuji*?

Omikuji are fortunes written on small pieces of paper and drawn at random from a box at a temple or shrine. Commonly there are six types, from "great blessing" to "curse." Those indicating good fortune can be taken home, but less fortunate ones are tied to the branch of a nearby tree.

第10章 文化 Culture

山古志の棚田 (新潟) ▶

1 学芸

Q: 日本人のノーベル賞受賞者は？

物理学賞が10名、化学賞が7名、医学生理学賞が2名、文学賞が2名、平和賞が1名です（2014年現在）。

物理学賞：湯川秀樹（1949年）、朝永振一郎（65年）、江崎玲於奈（73年）、小柴昌俊（02年）、小林誠・益川敏英・南部陽一郎（08年）、赤崎勇・天野浩・中村修二（14年）。

化学賞：福井謙一（81年）、白川英樹（00年）、野依良治（01年）、田中耕一（02年）、下村脩（08年）、鈴木章・根岸英一（10年）。

湯川秀樹

医学生理学賞：利根川進（87年）、山中伸弥（12年）。

文学賞：川端康成（68年）、大江健三郎（94年）。

平和賞：佐藤栄作（74年）。

1 Arts and Sciences

Q: How many Japanese have won the Nobel Prize?

There have been 10 winners in physics, 7 in chemistry, 2 in physiology of medicine, 2 in literature, and 1 for peace (as of 2014). The winners are as follows:

Physics: Hideki Yukawa (1949), Sin-Itiro Tomonaga (1965), Leona Esaki (1973), Masatoshi Koshiba (2002), Makoto Kobayashi, Toshihide Masukawa, and Yoichiro Nambu (2008), and Isamu Akasaki, Hiroshi Amano, and Shuji Nakamura (2014).

Chemistry: Kenichi Fukui (1981), Hideki Shirakawa (2000), Ryoji Noyori (2001), Koichi Tanaka (2002), Osamu Shimomura (2008), and Akira Suzuki and Ei-ichi Negishi (2010).

Physiology of medicine: Susumu Tonegawa (1987) and Shinya Yamanaka (2012).

Literature: Yasunari Kawabata (1968) and Kenzaburo Oe (1994).

Peace: Eisaku Sato (1974).

Q: 文化勲章とは?

文化勲章とは、学術・芸術分野で貢献した人に与えられる、最も権威のある勲章です。学術分野では学士院会員など、芸術分野では芸術院会員などから選ばれるのが恒例ですが、ノーベル賞受賞者や外国人なども対象になります。1937年の創設以来、受章者は384名(2014年)で、うち外国人が5名(いずれも米国人)。

毎年、文化の日(11月3日)に皇居で授章式が行われています。

Q: 日本の代表的なマンガ家・アニメ作家は?

今やマンガとアニメーションは、日本文化の象徴の一つです。日本のマンガ家やアニメ作家に大きな影響を与えた人物としては、手塚治虫(1928-89)が挙げられます。代表作の一つの『鉄腕アトム』はアニメ化されて、米国では『アストロボーイ』というタイトルでテレビ放映され、人気を博しました。その後、日本のアニメ作品が世界各地で評判になり、"anime"という言葉が英語として定着するまでになりました。

アニメ作家として傑出しているのは宮崎駿(1941-)で、2001年に発表した『千と千尋の神隠し』は観客動員2350万人、興行収入304億円という日本映画史上での最高記録を樹立しました。

この作品はベルリン国際音楽祭で金熊賞

Q: What is the Order of Culture?

The Order of Culture is the most prestigious Japanese award for contributions to Japanese art, literature, and culture. In the sciences it is customary for candidates to be chosen from among members of the Japan Academy, and in the arts from the Academy of Arts, but non-Japanese and Nobel Prize winners are also considered. The Order was established in 1937, and to date (2014) 384 people have received the award, among whom there have been 5 foreigners (all citizens of the United States).

The awards ceremony is held every year in the imperial palace on Culture Day (November 3).

Q: Who are the most famous Japanese manga and anime artists?

Without a doubt, manga and anime have now become two of the most representative arts of Japan. The person who had the greatest impact on these arts is Osamu Tezuka (1928-89). His celebrated manga *Tetsuwan Atomu* was made into an anime and telecast in the United States under the title *Astro Boy* to great acclaim. Subsequently, Japanese animation won kudos throughout the world to such an extent that "anime" became a part of the English language.

Today the most outstanding anime artist is Hayao Miyazaki (b. 1941). His *Spirited Away* (2001) attracted 23,500,000 theatergoers and grossed ¥30.4 billion, making it the most successful film in Japanese history.

It won the Golden Bear at the 2002 Berlin International

(2002年)、アカデミー賞長編アニメ賞(2003年)を受賞し、日本人で二人目のアカデミー名誉賞(2014年)に輝きました。

Q: 世界的に有名な映画監督は?

日本人初のアカデミー名誉賞(1990年)を受賞した黒澤明(1910 – 98)は、S・スピルバーグ、J・ルーカス、F・コッポラなどの海外の映画人にも大きな影響を与え"世界のクロサワ"と呼ばれました。黒澤作品はダイナミックな映像表現とヒューマニズムあふれる作風で『羅生門』(1950年)以降、『生きる』(52年)、『七人の侍』(54年)など約30作が発表されました。

映画手法で世界的に影響を与えたのが小津安二郎(1903 – 63)で、代表作は『晩春』(49年)、『東京物語』(53年)です。

日本映画は1960年代からテレビに押されて低調になり、人気はアニメ作品に移ってきていますが、近年は新しい映像作家も出現しています。海外で高い評価をされているのは北野武(1947 –)で、コメディアンとして活躍する一方、1989年に映画監督としてデビュー後、『HANA – BI』でベネチア国際映画祭でグランプリ(97年)を獲得するなど、日本を代表する映画人の一人とされます。

Q: 世界で評価が高い音楽家は?

戦後、多くの若い音楽家が海外のコンクール

Film Festival and the 2003 Academy Award for Best Animated Feature, with Miyazaki becoming the second Japanese to win an Honorary Academy Award in 2014.

Q: Who is the most famous Japanese film director?

Akira Kurosawa (1910-98) was the first Japanese to win an Honorary Academy Award (1990) and is known for the influence he exercised on Steven Spielberg, George Lucas, and Francis Ford Coppola. It was said at the time that Kurosawa was not just a Japanese director but a director for the whole world. His works are characterized by their dynamism and humanitarianism, starting with *Rashomon* (1950), *Ikiru* (1952), and *Seven Samurai* (1954). In all, he directed some 30 movies.

The director who exercised great global influence in terms of technique was Yasujiro Ozu (1903-63). His most memorable works are *Late Spring* (1949) and *Tokyo Story* (1953).

In the 1960s the film industry began to lose ground to television, with anime gaining in popularity, but just recently new film creators have come to the fore. Abroad, Takeshi Kitano (b. 1947) is highly rated. While continuing his career as a comedian, he debuted as a movie director in 1989 and won the Golden Lion at the Venice Film Festival for *Hana-bi* (Fireworks) in 1997, among others. He is now one of Japan's most renowned directors.

Q: Who are Japan's most acclaimed world musicians?

Since the end of the war, while many Japanese young

に挑戦してきましたが、その先駆者として挙げられるのが指揮者の小沢征爾（1935-）です。73年から30年間にわたってボストン交響楽団（米国）の音楽監督を務めたほか、2002年にはウィーン国立歌劇場（イタリア）の音楽監督に就任し、世界の音楽界で話題になりました。

ウィーン国立歌劇場

クラシック界では、米国を拠点に活動しているバイオリンの五嶋みどり（1971-）、英国在住のピアノの内田光子（1948-）、イタリアで高い評価を得ているソプラノの中丸三千繪（1960-）などがいます。また、日本人初のアカデミー賞作曲賞を受賞（1987年）した坂本龍一（1952-）、シンセサイザーによる作曲や演奏を行っている冨田勲（1932-）などが世界的に知られています。

Q: 代表的なマスメディアは？

新聞とテレビが大きな影響力を持っています。日本の新聞発行の特徴は、全国紙と地方紙が共存し、各家庭に配達されていることです。中でも全国紙5紙は巨大な発行部数を持ち、地上波のキー局といわれるテレビ局を系列下に置いています。その関係を列記します。

① 読売新聞（発行部数約926万部）
　　　日本テレビ放送網（NTV／AX）
② 朝日新聞（同約710万部）
　　　テレビ朝日（EX）
③ 毎日新聞（同約329万部）
　　　TBSテレビ（TBS／RX）

people have gone abroad to enter music competitions, the forerunner of them all is surely the conductor Seiji Ozawa (b. 1935). He became the music director of the Boston Symphony Orchestra in 1973 and served in that position for nearly 30 years. From 2002 to 2010 he was the principal conductor of the Vienna State Opera.

In classical music, there is the US-based violinist Midori Goto (b. 1971), the naturalized-British pianist Mitsuko Uchida (b. 1948), and the Italy-acclaimed soprano Michie Nakamaru (b. 1960). Ryuichi Sakamoto (b. 1952) won an Academy Award for the Best Original Score in 1987, and Isao Tomita (b. 1932) is known globally for his composing and playing on the synthesizer.

Q: What are the principal mass media outlets?

Television and newspaper media have enormous influence. One characteristic of newspapers is that there are nationwide newspapers and regional newspapers, both existing in harmony and delivered to individual households. The five main nationwide newspapers have huge circulations, and each has a terrestrial TV station under its umbrella. The affiliations between newspapers and television stations is as follows:

① *Yomiuri Shimbun* (circulation: approximately 9.26 million)
    Nippon Television (NTV, AX)
② *Asahi Shimbun* (circulation: approximately 7.1 million)
    TV Asahi (EX)
③ *Mainichi Shimbun* (circulation: approximately 3.29 million)
    TBS Television (TBS, RX)

④ 日本経済新聞（同約275万部）
　　テレビ東京（TX）
⑤ 産経新聞（同約161万部）
　　フジテレビジョン（CX）

（新聞の発行部数は2014年下期ABC協会調べ）

　近年、放送のデジタル化が進み、1台の受像機で放送、通信、コンピュータの使用ができるようになりました。同時に本格的な多チャンネルの時代を迎え、海外メディアの日本進出の動きも加速され、民間放送局は生き残りをかけた競争の渦中にあります。

Q: NHKの経営者は？

　日本放送協会という特殊法人で、英国のBBCと並ぶ公共放送局です。国民の受信料で運営されているため、報道に公平さが求められ、民間局のように特定企業のコマーシャルを入れることはできません。

　NHKの放送波は、テレビが総合・教育・BS1・BSプレミアムの4波、ラジオが第1・第2・FMの3波です。国内には54放送局・14支局があり、海外では4つの総局（アメリカ・ヨーロッパ・中国・アジア）のもとで取材活動などを行っています。

Q: テレビの長寿番組は？

　テレビ放送で最も歴史が古いNHKの場合は、

④ *Nikkei Shimbun* (circulation: approximately 2.75 million)
   TV Tokyo (TX)
⑤ *Sankei Shimbun* (circulation: approximately 1.61 million)
   Fuji Television (CX)

  * Figures for second half-year 2014 provided by Japan Audit Bureau of Circulations.

With the recent increase in digital broadcasting, it has become possible to broadcast, communicate, and perform computer functions using only one device. At the same time, full-fledged multichannel broadcasting has appeared on the scene, and foreign media are making incursions into the Japanese market. Commercial stations are caught in a cutthroat fight for survival.

Q: What is NHK?

NHK is Japan's national broadcaster, comparable to BBC in the United Kingdom. Since it is funded by viewers' license fees, it is expected to be fair in its coverage and cannot broadcast commercials as commercial stations do.

In covering the news NHK operates two terrestrial television services (NHK General TV and NHK Educational TV), two satellite television services (NHK BS-1 and NHK BS Premium), and three radio networks (NHK Radio 1, NHK Radio 2, and NHK FM). Domestically NHK has 54 broadcasting stations and 14 branches, and overseas there are 4 head offices (United States, Europe, China, and Asia).

Q: What are the longest running TV programs?

On NHK, which has the oldest history as a broadcaster, the

素人の歌声コンテストの「のど自慢」(1953年〜)、シンプルなレシピを紹介する「きょうの料理」(57年〜)、幼稚園の子どもを対象にした「おかあさんといっしょ」(59年〜)などです。

一方、民間放送局のテレビ番組は通常、三カ月単位で変更されます。スポンサーは視聴率第一のため、視聴率が悪い番組はすぐに消える運命にあります。したがって、民間放送局の長寿番組は、NHKのそれよりも過酷な競争を生き抜いてきたと言えるでしょう。

民間放送局の三大長寿番組は、皇室関連のニュースを流す「皇室アルバム」(毎日放送：59年〜)、演芸ショーの「笑点」(日本テレビ：66年〜)、「サザエさん」(フジテレビ：69年〜)です。なお、サザエさんは、最も長く続いているテレビアニメ番組として、2013年にギネスブック認定されました。

Q: 日本画は西洋の絵とどう違うの？

日本画という言葉は、明治以降に西洋の絵を洋画といったことに対してつくられたものです。最大の違いは材料で、鉱物をくだいて粉末状にした岩絵の具を、にかわを媒材にして紙や絹に描きます。使う材料によって色彩のぼかし方などの表現方法が異なるため、油絵など西洋の絵と比

平山郁夫の日本画

longest running programs are *Nodo Jiman* (Proud of My Voice; 1953–), which is an amateur singing contest, *Kyo no Ryori* (Today's Meal; 1957–), which features simple recipes, and *Okasan to Issho* (Together with Mom; 1959–), which targets kindergarten children.

In contrast to NHK, commercial stations regularly change their programming every three months. Since sponsors place viewership above everything else, any program that is not performing is soon discontinued. For that reason, any long running program on a commercial station has survived competition much tougher than on NHK.

The three longest running programs on commercial television are *Koshitsu Arubamu* (Imperial Album; news on the imperial family, TBS, 1959), *Shoten* (Laughing Point; traditional comedy, Nippon TV, 1966), and *Sazae-san* (anime; Fuji TV, 1969). In 2013 *Sazae-san* was recognized by Guinness World Records as the longest running anime film.

Q: What is the difference between Japanese painting and Western painting?

The term "Japanese painting" (*Nihonga*) was coined in the Meiji period (1868-1912) to distinguish Japanese-style painting from Western-style painting (*Yoga*). The most telling difference is in the materials used. Japanese painting makes use of minerals and other natural materials that have been powdered into fine pigments, which are applied to Japanese paper (*washi*) or silk with a glue binder made of hide. Depending on the materials used, the way in which shading and gradation is created differs, meaning that,

べて技法を習得するまでに修練が必要です。

日本画は花鳥風月といわれるように、自然を主題にしたものが多く見られます。しかし、こうした伝統を受け継ぎながらも、新しい日本画をつくろうという試みもされてきました。

国内外で高く評価されている現代の日本画家の一人が平山郁夫(1930 - 2009)で、仏教に関わる作品を数多く発表しました。フランス、中国、フィリピン、韓国などの国家顕彰も受けています。

2　伝統技芸

Q: 歌舞伎はいつから始まったの？

17世紀初め、出雲大社の巫女と称する阿国が京都で演じた「かぶき踊り」が起源とされます。しかし、これが奇抜で煽情的だったため、風俗を乱すとして幕府が禁じました。後年、女性役を演じる男優(女形)を配することで存続を図ろうという動きが出て、元禄期(1688～1704年)に現在のスタイルが確立しました。

歌舞伎役者は原則的に世襲制で、3歳頃から子役としてデビューし、役柄や名前も伝統的に引き継ぐ慣わしです。例えば、歌舞伎界で権威が高い市川家の場合は、新之助〜海老蔵〜団十郎という形で襲名し、荒々しく豪快な役柄を演じる「荒事」を得意とします。

compared to Western oil painting, considerable training and practice are required for mastery.

Japanese painting most often takes nature as its theme, as indicated by the phrase *kachofugetsu* (flowers, birds, wind, and moon), a common literary reference to nature. While this traditional approach is still being followed, there are also endeavors to create something new.

Within Japan Ikuo Hirayama (1930-2009) garnered recognition for his many depictions of Buddhist themes. He also won awards in France, China, the Philippines, South Korea, and elsewhere.

2 Traditional Theater and Handicrafts

Q: What are the roots of the Kabuki theater?

Kabuki is said to have been first performed in Kyoto by a maiden (or shaman) named Okuni from the Izumo Shrine at the beginning of the 17th century. However, since Kabuki was viewed not only as bizarre but as erotic and disruptive of social norms, the government soon banned it. Subsequently, efforts were made to preserve Kabuki by having men play the female roles, and in the Genroku era (1688-1704) Kabuki as we know it today came into being.

As a rule, Kabuki is based on hereditary succession, with a child first appearing on the stage at the age of three and inheriting the type of role played and eventually the name of his father. For example, in the famous Ichikawa family, the names Shinosuke, Ebizo, and Danjuro have been passed on from generation to generation, along with its dynamic,

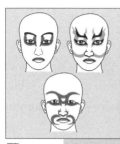

> ▶ 隈取
>
> 歌舞伎は様式性が高い演劇で、それを端的に表現しているのが役の化粧。主役が顔に描く「隈取(くまどり)」は、役柄を観客が理解しやすいようにした舞台芸術の一つです。

隈取

Q: 歌舞伎はどこでやっているの？

歌舞伎座(東京)

歌舞伎公演のメッカは、東京の歌舞伎座です。2013年に改築オープンした新劇場は、座席数約1800のバリアフリー設備が整った施設です。興行は月ごとに演目が変わり、原則として昼の部、夜の部の一日2公演が行われます。

また、新橋演舞場(東京)、大阪松竹座、京都四條南座などでも定期的に公演されています。

Q: 能と狂言はどんな関係なの？

能

いずれも奈良時代頃に中国から渡来した、滑稽な仕草をするサーカスのような芸能である「散楽(さんがく)」がルーツで、そのうちの歌舞が能、物まねが狂言に発展したとされます。

能は鎌倉時代に現在の原型が整い、14世紀後半に観阿弥(かんあみ)・世阿弥(ぜあみ)父子によって芸術性の高い演劇へと昇華しました。主役(シテ)がつける面は、演者の表情を隠すことで非日常性と様式美

exaggerated style of acting known as *aragoto*.

> ▶ *Kumadori* **Makeup**
> Kabuki is highly stylized, and this is clearly seen in the actor's makeup (*kumadori*). Through this distinctive makeup, the audience is able to easily identify the character of the actor.

Q: Where is Kabuki performed?

The Mecca of Kabuki performance is the Kabuki-za in Tokyo. The new theater, rebuilt and opened to the public in 2013, is a barrier-free structure that accommodates 1,800 people. The program changes every month, with different plays comprising the afternoon and evening performances.

Performances are also held regularly at Tokyo's Shimbashi Enbujo, the Osaka Shochiku-za, and the Kyoto Shijo Minami-za.

Q: What is the relationship between Noh and Kyogen?

Both Noh and Kyogen are forms of classical drama originating in circus-like antics called *sangaku* that made their way to Japan from China in the Nara period (710-784). It is speculated that the singing and dancing aspects of *sangaku* developed into Noh, and the pantomime aspects became Kyogen.

Noh assumed its present-day form in the Kamakura period (1185-1333) and in late 14th century under the father and son Kan'ami and Zeami, who raised it to a highly artistic form of theater. The mask worn by the protagonist (*shite*)

を高める効果をねらっています。

狂言

能が非日常的な悲劇をテーマにしているのに対し、狂言は風刺や滑稽を強調した写実的な喜劇です。能と狂言は表裏一体の関係で、能舞台ではたいてい能、狂言、能という順序で上演されます。

Q: 文楽とはどんな芸能なの？

文楽人形

日本特有の人形芝居です。浄瑠璃という音楽と語りに合わせ、1体の人形を3人で操ります。文楽は江戸時代に全国的に流行し、17世紀終わり頃に竹本義太夫によってさらに高度な芸能として確立しました。2002年にはユネスコの世界無形文化遺産に登録されました。現在、東京では国立劇場、大阪では国立文楽劇場で定期的に公演が行われています。

Q: 落語と講談の違いは？

話芸を職業とする人が登場したのは江戸時代で、それは戦乱のない平和な世の中になったことの反映でした。落語は噺家と呼ばれる人が滑稽な話をして客を笑わせ、講談は講釈師が戦記や人情話で客を泣かせるといった違いがあります。

また、落語と講談はそれぞれ江戸（東京）と上

has the effect of concealing the actor's individual features and lending an otherworldly mystique to the performance.

In contrast to Noh's otherworldliness, Kyogen is realistic and deals in satire and comedy. Kyogen and Noh are, so to speak, two sides of the same coin, and the order in which they are performed is Noh, Kyogen, Noh.

Q: What is Bunraku?

Bunraku is a type of puppet theater unique to Japan. Accompanied by music and narration called *Joruri*, each puppet on the stage is worked by three puppeteers. Bunraku achieved wide popularity in the Edo period (1603-1868), and near the end of the 18th century Takemoto Gidayu elevated it to the highly refined art it is today. In 2002 UNESCO recognized Bunraku as an Intangible Cultural Heritage of Humanity. Performances are periodically held at the National Theater in Tokyo and the National Bunraku Theatre in Osaka.

Q: What is the difference between Rakugo and Kodan?

Verbal or oral arts first made their appearance in the Edo period (1603-1868). They were a product of newly arrived peace, after more than a century of civil war. In Rakugo, the performer tells a humorous story that makes the audience laugh; in Kodan, the performer narrates war stories and sentimental tales that make the audience cry. This is the principal difference in terms of content.

There are also differences between Osaka and Tokyo.

方(大阪)でも違いがあります。その一例が、演者が使う道具です。江戸落語の噺家は扇子と手ぬぐいを小道具に使いますが、上方落語では小拍子(拍子木)も小道具として使うほか噺家の前に見台(机)・膝隠し(衝立)を置きます。講談でも、東京の講釈師は張り扇を小道具にしますが、大阪では張り扇と拍子木を併用します。

Q: 生け花って、なに？

生け花

植物を主に、さまざまな材料と組み合わせて構成して鑑賞をする、日本発祥の芸術です。室町時代中期頃から僧侶が仏前に供える献花として考案したものが、後に華道として伝承されるようになり、江戸時代後期に多くの流派が生まれました。現代では、伝統様式や技法にこだわらない生け花も登場しています。

Q: 日本人は誰でも茶道の心得があるの？

茶道

生け花(華道)と共に江戸時代から戦前までの日本女性必須のたしなみとされてきた茶道は、現代では一部の人が行っていて一般的ではありません。したがって、茶道のしきたりなどを心得ている日本人はごく少数です。

現代に継承されている茶道の原点は、16世紀後期に簡素な美を追求することをめざした千利

One example of this is the difference in props. In Tokyo the Rakugo performer uses a folding fan and a small towel, whereas in Osaka the performer adds to this a pair of wooden clappers as well as a lectern in front of him and partition before the knees. In Tokyo the Kodan performer uses a pleated paper fan to establish rhythm, but in Osaka both clappers and pleated fans are used.

Q: What is ikebana?

Ikebana is the uniquely Japanese art of arranging flowers and sometimes other material in a form worthy of aesthetic appreciation. It began in the mid Muromachi period (1336-92) with monks arranging flowers before Buddhist statues, to be transmitted to later generations as *kado* (the way of flowers), producing a proliferation of different schools in the late Edo period (1603-1868). Now, in addition to the traditional forms of arrangement, entirely new styles have come into being.

Q: Is every Japanese familiar with the principles of the Way of Tea?

From the Edo period until the Pacific War, the Way of Tea—that is, the Japanese tea ceremony—was one of those cultural refinements that all Japanese women were expected to possess, along with the art of flower arranging. Now, however, it is carried out by only a small minority, its principles no longer widely known.

The tea ceremony practiced today has its roots in the work of Sen no Rikyu (1522-91), who stressed rustic simplicity

休の侘び茶です。

茶道は客をもてなす作法で、主人は茶室で沸かした湯で抹茶(茶葉を粉末にしたもの)をかき混ぜ客に飲んでもらいます。そのプロセスを点前と言い、この所作が茶道の極意とされます。茶室は、主人と客との心の交流の場なのです。

Q: 家元制度って、なに?

茶道や華道などの日本の伝統技芸には、それを代々継承してきた家元が存在します。例えば茶道では、千利休を祖とする表千家、裏千家、武者小路千家の3家があります。

伝統技芸は相伝といって師匠が弟子に一対一で極意を伝えるのを原則とします。家元制度は相伝において血縁を重視しています。

Q: 陶磁器と漆器の違いは?

陶磁器

日本の伝統工芸品といえば陶磁器と漆器です。その違いは、器の素材にあります。陶磁器は土、漆器は木がベースで漆でコーティングされています。また、陶磁器は粘土を焼き、漆器は木に漆を塗り重ねるため、それぞれ「焼き物」「塗り物」と呼ばれます。

陶磁器は、有色粘土で形を作り釉薬を塗って

and directness of approach (*wabicha*).

The tea ceremony consists of the interplay between host and guests: the host boils the water, mixes in powdered green tea leaves, and has the guests drink the resultant tea. This process is called *temae* and represents the essence of the Way of Tea. The tearoom is the venue for this harmonious meeting of minds between host and guest.

Q: What is the *iemoto* system?

In ikebana, the Way of Tea, and other traditional arts, there is a "house" (*iemoto*), or more broadly a grand master, who carries on the tradition from one generation to another. For example, in the tea ceremony there are three houses: the Omote Senke, Ura Senke, and Mushanokoji Senke, all of which trace their history back to Sen no Rikyu.

In this system the essence of the tradition is passed down from master to disciple in a strictly hereditary fashion, placing ultimate emphasis on bloodline.

Q: What is the difference between ceramic ware and lacquer ware?

Among Japanese handicrafts, ceramic and lacquer wares are two of the stars. The difference between them lies in the materials used. Ceramics are made of clay, while lacquer ware is built on a wooden base on which coatings of lacquer are applied. Further, since ceramics is made of fired clay, it is called "fired ware" (*yakimono*), while lacquer ware is made of multiple coatings of lacquer and is therefore called "coated ware" (*nurimono*).

Ceramics created from colored clay, glazed, and fired at

漆器

1100〜1300℃で焼いた陶器と、白色粘土で形を作り1300〜1400℃で焼いた磁器があり、これらは中国伝来の技術をもとに発展しました。かつて欧米では陶磁器を"China"、漆器を"Japan"と呼びました。

Q: 日本刀の特徴は？

日本に鉄器の製法が伝来したのは古墳時代以前で、砂鉄を原料にした「たたら製鉄」という技法がもとになって、武器としての刀がつくられるようになりました。現在、日本刀と呼ばれるものは平安時代末期以降の刀剣で、長さによって太刀（刀）、脇差、短刀に大別されます。

日本刀には殺傷力を高めるために鉄を鍛錬して堅固なものにする技術と共に、形やデザインの美しさも求められました。実用性と芸術性を併せ持つことが、日本刀の特徴なのです。

戦乱がおさまった江戸時代、刀は実用性よりも芸術性を追求するようになったため、慶長年間（1596〜1614年）以前のものを古刀、それ以後から明治8年までのものを新刀、明治9年（廃刀令が出た年）以降につくられたものを現代刀と称しています。

日本刀

temperatures between 1100 and 1300 degrees is earthenware (*toki*), and that made of white clay and fired between 1300 and 1400 degrees is porcelain (*jiki*). Both of these were introduced from China and further developed in Japan. In the past, porcelain was often referred to as "China" in Western countries, and lacquer ware as "Japan."

Q: What are the outstanding characteristics of a Japanese sword?

The techniques for manufacturing ironware first came to Japan sometime before the Kofun period (around 250-538) and made use of iron sand in a furnace called a *tatara*. From this emerged the first swords. What is now called the Japanese sword (*Nihon-to*) appeared on the stage of history in the late Heian period (794-1185), and can be classified according to length (from long to short) as *tachi*, *wakizashi*, and *tanto*.

The Japanese sword not only requires proper tempering to make it a lethal weapon but is also expected to have an aesthetically pleasing form and design. This combination of practicality and beauty is what distinguishes the Japanese sword.

With the coming of peace in the Edo period, the aesthetic element came to be more valued than the practical. As a result, swords made before the Keicho era (1596-1614) are now called Old Swords (*Koto*); those made thereafter until 1875 are called *Shinto* (New Swords). Swords made after the wearing of swords in public was banned in 1876 are called Modern Swords (*Gendai-to*).

江戸時代の刀工

> ▶刀工
> 日本刀は現代でも美術工芸品としてつくられていて、なかには人間国宝に認定される刀工もいます。

Q: 人間国宝って、なに？

文部科学大臣が指定する重要無形文化財保持者（個人、団体）の通称で、芸能部門では延べ177名、工芸技術部門では延べ173名が認定されています（2014年）。ちなみに、これまでに刀工は6名、落語家は3名が人間国宝に認定されました。

Q: 大相撲はいつから始まったの？

力比べという形で神意（神様の意思）をうかがう儀式として古代から行われ、史実に記録されている最初は642年とされます。平安時代には天皇の前で相撲大会（節会）が開催されました。

江戸時代になると、神社の祭礼の際の興行として催されるようになりました。大名が力自慢の人を家来にして競わせ、力士番付が流行しました。明治時代の「裸体禁止令」で存続の危機を迎えましたが、相撲好きの明治天皇によって国技とされ現在に至っています。

Q: 大相撲はいつ、どこでやっているの？

本場所（15日間興行）は、年6回開催されてい

> ▶ **Swordsmiths**
> Swords are still being made in modern Japan as one of its highly valued arts and crafts. In fact, some swordsmiths have been designated living national treasures by the government.

Q: What is a Living National Treasure?

A Living National Treasure refers to an individual or group considered as possessing an important intangible cultural property as designated by the Minister of Education. In the performing arts there are 177 holders of this title, and in arts and crafts 173 (as of 2014). Six swordsmiths and three Rakugo performers are among this number.

Q: When was the first sumo bout?

As a type of wrestling, sumo was practiced in ancient times as a means of divining the will of the gods. It is first mentioned in historical documents in 642. It is said that in the Heian period (794-1185), sumo tournaments (called *sechie*) were held before the emperor.

In the Edo period (1603-1868) sumo became one of the events conducted at Shinto festivals. Feudal lords of the time would compete by having the strongest of their vassals battle it out in the ring, and published rankings of the strongest wrestlers became popular. In the Meiji period (1868-1912) sumo faced a crisis when public nakedness was banned, but that was overcome when Emperor Meiji named sumo the national sport.

Q: When and where are sumo tournaments held?

Fifteen-day tournaments are held six times a year. Three

両国国技館

ます。国技館(東京)では1月・5月・9月の3場所が、他は大阪場所(3月)、名古屋場所(7月)、九州場所(11月)です。本場所以外は、地方巡業やチャリティ興行などが行われています。

Q: 力士になるには?

新弟子検査に合格しなければなりません。原則として身長173cm以上、体重75kg以上の体格が必要で、外国人も対象になります。新弟子は国技館内の相撲教習所で6カ月間教習を受けますが、試験はありません。序ノ口から幕下までの4階級は養成員とされ、所属部屋に養成費(月額20万円程度)が相撲協会から支給されます。十両から横綱までの6階級(定員70名)の関取には月給(100〜282万円)と賞与や場所ごとの報奨金などが支給されます。

土俵入り

Q: 柔道と空手の違いは?

柔道は、柔術という古武道をもとに1882年に加納治五郎によって創始され、投げ技、固め技があります。試合時間は3〜20分間で、延長もあります。一本、技あり、有効、効果の順でスコアがつき、勝負が決まります。1964年の東京五輪で正式種目に採用されて以来、国際競技になりました。柔道着は元は白一色でしたが、近年

tournaments are held at the Kokugikan in Tokyo (January, May, and September), one in Osaka (March), one in Nagoya (July), and one in Fukuoka, Kyushu (November). Bouts also take place as exhibitions in the provinces and as charity events.

Q: What are the requirements for becoming a sumo wrestler?

First of all, new hopefuls must pass a physical exam, proving they are at least 173 centimeters tall and not less than 75 kilograms in weight. The same applies to foreign applicants. New recruits must then attend a sumo school within the Kokugikan in Tokyo for six months, although there are no tests. Wrestlers in the first four of the six divisions in sumo are considered trainees, and the Sumo Association pays the stables to which they belong a monthly fee of some ¥200,000. The 70 wrestlers in the six ranks from *juryo* to *yokozuna* receive a monthly salary of from ¥1,000,000 to ¥2,820,000 plus a bonus for each tournament they participate in.

Q: What is the difference between judo and karate?

Judo was created by Jigoro Kano in 1882 on the basis of an old martial art known as jujutsu. It consists of throwing and grappling techniques. The time of the match is from three to twenty minutes, with extensions possible. Scoring is based on, in descending order, *ippon*, *waza-ari*, *yuko*, and *koka*. Since being chosen as one of the events in the 1964 Tokyo Olympics, judo has become an international sport. The judo

は青色の柔道着も普及しています。

空手は、沖縄で発達した護身用の武技で、中国拳法の影響を受けたことから"唐手"とも呼ばれました。突き、打ち、当て、蹴りを技の基本とし、競技は3分間で3本先取による「組手試合」、攻防の技の組合せを競う「型試合」の2種があります。空手着は、柔道着を改良したものです。

柔道

空手

Q: 剣道の勝負はどうつけるの?

剣道は、江戸時代に武士が鍛錬のために行っていた剣術が競技として発展したものです。竹刀で相手の防具の面・胴・小手を打つか、喉を突くかすれば「一本」となります。試合では5分間で二本先取りの勝負が3回行われ、勝敗を決めます。

剣道

剣道で強調される「礼に始まって礼に終わる」は、他の伝統技芸でも共通の基本精神です。

uniform (*judogi*) was formerly exclusively white in color, but recently blue has also come into use.

Karate ("empty hand") is a martial art that developed in Okinawa as a means of self-defense. From the fact that it was influenced by Chinese *kenpo*, the name is sometimes written with the Chinese characters that mean "Tang (dynasty) hand." Its principal techniques are punching, striking, and kicking. A bout runs for three minutes, with the winner decided by the first to get three points. There are two modes in karate: *kumite* (contact sparring) and *kata* (a formalized sequence of movements representing various offensive and defensive postures). The uniform (*karategi*) is a modification of the judo uniform.

Q: How is the winner decided in kendo?

Kendo (Way of the Sword) is a martial art that developed in the Edo period (1603-1868) as a way for samurai to practice sword fighting (*kenjutsu*). It uses bamboo swords (*shinai*) and protective armor, and a point is scored when the opponent is struck on the headpiece, breastplate, or *kote* (covering for forearms, wrists, and hands) or when a successful thrust is made to the throat. One bout consists of five minutes (there are three bouts in all), and the winner is the first to win two points.

As in the other traditional martial arts, kendo emphasizes respect for one's opponent: "A match commences with a show of respect and concludes with a show of respect."

Q: アーチェリーと弓道の違いは？

弓で矢を射て的に当てる、という点では同じですが、弓の構造が違います。アーチェリーの弓は、弓道の和弓とは異なって精度を向上させる機械的な構造を持っていて、日本では洋弓とも呼ばれます。

また、競技のうえではアーチェリーが的中率のみを重視するのに対して、弓道では射手のフォームも得点の対象になります。弓道の試合は、主に屋内で行う「近的」(射距離28m、的径36cm)、主に屋外で行う「遠的」(射距離60m、的径1m)の2種に大別されます。

弓道

Q: 囲碁、将棋のプロ棋士とは？

日本では、趣味として囲碁や将棋を楽しむ人が大勢います。一方、職業として行っているのが「棋士」です。では、プロ棋士になるにはどうすればよいでしょうか。

囲碁の場合は、まず入段試験に合格しなければなりません。受験者のほとんどは子どもの頃から師匠のもとで修業をしてきた人で、合格率は例年約60名の受験者の1割程度です。試験に合格して初段になった後は、棋戦での勝星数・タイトル戦でのタイトル獲得数・賞金ランキングによって昇段し、九段まで昇段できるのは一部の人です。

Q: What is the difference between Japanese archery (*kyudo*) and Western archery?

The aim of both is to hit a target, but the structure of the bow is different. In contrast to the unadorned Japanese bow (*wakyu*), Western bows (*yokyu*) are often equipped with mechanical aids to improve accuracy.

In competition, Western archery is scored on accuracy alone, but Japanese archery also takes form into account. Matches can be classified into whether they take place indoors (distance 28 meters, target diameter 36 centimeters) or outdoors (distance 60 meters, target diameter 1 meter).

Q: What does it take to become a professional go or shogi player?

Go and shogi are two popular board games with many hobbyist followers, but there are also professional players called *kishi*. How does one become a professional?

In go, the first step is to pass an entrance exam. Even though most examinees have been training under a professional since childhood, only about 10% pass the test on a typical year, with some 60 taking the exam. Successful applicants are then ranked as a first *dan* (rank), and further advancement depends on games won, victories in title matches, and prize money ranking. The highest rank is 9th *dan*, which very few people reach.

将棋の場合は、まず日本将棋連盟の養成機関である「奨励会」に入ることが条件です。会員同士の対局成績によって、満21歳までに初段、満26歳までに四段にならないと退会となり、プロ棋士への道は閉ざされます。プロ棋士は四段から九段までの段位の人で、毎年、戦績に応じて5段階に分かれたリーグ戦で順位が付けられます。最上位のA級のリーグ戦の優勝者には名人への挑戦権が与えられます。

囲碁

Q: 競技かるたは、どんなゲームなの？

小倉百人一首

100枚ずつ対になった200枚の札を使う集中力を必要とするゲームです。読み札（絵札）には、13世紀の和歌集から選ばれた和歌と絵が、対の取り札（文字札）には下の句が記されます。読み札が読まれると、対戦する2人が取り札を取り合う競技で、優れた記憶力と反射神経が求められます。女性は和服に袴を着けて対戦しますが、そのしとやかさは競技の場ではバトルモードに一転します。

段位は初段から十段まであり、四段以上（A級）が全国大会への出場資格があります。競技かるた人口は小学生からお年寄りまで幅広く、毎年1月に開催される名人位・クイーン位決定戦では、頂点となる男女2名が決まります。

In shogi, the first requirement is to gain entrance to the Shoreikai, an organization that trains professional shogi players and is run by the Japan Shogi Association. Members play against one another until they reach the 1st *dan* level by the age of 21 and 4th *dan* level by the age of 26. Barring this, they must leave the Shoreikai and the road to becoming a professional player is closed. Professional players are ranked from 4th to 9th *dan*. Winners of A-league tournaments gain the right to challenge the current holder of the title of Meijin, the most prestigious title in Japanese professional shogi.

Q: What is competitive *karuta*?

Karuta is a card game of concentration. There are 200 cards in groups of 100 cards each. One card (the reading card) has the text from a poem taken from a 13th-century poetry anthology (*Hyakunin Isshu*) and an illustration. The other card (the grabbing card) has the last part of the poem. When the text is read from the reading card, two competing players strive to see who can touch the appropriate grabbing card first. The game is a test of the powers of concentration as well of quick response. Women wear graceful kimonos, but quickly go into battle mode.

In tournament or competitive *karuta*, rankings are from 1st *dan* to 10th, and players with a 4th *dan* or higher can take part in national tournaments. The large competitive *karuta* population ranges from elementary school children to the elderly, and every year in January a tournament is held to see who will be honored with the title of Meijin (for men) or Queen (for women).

第10章 文化

Q: けん玉って、なに?

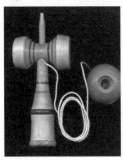
けん玉

遊具としてのけん玉の原型は世界各地に見られますが、日本では江戸時代から行われ、大正時代に日月ボールという呼称で普及しました。木製の「けん」という器具とひもでつないだ球を、けんに乗せたり刺したりするゲームで、近年は高度な技がたくさん生まれています。

これを競技として確立したのは日本独自で、課題の技とその回数によって級段位が認定されます。段位は初段から十段までありますが、競技による認定は六段までで、それ以上は功績に応じて与えられます。

3 芸能

Q: 人気が高い芸能は?

演芸ではコント、音楽ではJ-POPです。

コントは二人で掛け合いをする漫才、一人で演じる芸などがあり、聴衆を笑わせるのが目的です。漫才は平安時代から行われてきた新年を祝う歌舞「万歳」に由来し、昭和初期に主に関西でお笑い芸として定着したものです。

Q: What is *kendama*?

A *kendama* is a traditional Japanese toy consisting of a wooden cross-shaped implement with three cups and a spike, to which a ball with a hole in it is attached by a string. The basic goal of the game is to catch the ball in the cups or on the spike, although in recent years more sophisticated techniques have emerged. Similar toys can be seen throughout the world, and in Japan *kendama* first appeared in the Edo period (1603-1868), achieving great popularity in the following Meiji period under the name *jitsugetsu* ball ("sun moon ball").

Japan is the only country in which *kendama* has developed into a competitive sport, in which ranking is determined by speed and technique. The two highest ranks are awarded to those who have contributed to the sport, not solely on their competitive skills.

3 Performing Arts

Q: What are the most popular performing arts?

The most popular form of variety entertainment is standup comedy, and the most popular form of music is J-Pop.

Standup comedy includes skits performed by single performers and routines performed by two comedians, commonly called *manzai*. *Manzai* has its origins in the Heian period (794-1185) when "messengers" would deliver felicitations on New Year's Day. It became established in the early Showa period (1926-89) as part of the comic culture of the Osaka region.

J-POPは日本で制作されたポピュラー音楽全般を指す和製英語で、1990年代頃からミリオンセラーが続々誕生しました。現在は、多人数のユニットが歌と踊りでパフォーマンスをする手法が流行しています。

Q: 演歌って、なに？

日本の風土、日本人の情緒に根ざした歌で、情感に訴える歌詞と哀愁に満ちたメロディーが特徴。大衆に普及するようになったのは1930年代頃からで、敗戦後は美空ひばり（1937 – 89）をはじめ多くの演歌歌手が登場し、60〜70年代に黄金期を迎えました。その後はJ-POPなどに押されて低調になりましたが、お年寄りには演歌ファンがたくさんいます。

Q: 宝塚歌劇団とは？

宝塚は1913年に女性のみで編成された歌劇団で、華やかなブロードウェイのようなショーが特徴です。団員になるには、宝塚音楽学校（2年制）に入学しなければならず、競争率が25倍前後という難関です。卒業後、団員は生徒と呼ばれ、身分は阪急電鉄の社員です。

入団年次や試験席次により名簿順位が決められ、5組に分かれて公演を行っています。組のトップスターは男役で、本公演（2作）は年10回、5組が持ち回りで宝塚大劇場（兵庫県宝塚市）と東京宝塚劇場（千代田区有楽町）で行います。

J-Pop refers to a type of music that combines traditional Japanese music with rock, often accompanied by dance. It became particularly popular in the 1990s and produced many million-sellers. Presently dance-vocal groups are the fad.

Q: What is *enka*?

Enka is a type of singing that particularly appeals to Japanese sentiments in its sentimental lyrics and plaintive music. It began spreading among the general public in the 1930s, and with the postwar appearance of Hibari Misora (1937-89) and others, it entered its golden age in the 60s and 70s. Thereafter its position was threatened by J-Pop and lost popularity, but it is still much favored by senior citizens.

Q: What is the Takarazuka Revue?

Takarazuka, an all-female musical theater troupe formed in 1913, puts on lavish, Broadway-style productions in which all the roles are played by women. Those wishing to become a member of the troupe must first attend the competitive Takarazuka Music School for two years, the number of applicants being 25 times that of those accepted. Graduates become employees of the Hankyu Railway company, the owner of the troupe.

The troupe is divided up into five acting groups according to year of entrance and test scores, and major productions are held 10 times a year (consisting of two plays each). Each group takes turns presenting productions at the Takarazuka Grand Theatre (Takarazuka City, Hyogo Prefecture) and the

Q: 民間テレビ局の広告収入は、いくら？

経済産業省の調査データでは、年間広告費約5.7兆円のうち民間テレビ局の広告収入の総額は約1.5兆円とされます（2014年）。ここ10年ほど横這い状況が続き、民間テレビ局の経営を圧迫しています。一方、インターネットの広告収入総額は約5000億円で06年と比べ4倍に増えています。

Q: タレントの出演料の相場は？

民間テレビ局のゴールデンタイムのドラマの主演女優の出演料は、トップクラスで1時間（1本）300〜350万円、若手が同100〜150万円で、NHKの場合はその3分の1程度と言われます。また、テレビCMのギャラの最高額は年間契約で1社5000万円。10社と契約する人気女優もいます。

ちなみに、2014年推定CMギャラのトップは女優の綾瀬はるか（1社4000〜5000万円）、男性はプロテニスプレイヤーの錦織圭（1社6000万円以上）というのが業界での通説です。

Takarazuka Theatre (Yurakucho, Chiyoda Ward, Tokyo).

Q: What is the advertising revenue of commercial TV stations?

According to statistics provided by the Ministry of Economy, Trade and Industry, total advertising revenue in 2014 amounted to ¥5.7 trillion, of which commercial TV accounted for ¥1.5 trillion. This figure has been stagnant for the last 10 years, impacting the stations' finances. On the other hand, Internet advertising revenue has risen to about ¥500 billion, four times what it was in 2006.

Q: What is the going appearance fee for TV performers?

The appearance fee for a leading actress in a TV drama on a commercial station during prime time is ¥3,000,000 to ¥3,500,000; for a young aspiring actress, ¥1,000,000 to ¥1,500,000; and about 1/3 of those figures for NHK. The highest annual revenue for a TV commercial contracted with one company is ¥50,000,000. Some popular actresses may contract with as many as 10 companies.

According to reliable sources in the industry, the highest paid actress for TV advertising in 2014 was Haruka Ayase (¥40,000,000 to ¥50,000,000 per contract); the highest paid male celebrity was the tennis player Kei Nishikori (over ¥60,000,000 per contract).

4 現代の文化の特徴

Q: 今の日本文化の特徴は？

昔からの伝統文化と欧米風の生活習慣が混在するのが、現代の日本文化の特徴です。日本人は昔から外来の文化を取り入れつつ自国なりの文化をつくり上げるのが上手で、戦後の発展もそうした民族性に支えられてきました。

しかし、高度経済成長期の東京への一極集中化と、それに準じた地方の急速な都市化がさまざまなひずみを招いています。例えば、地方都市の没個性化です。駅前の商店街はどこも同じような街並みに再開発され、住民が主体的に関わる伝統行事もめっきり少なくなりました。

その反省から今、各地で地方発信の文化事業が計画、実行されています。その象徴がB級グルメで、あえて一流のA級としない点が地方の食文化の独自性を際立たせようとの試みと言えます。

Q: 日本人はコメを食べなくなったの？

戦後の日本人が、欧米風の生活習慣を取り入れた最大のものが食文化です。1980年代後期には、家庭で主食としていたコメがパン・菓子類に取って代わられ、日本人のコメ離れが顕著になりました。この傾向はその後も続き、2013年には購入額で2〜3倍もの差がついてしまっています（家計調査年報）。

4 Modern-day Culture

Q: What are the features of Japanese culture today?

Present-day Japanese culture is a mixture of traditional culture and Western lifestyles. From the distant past the Japanese have been adept at adopting foreign influences and adapting them in a Japanese way. The postwar development of Japan owes its success to that trait.

However, the focus on Tokyo following the period of rapid economic development, as well as the urbanization of outlying areas, has produced certain stresses and strains in Japanese life. One of these is the homogenizing of provincial cities. The shopping areas in front of local train stations have been "developed" so that they all look the same, and the number of traditional events in which locals play an active role has dwindled dramatically.

In reaction to this, plans have been drawn up for promoting local cultures and are now being put into effect. One example of this is the promotion of so-called B-class cuisine, making the local specialties stand out by purposely not ranking them as A class.

Q: Is rice no longer eaten?

Postwar Western influence can be seen most clearly in the food Japanese now eat. Toward the end of the 1980s, what had until then been the staple food, rice, began to be replaced by bread and various confectionaries. The movement away from rice became an undeniable fact. By 2013 the purchase of bread etc. had become two to three times that of rice (Family Income and Expenditure Survey).

松花堂弁当

▶世界文化遺産になった「和食」

2014年12月、ユネスコが「和食」を世界文化遺産に登録しました。ご飯に汁もの、おかず三種で構成された「和食」は、栄養バランスに優れた食事として評価されたのですが、"遺産"というのが気になります。

Q: コンビニはいくつあるの？

利便性が、現代の日本人の暮らしぶりの基本になっています。その一つの象徴がコンビニエンス・ストア、いわゆる「コンビニ」です。ここでは食料、飲料、本、文具などの日常必需品が数多く揃っているほか、公共料金の支払いや荷物を送ったりできます。24時間営業をしている店も多く、全国に5万店あります。最大規模のセブンイレブンは1万7177店、年間総売上3.78兆円です。（2015年1月現在）。

今やコンビニは日本の文化現象とも言われますが、小売店がコンビニに取って代わられることによる地方都市の没個性化を促進している一面も指摘されています。

Q: スマホって、なに？

スマホとは、スマートフォンの短縮語です。コンビニと同様に近年の文化現象として特筆されるのが、「ケータイ」（携帯端末）です。音声による通信機能のみならず、メッセージの送信、情報収集、撮影、ゲーム、ショッピングなど、携帯とオンラインサイトは日本人に新たなライフスタイルと文化をもたらしています。

> **Japanese Cuisine: An Intangible Cultural Heritage**
> In December 2014 UNESCO designated Japanese cuisine (*washoku*) an Intangible Cultural Heritage. The traditional Japanese meal consisting of a soup and three dishes was ranked highly for its nutritional value. However, the word "heritage" is troubling in that it seems to indicate something of merely historical interest.

Q: How many convenience stores are there?

Convenience might be a byword of modern Japan, and its icon might be the convenience store (or *konbini* as it is familiarly known). There you can buy most of the items needed for everyday life, such as food, drink, books, stationary, and much more; you can also pay your utility bills and post packages for speedy delivery. Most of the 50,000 stores located nationwide are open 24/7. The largest chain, Seven-Eleven, has 17,177 stores and annual sales of ¥3.78 trillion (January 2015).

Convenience stores can be viewed as a positive symbol of the pace of life today, but it is also true that they have forced many small, regional retailers out of business, contributing to the homogenization of local areas.

Q: What is a *sumaho*?

Sumaho is an abbreviation for smartphone. In addition to the convenience store, the mobile or cell phone has become a symbol of modern life, and the smartphone stands at the apex of that phenomenon. Needless to say, with a smartphone you can not only communicate with people by the spoken word but also send messages, collect data, take pictures, play games, shop, etc. It is the ultimate in convenience.

スマホのサービスの一つがライン(LINE)で、24時間、無料で通話ができ、メール、写真、動画、音声を送ることもできます。そのため、若い世代がこれを利用することが多く、(しばしば中毒といえるほど依存する)日常的なネットワークツールになっています。しかし、ラインというバーチャル世界でのつながりはもろく、依存症やいじめの原因になっているとして、未成年者の利用制限を求める意見も多いのです。

One of the services available on a smartphone in Japan (and elsewhere as well) is called Line. Line allows the user to exchange texts, images, video and audio, and conduct free VoIP conversations and video conferences. It is a free service available 24 hours a day. Line has many followers among young people (often to the extent of addiction), who like its ability to create networks of friends. On the con side, the connection between such virtual friends is often very tenuous and can lead to bullying. This has led to calls for restrictions on usage by young people.

第11章 レジャー・スポーツ
Leisure and Sports

1 レジャー

Q: 日本人の余暇の過ごし方は？

『レジャー白書』（日本生産性本部）の余暇市場動向（2014年）によると、日本人が参加した余暇活動ベスト5は以下のとおりです。

1位	国内観光旅行	5590万人
2位	ドライブ	4690万人
3位	外食（余暇中）	4470万人
4位	読書	4440万人
5位	映画（映画館）	3780万人

その他、ショッピング、カラオケ、ウオーキングなどがベスト10内にランクされています。また、遊園地・テーマパークの入園者（2100万人）も増加傾向にあります。

近年の余暇活動の傾向としては、お金がかかるものは敬遠する人が増えています。また、満足度は10～40代は低く、50代から上昇して70

1 Leisure

Q: How do Japanese spend their free time?

According to the white paper produced by the Japan Productivity Center (2014), the top five ways Japanese spend their free time are as follows (number of people in parentheses):

1. Tourism within Japan　　　　　(55.9 million)
2. Driving　　　　　　　　　　　(46.9 million)
3. Eating out (during leisure time)　(44.7 million)
4. Reading　　　　　　　　　　　(44.4 million)
5. Movies at theaters　　　　　　(37.8 million)

In the top ten we also find shopping, karaoke, and walking. The number of people visiting amusement and theme parks is also on the rise (21 million).

The recent trend is to avoid expensive activities. As for the amount of satisfaction gained from free-time activities, the lowest level is recorded for those aged from 10 to 40 and

代は最高という結果が出ています。

Q: 海外旅行で人気がある国は？

日本人は年間約1000万人以上が、海外旅行をしています。人気が高いのはアジアでは韓国、台湾、香港、タイ、ベトナムなど、欧米ではハワイ、グアム、フランス、イタリアなどです。

Q: 日本独特のレジャー施設は？

外国人が驚くのは、パチンコ店とカラオケボックスの多さです。この2つは、日本で生まれて発展したレジャー施設の雄と言ってもよいでしょう。その他、日本独特のレジャー施設として健康ランドやスーパー銭湯などの温浴施設があります。また、公営ギャンブル施設としての競輪場、競艇場、オートレース場も日本だけに存在します。

Q: ゲームや漫画に熱中する大人がいるって、ほんとう？

日本では、ゲームや漫画は子ども達だけの楽しみではありません。20代、30代まで幅広い層に楽しまれています。例えば、週刊漫画雑誌は数百万部発行され、単行本になるとシリーズで数千万部発行される作品も少なくありません。ゲームは従来はテレビゲームが主流でしたが、近年は携帯端末でできるゲームの支持者が増加しています。電車の車内で、下を向いてゲームをしている若者の姿を見かけることも多いはず

the highest for those of 50 or older, peaking at 70.

Q: What are the most popular destinations for foreign travel?

Some 10 million Japanese travel abroad every year. The most frequented Asian countries are South Korea, Taiwan, Hong Kong, Thailand, and Vietnam. The Western destinations most visited are Hawaii, Guam, France, and Italy.

Q: Are there any uniquely Japanese leisure facilities?

What often comes as a surprise to visitors to Japan is the huge number of karaoke boxes and pachinko pinball parlors. These two leisurely activities—Japan born and raised—stand head and shoulders above the rest. Other facilities characteristically Japanese include health spas, super hot springs, and other multipurpose therapeutic centers. There are also forms of legal gambling, such as cycling, boating, and motorcycle racing, that are only found in Japan.

Q: Is it true that mature adults are just as enthusiastic about comics and video games as young people?

In Japan, comics (manga) and video games are not the exclusive province of the young. There is also a wide following among people in their twenties and thirties. An indication of this fact is that manga weekly magazines often have print-runs in the several hundreds of thousands, and when a manga comes out in serialized book form, it may sell several million copies. Video games were originally made to be played on a TV monitor but now the mobile phone is becoming the device of choice. In the trains you will notice a

です。

> ▶ おたく
>
> 漫画（アニメ）やゲームの愛好者のなかでも際だって嗜好性が強い人の蔑称。1970年代に生まれた言葉で、電気街で知られる秋葉原（東京）は「おたく族のメッカ」とも呼ばれています。

秋葉原

Q: カラオケはいつからブームになったの?

ハンブルクのカラオケパブ

　カラオケは「空」と「オーケストラ」を合体した略語です。「空」はリードヴォーカルのトラック部分がないことを意味しています。カラオケ機器の原型は、1970年代初期に登場しました。主流は、ビルのフロアを細かく仕切り個室にして時間貸しで楽しめるカラオケボックスで、全国に約9300施設あるとされます（カラオケ白書2014）。

　機器の多機能化も進み、音声変換や歌の採点などもできるようになっています。家庭向けのカラオケ内蔵マイクも普及していますが、他人の前で歌うところにこそカラオケの楽しさがあるのです。

Q: パチンコはどんな遊技なの?

　ピンボールと似たゲームで、多くの釘が打たれた盤面上に鋼球を打上げ、それが落下して特定の入賞口に入ると賞球が得られる遊技です。賞球は景品と交換できます。パチンコ店が登場したのは1930年代ですが、戦時中は全面禁止さ

good number of young heads bent over their mobile phones.

> ▶ **Otaku**
>
> *Otaku* refers to someone who takes his or her liking for anime, manga or video games to extraordinary lengths. The word emerged in the 1970s when the Akihabara district, known for its plethora of electronic and other geeky goods, came to be called the *Otaku* Mecca.

Q: When did karaoke begin to boom?

The word karaoke combines the Japanese word for empty with a shortened version of orchestra. "Empty" refers to the fact that the track for the lead vocal is empty. The first karaoke device appeared at the beginning of the 1970s. The usual arrangement is for one floor of a building to be divided up into many small karaoke boxes for rent. There are said to be some 9,300 such facilities nationwide (Karaoke White Paper).

The karaoke device has become more sophisticated over time, with the addition of voice distortion and even the awarding of points for performance. Home karaoke devices with a built-in microphone are also available, but the ultimate pleasure of karaoke is still singing before an audience.

Q: What is pachinko?

Pachinko refers to a pinball-like game in which a ball is shot onto a vertical board, falls through many pins, and produces extra balls when the launched ball falls into the appropriate slots. These newly won balls can be exchanged for prizes. The first pachinko parlors appeared in the 1930s, only to

れ、戦後に復活しました。70年代後半頃までは鋼球を手動で打っていましたが、その後は自動式になり、射出は0.6秒に1発以内と制限されています。

現在のパチンコ台は、アニメなどの作品を題材とした「タイアップ機」が主流で、入賞時に興奮させたり大当たりの期待感を高めるさまざまな機能を備えています。景品の換金も行われているため、射幸心をあおるギャンブル要素が強いと指摘され、パチンコ依存症が社会問題になっています。

パチンコ

2 スポーツ

Q: 日本人がよくするスポーツは？

文部科学省の調査（体力・スポーツに関する世論調査2013年1月）によると、1年間に行ったスポーツのベスト10は、①ウオーキング、②体操、③ボウリング、④ジョギング、⑤水泳、⑥ゴルフ、⑦テニス、⑧室内運動、⑨キャッチボール・ドッジボール、⑩登山でした。

野球やサッカーは人気が高いスポーツのわりに上位にランクされないのは、プレイをする場所が少ないのが原因です。また、高齢者の間では日本で生まれたゲートボールという球技が人気があります。これは、5人ずつの2つのチームがT字型のスティックでボールを打ち、3つのゲートを通過させる競技で、チームワークの駆け引

be banned during the war and then reappear in the postwar period. The balls were released manually until near the end of the 1970s, when automatic firing came into use, with the restriction that a shot could only be fired every 0.6 seconds.

The majority of pachinko machines today are video-oriented with tie-ups to anime creators and other visual artists. They have a good many features that heighten the moment, or the expectation, of winning a jackpot. Since the prizes can be exchanged for money, pachinko is actually an addictive form of gambling, and for that reason its social value has been questioned.

2 Sports

Q: Which sports are most actively engaged in?

According to the Ministry of Education's Physical Strength and Sports Survey of January 2013, the top ten sports that Japanese engaged in were: 1) walking, 2) gymnastics, 3) bowling, 4) jogging, 5) swimming, 6) golf, 7) tennis, 8) indoor sports, 9) catch-ball, dodgeball, 10) mountain climbing.

The fact that baseball and soccer, while admittedly popular, are not ranked in the top ten is probably due to the lack of adequate space. Among the elderly, gateball is particularly popular, a game that was invented in Japan. Gateball consists of two teams of five members each, who use T-shaped mallets to hit balls through three gates. It involves both strategy and teamwork. In winter, skiing and

きが勝敗に結び付きます。冬には、スキーやスノーボードを楽しむ人が増えてきています。

Q: 観戦するのが好きなスポーツは?

競技場へ足を運んだり、テレビ中継を楽しむ人が多いスポーツは野球、サッカー、ゴルフ、大相撲です。また、バレーボール、ラグビー、ボクシング、マラソン、卓球、柔道、水泳も人気が高い競技です。

野球はプロ野球のほかに、春と夏の2回、甲子園(兵庫県)で行われる高校野球全国大会を楽しみにしている人もたくさんいます。マラソン競技で観戦者が多いのは、お正月に開催される大学対抗の箱根駅伝です。

Q: プロ野球のチームは、いくつあるの?

日本のプロ野球は、セントラルとパシフィックの2リーグにそれぞれ6球団、計12球団あります。各球団にはマイナーリーグに当る二軍があり、イースタンリーグとウエスタンリーグがあります。

また、2009年に女子プロ野球リーグが創設され、4チームが活躍しています。

Q: プロサッカーチームは、いくつあるの?

日本のプロサッカーは、1993年に創設された「Jリーグ」(10クラブチーム)を出発点にしています。99年にJ1とJ2の2リーグ制となり、

snowboarding are attracting more followers.

Q: What sports are the most watched?

The sports that people most enjoy watching, either in person or on TV, are baseball, soccer, golf, and sumo. Also popular are volleyball, rugby, boxing, marathons, table tennis, judo, and swimming.

Aside from professional baseball, there is also the national high school baseball tournament, which is held in spring and summer every year at the Koshien stadium in Hyogo prefecture and is hugely popular. Among the various marathons, that most watched is the Hakone *ekiden* (relay race) held during New Year's, featuring competing university teams.

Q: How many professional baseball teams are there?

The highest level of Japanese professional baseball (Nippon Professional Baseball) has two leagues, the Central and the Pacific, with six teams each. Each of these 12 teams has what is equivalent to a minor league team, forming the Eastern and Western leagues.

In 2009 the Japan Women's Baseball League was established with four teams.

Q: How many professional soccer teams are there?

Japanese professional soccer (football) got underway in 1993 with the establishment of the J. League with 10 club teams. In 1999 J. League was split into the J1 division and J2 division.

2014年にJ3リーグが新たに発足しました。現在、クラブチームはJ1リーグが18、J2リーグが22、J3リーグが12です（2015年）。

また、1989年に日本女子サッカーリーグが創設されました。社会人・大学生主体の「なでしこリーグ」には1部（10クラブ）と2部（10クラブ）があり、「チャレンジリーグ」と呼ばれる3部（12クラブ）には高校生・中学生もいます（2015年）。

Q: サッカーくじって、なに？

日本プロサッカーリーグなどの試合結果、あるいは各チームの得点数を予想して投票し、的中すると当選金が受け取れる公営ギャンブルです。1998年5月に成立した法律に基づき、日本スポーツ振興センターが運営しています。

投票券は「totoチケット」と呼ばれ、指定窓口の他、コンビニ、インターネットでも購入できます。ちなみに2014年度の総売上額は約1108億円で、このうち約190億円が地方自治体やスポーツ団体へ助成金として配分されます。当選者が出ない場合はキャリーオーバーとして累積されるしくみで、最高当選額はキャリーオーバー時が5億円、それ以外は1億円です。

In 2014 J3 was added. As of 2014, there are 18 club teams in J1, 22 in J2, and 12 in J3.

In women's soccer, the L. League was established in 1989. The league consists of three divisions, the Nadeshiko League (with both professional and amateur players in two divisions) and the Challenge League (with junior high and high school players). There are 32 club teams in all (2015).

Q: What is the soccer lottery?

The soccer lottery is a form of legal gambling in which participants predict the outcome of matches or the number of points scored and win a monitory prize when correct. It is based on a law passed in May 1998 and is run by the National Agency for the Advancement of Sports and Health.

The tickets (called Toto tickets) needed to take part in the lottery are sold at appointed booths, convenience stores, and online. In 2014 total sales amounted to ¥110.8 billion, of which ¥19 billion went to the local governments running the lottery and to sports organizations to promote their activities. When there is no winner, the prize money is carried over to the next lottery. Counting money carried over, the largest amount is ¥500 million; otherwise, ¥100 million is the maximum.

第12章 観光・イベント
Chapter 12 Tourism and Special Events

伏見稲荷大社 ▶

1 観光

Q: 日本への観光客が多い国は？

来日する外国人は年間約1340万人で、その8割がアジアの国々からの来客です。ベスト3は、台湾（約283万人）、韓国（約275万人）、中国（約241万人）。

中国人観光客が多いのが春節の大型連休がある2月で、日本の観光地は中国人の観光ツアーで混雑します。近年、観光客が急増しているのがタイで、65万人強（前年比伸び率45％）。タイでは、4月の連休を利用した訪日ツアーが流行しています。（数値は2014年、日本政府観光局調べ）。日本政府は、2020年の東京五輪までに年間2000万人を目標にしています。

● 訪日観光客が多い国・地域ベスト10 (2014年1月～12月)

① 台湾 Taiwan	② 韓国 South Korea	③ 中国 China	④ 香港 Hong Kong	⑤ 米国 United States
2,829,800人	2,755,300人	2,409,200人	925,900人	891,600人

1 Tourism

Q: What countries send the most visitors to Japan?

The number of tourists coming to Japan every year is about 13.4 million, of which 80% are from Asia. The top three are Taiwan (about 2.83 million), South Korea (about 2.75 million), and China (about 2.41 million).

Chinese tourists are particularly prominent in February during the Chinese Spring Festival, when there are a number of consecutive holidays. During this time the Japanese tourist attractions are crowded with Chinese tour groups. Thailand, on the other hand, has shown remarkable increases in recent years (over 650,000; up more than 45% over the previous year), taking advantage of consecutive holidays in April. The government has set a goal of 20,000,000 annual visitors by the

The top 10 countries and regions sending visitors to Japan are:
(All figures provided by the Japan National Tourist Organization, 2014.)

⑥ タイ Thailand	⑦ オーストラリア Australia	⑧ マレーシア Malaysia	⑨ シンガポール Singapore	⑩ 英国 United Kingdom
657,600 人	302,700 人	249,500 人	227,900 人	220,100 人

第12章 観光・イベント

Q: 外国人に人気がある観光地は?

　外国人観光客が集中するのは、東京、京都、大阪の3都市で約8割と言われます。最も人気があるのが京都で、ついでに奈良を巡る古都観光です。京都では伏見稲荷大社、金閣寺、清水寺、祇園などが人気スポット。東京ではスカイツリーや浅草寺などの下町を巡るバスツアーを楽しむ観光客が多く、新宿のゴールデン街や渋谷のスクランブル交差点も人気があります。

清水寺

白川郷

　また近年、外国人観光客が増えているのが、日本の里山の原風景ともいえる白川郷(世界遺産、岐阜県)、平成の大修理を終えた国宝・姫路城(世界遺産、兵庫県)をはじめとする城巡りです。北陸新幹線の開業で行きやすくなった古都・金沢は今後、外国人観光客が増加すると見られています。

Q: 宿泊施設にはどんなものがあるの?

　日本の観光客向け宿泊施設は、旅館と観光ホテルに大別されます。旅館は純日本式、温泉地に多い観光ホテルは和洋ミックスです。「政府登録」の旅館やホテルがありますが、これは政府

2020 Tokyo Olympics.

Q: What are the most popular tourist sites?

Approximately 80% of visitors to Japan concentrate their time in the three big cities of Tokyo, Kyoto, and Osaka. Kyoto is the most popular, with many people making a side trip to nearby Nara. Kyoto is especially noted for Fushimi Inari Shrine, Kinkaku-ji (Golden Pavilion), Kiyomizu-dera temple, and the Gion district. In Tokyo, many visitors take the bus tour to the Skytree tower, Senso-ji temple, and the surrounding area that preserves the plebeian atmosphere of old Tokyo. The cramped Shinjuku Golden Gai area, famous for its architectural interest and nightlife, and the Shibuya scramble crossing are also attractions.

Of late, visitors hoping to get a taste of "good old" Japan have increasingly visited Shirakawa-go, an old farming village with a distinctive type of architecture in Gifu prefecture (World Heritage Site), and the recently renovated Himeji Castle in Hyogo prefecture (World Heritage Site), among other castles. With the new Hokuriku Shinkansen now in operation, the well-preserved historical town of Kanazawa can be easily reached from Tokyo and will surely become a favorite tourist destination.

Q: What kinds of accommodations are there for tourists?

Accommodations for foreign visitors can be broadly divided into tourist hotels and Japanese inns. Inns are purely Japanese in their arrangements and layout, while the tourist hotels found near hot springs are a mixture of Japanese and Western

が定める基準を満たした施設ということで、ステイタスではありません。日本では欧米のようなホテルの公的格付けがないため、料金を基準に施設を選ぶ必要があります。

Q: 世界遺産に登録されているのは、どこ?

ユネスコが、自然のままの地や歴史的建造物・遺跡などを指定して「世界遺産リスト」に登録した件数は1007件(2014年12月現在)。

日本の「世界遺産」は、以下のとおりです。

自然遺産
❶ 白神山地
　　(青森県・秋田県、1993年12月登録)
❷ 屋久島
　　(鹿児島県、1993年12月)
❸ 知床
　　(北海道、2005年7月)
❹ 小笠原諸島
　　(東京都、2011年6月)

文化遺産
① 姫路城
　　(兵庫県、1993年12月登録)
② 法隆寺地域の仏像建造物
　　(奈良県、1993年12月)
③ 古都京都の文化財
　　(京都府・滋賀県、1994年12月)
④ 白川郷・五箇山の合掌造り集落
　　(岐阜県・富山県、1995年12月)

fixtures. Some inns and hotels are "officially registered" by the government, but since Japan does not have hotel rankings like in the West, this simply means that the hotel or inn has met basic government standards. In the end, you must choose based on price and your own taste.

Q: How many World Heritage Sites are there?

World Heritage Site is a building, city, complex, desert, forest, island, lake, monument, or mountain that is listed by UNESCO as being of special cultural or physical significance. As of December 2014, there are 1,007 such sites. The Japanese sites are as follows:

Natural Sites

❶ Shirakami-Sanchi
   (Aomori and Akita prefectures; listed December 1993)
❷ Yakushima
   (Kagoshima prefecture; listed December 1993)
❸ Shiretoko
   (Hokkaido prefecture; listed July 2005)
❹ Ogasawara Islands
   (Tokyo Metropolis; listed June 2011)

Cultural Sites

① Himeji-jo
   (Hyogo prefecture; listed December 1993)
② Buddhist Monuments in the Horyu-ji Area
   (Nara prefecture; December 1993)
③ Historic Monuments of Ancient Kyoto
   (Kyoto and Shiga prefectures; listed December 1994)
④ Historic Villages of Shirakawa-go and Gokayama
   (Gifu and Toyama prefectures; listed December 1995)

⑤ 厳島神社
（広島県、1996年12月）
⑥ 原爆ドーム
（広島県、1996年12月）

厳島神社

⑦ 古都奈良の文化財
（奈良県、1998年12月）
⑧ 日光の社寺
（栃木県、1999年12月）
⑨ 琉球王国のグスク及び関連遺産群
（沖縄県、2000年12月）
⑩ 紀伊山地の霊場と参詣道
（三重県・奈良県・和歌山県、2004年7月）
⑪ 石見銀山遺跡とその文化的景観
（島根県、2007年7月）
⑫ 平泉――仏国土（浄土）を表す建築・庭園及び考古学的遺跡群
（岩手県、2011年6月）
⑬ 富士山――信仰の対象と芸術の源泉
（静岡県・山梨県、2013年6月）
⑭ 富岡製糸場と絹産業遺跡群
（群馬県、2014年6月）

富岡製糸場

なお、明治日本の産業革命遺産（福岡県など8県）を文化遺産として登録勧告中（2015年5月現在）。

Q: 温泉って、なに？

火山列島の日本には、地下にたくさんの温泉・鉱泉が存在します。摂氏25度以上が温泉で、それ未満を鉱泉と言います。

温泉施設は2万以上もあるとされますが、天

⑤ Itsukushima Shinto Shrine
   (Hiroshima prefecture; listed December 1996)
⑥ Hiroshima Peace Memorial
   (Genbaku Dome, Hiroshima prefecture; listed December 1996)
⑦ Historic Monuments of Ancient Nara
   (Nara prefecture; listed December 1998)
⑧ Shrines and Temples of Nikko
   (Tochigi prefecture; listed December 1999)
⑨ Gusuku Sites and Related Properties of the Kingdom of Ryukyu
   (Okinawa prefecture; listed December 2000)
⑩ Sacred Sites and Pilgrimage Routes in the Kii Mountain Range
   (Mie, Nara, Wakayama prefectures; listed July 2004)
⑪ Iwami Ginzan Silver Mine and its Cultural Landscape
   (Shimane prefecture; listed July 2007)
⑫ Hiraizumi—Temples, Gardens and Archaeological Sites Representing the Buddhist Pure Land
   (Iwate prefecture; listed June 2011)
⑬ Fujisan, sacred place and source of artistic inspiration
   (Shizuoka and Yamanashi prefectures; listed June 2013)
⑭ Tomioka Silk Mill and Related Sites
   (Gunma prefecture; listed June 2014)

Further, eight sites in Fukuoka prefecture and elsewhere that are connected with industrial development in the Meiji period (1868-1912) are now on the Tentative List (as of May 2015).

Q: What distinguishes Japanese hot springs?

Japan being a volcanic archipelago, it has many hot springs and mineral water sites. Water above 25 degrees Celsius is considered a hot spring; below that, it is mineral water.

There are said to be over 20,000 hot spring resorts

然温泉はその3割ほどで、有名な温泉地でも施設が増えたことで源泉から供給される湯量が不足ぎみになり、水増し湯や循環湯でカバーしているケースが目立ちます。湯船からあふれたお湯を流しっぱなしの「源泉かけ流し」かどうかが、適正な天然温泉かそうでないかを見分けるポイントです。

Q: 有名な温泉地は、どこ？

数多い温泉地の中から選ぶのは難しいのですが、温泉ランキングなどを参考にすると、以下の温泉地が挙げられます。

東日本：
登別（北海道）
秋保（宮城県）
那須・鬼怒川（栃木県）
草津・伊香保（群馬県）
強羅・箱根（神奈川県）
熱海・湯河原・伊東（静岡県）など。

西日本：
下呂（岐阜県）
有馬・城崎（兵庫県）
白浜（和歌山県）
山中（石川県）
玉造（島根県）
道後（愛媛県）
黒川（熊本県）
別府・湯布院（大分県）
指宿（鹿児島県）など。

nationwide, but only one-third of them use natural hot spring water. The number of resorts has grown to such an extent that even in the most famous hot spring areas, there is a lamentable shortage of natural thermal water, meaning that it has to be augmented from other sources or recycled. You can tell if the water is from a natural hot spring by whether it is allowed to run freely out of the bathing area.

Q: Which hot spring areas are the most well-known?

While it is difficult to come up with an impartial list, a comparison of various listings and rankings produces the following.

Eastern Japan

Noboribetsu (Hokkaido)
Akiu (Miyagi prefecture)
Nasu and Kinugawa (Tochigi prefecture)
Kusatsu and Ikaho (Gunma prefecture)
Gora and Hakone (Kanagawa prefecture)
Atami, Yugawara, and Ito (Shizuoka prefecture)

Western Japan

Gero (Gifu prefecture)
Arima and Kinosaki (Hyogo prefecture)
Shirahama (Wakayama prefecture)
Yamanaka (Ishikawa prefecture)
Tamatsukuri (Shimane prefecture)
Dogo (Ehime prefecture)
Kurokawa (Kumamoto prefecture)
Beppu and Yufuin (Oita prefecture)
Ibusuki (Kagoshima prefecture)

熱海

▶熱海温泉

1200年以上の歴史を持つ日本有数の温泉地。東京から新幹線で35〜50分、車で約2時間という至便性から観光客が多く、60軒以上のホテルや旅館があります。夏と冬は花火大会が開催されます。

Q: 日本のおみやげで人気があるのは?

円安や東南アジア、中国向けのビザ緩和を追い風に、訪日外国人客数が急増しています。外国人旅行者を対象に消費税抜きで商品を販売できる免税店も増加し、1万8000店になりました（2015年5月）。2014年10月には、家電・バッグ・衣料品などに加え、食料品・医薬品・化粧品も対象にされました。

ちなみに、中国人観光客は医薬品・化粧品・家電・バッグなどを"爆買い"することで話題になっていますが、意外な人気商品は温水洗浄便座だそうです。

市松人形

東京でのおみやげを買う場所としては、浅草仲見世、秋葉原電気街、上野アメ横商店街などが主で、それぞれ日本人形、電気炊飯器、タラバガニが人気商品です。

> ▶ **Atami Hot Springs**
> With a history of over 1,200 years, Atami is one of Japan's most famous hot spring resorts. It can be conveniently reached from Tokyo by shinkansen in 35 to 55 minutes, or by car in about 2 hours, accounting in part for its many visitors. It boasts over 60 hotels and inns. There is a magnificent fireworks display in both summer and winter.

Q What are the most popular souvenirs?

What with the appreciation of the yen and the loosening of tourist visa restrictions for Southeast Asia and China, the number of tourists coming to Japan has shown a dramatic increase. The number of tax-free shops where tourists can make purchases without paying the consumer tax has also grown to 18,000 shops (as of May 2015). In October 2014, in addition to electric appliances, handbags, and clothing, foodstuffs, pharmaceuticals, and cosmetics were also added to the list of tax-free items.

A much-talked-about recent event is the splurge buying of pharmaceuticals, cosmetics, electric appliances, and handbags by tourists from China, among which items is the popular toilet seat that both heats the posterior and washes it with water.

The principal places to buy souvenirs in Tokyo are Asakusa's Nakamise, Akihabara's Electric Town, and Ueno's Ameya Yokocho, where you can buy things like Japanese dolls, electric rice cookers, red king crab, and a multitude of other items.

Q: 国宝って、どのように決めるの？

国宝は、文字どおり日本の「国の宝」です。国が指定した重要文化財のなかで特に世界文化の見地から価値の高いものが選ばれ、文部科学大臣が指定します。2014年現在、国宝の指定件数は以下のとおりです。

建造物221件、絵画159件、彫刻128件、工芸品252件、書跡・典籍224件、古文書60件、考古資料46件、歴史資料3件。

国宝を多く収蔵して展示しているのが国立博物館で、東京・京都・奈良・九州（福岡県）の4館があります。なかでも東京国立博物館（上野）は収蔵件数が多く、常設展示も行っています。

Q: 仏像にはどんな種類があるの？

仏像は、仏教での信仰の対象としてつくられました。中国や韓国から渡来した像をもとに日本の仏師が独自に制作するようになったのは奈良時代前後で、平安時代や鎌倉時代には芸術的に優れた仏像が生み出されました。

仏像は、①如来像、②菩薩像、③明王像、④天部像の4種に大別されます。如来像は仏の姿を現したもので、仏教の世界観では釈迦だけでなく、たくさんの仏がいるとしています。菩薩像は仏になるための修行中の姿、明王像は悪魔から仏を守る神々、天部像はインドのバラモン

Q: How is a National Treasure designated?

The Japanese word for National Treasure (*kokuho*) literally means "treasure of the nation." National Treasures are chosen from a list of Important Cultural Properties for their high value in terms of world cultural history, and are designated by the Minister of Education, Culture, Sports, Science and Technology. As of 2014, the number of National Treasures was as follows: buildings, 221; paintings, 159; sculpture, 128; crafts, 252; written materials, 224; ancient documents, 60; archaeological artifacts, 46; historical artifacts, 3.

Many of these National Treasures are housed in the national museums in Tokyo, Kyoto, Nara, and Kyushu (Fukuoka). The Tokyo National Museum in Ueno has an exceptionally large number of National Treasures, many of which are on permanent display.

Q: What kinds of Buddhist sculpture are there?

Buddhist statues were created as religious objects of worship. Buddhist sculpture first came to Japan from China and Korea, and working with these statues as models, Japanese sculptors began to add their own individual styles around the beginning of the Nara period (710-784). By the Heian period (784-1185) and Kamakura period (1185-1333) works of outstanding artistic merit were being created.

Buddhist statues can be broadly classified by the figure they depict: 1) Nyorai, 2) Bosatsu, 3) Myoo, and 4) Tenbu. Nyorai refers to those who have attained enlightenment or become a Buddha, not simply to the historical Buddha, Shakamuni. Bosatsu, or Bodhisattva, refers to a figure who is still undergoing ascetic practices to become a Buddha. Myoo

の神々を表現しています。

高徳院の大仏

> ▶大仏
>
> 日本には「大仏」と呼ばれる仏像が90ほどあり、なかでも高さ10m以上の像は30ほどです。奈良・東大寺の大仏は749年完成で金銅の仏像として世界最大（高さ約16m）、鎌倉・高徳院の大仏は13世紀中頃の造立、台座を含め高さ約13.3mです。

Q: お城は、いくつあるの？

記録に残っている城は2万5000もあったとされますが、現存する城跡はその1％にも足りません。日本の城と言えば天守閣のある城が好まれますが、観光名所としての城は60ほどで復元・復興したものも含まれます。

国宝に指定されている城は、姫路城（世界遺産、兵庫県）、松本城（長野県）、彦根城（滋賀県）、犬山城（愛知県）、松江城（島根県）です。

姫路城

refers to deities who protect Buddhas from devils. Tenbu refers to gods incorporated from Indian Brahmanism.

> ▶ **Great Buddha Statues**
>
> There are 90 statues that are classified as Great Buddhas, or Daibutsu. Of these, 30 are over 10 meters in height. The Great Buddha at Todai-ji in Nara, completed in 749, is the world's largest bronze statue of Dainichi Nyorai (Vairocana) at 16 meters. The Great Buddha at Kotoku-in in Kamakura, completed in mid 13th century, is 13.3 meters tall, including the base.

Q: How many castles are there?

According to historical records, there were once as many as 25,000, but now less than 1% survive in one form or another. Among the 60 castles most frequented by tourists are many that have undergone rebuilding or reconstruction.

The castles listed as National Treasures are as follows: Himeji (World Heritage Site; Hyogo prefecture), Matsumoto (Nagano prefecture), Hikone (Shiga prefecture), Inuyama (Aichi prefecture), and Matsue (Shimane prefecture).

2 イベント

Q: 有名な祭りは？

一般的に「日本の三大祭」と呼ばれているのが、神田祭(東京・神田明神、5月中旬)、天神祭(大阪・天満宮、6月下旬～7月25日)、祇園祭(京都・八坂神社、7月1カ月間)です。

その他、全国からたくさんの観光客が訪れる祭として有名なのが、よさこい祭り(8月9日～12日、高知県高知市、100万人)、青森ねぶた祭(8月2日～7日、青森県青森市、250万人)、さっぽろ雪まつり(2月5日～11日、北海道札幌市、240万人)などです。(会期・集客数は2014年のデータ)

京都　祇園祭り

Q: 祭りは、なんのためにやるの？

古くからの神事が、その由来です。日本人は豊作や豊漁を願って年1回、神社に祀られている神様の威光が増すようにと神輿に乗せて外へ連れ出しました。これが祭りに発展したのです。また、祭りは神道でのハレ(非日常性)の儀式で、日常生活を離れた世界で身を浄めるという意味合いもあります。

2 Special Events

Q: What are the most famous festivals?

The three known as the Three Great Festivals of Japan are the Kanda Festival (Tokyo: Kanda Myojin shrine, mid May), Tenjin Festival (Osaka: Tenman-gu shrine, from late June to late July), and Gion Festival (Kyoto: Yasaka shrine, July).

Other famous festivals that attract people from around the country (with number of attendants in parentheses) are: Yosakoi Festival (Kochi city, Kochi prefecture: August 9-12, 1 million), Aomori Nebuta Festival (Aomori city, Aomori prefecture: August 2-7, 2.5 million), and the Sapporo Snow Festival (Sapporo city, Hokkaido: February 5-11, 2.4 million). (Dates and statistics based on 2014 data.)

Q: What is the purpose of a festival?

The origin of the festival (*matsuri*) is found in Shinto religious rites stemming from the distant past. Once a year, in the hope of having a bountiful harvest and plentiful fishing, shrine parishioners would take the god out of the shrine in a sacred palanquin to spread the god's blessings far and wide. This custom eventually developed into the festivals we see today. This coincides with the Shinto notion of *hare* ("bright") rituals, which mark a time when participants are transported to a world of the extraordinary and purify themselves of the dross of everyday life.

奇祭と言われるものも多くあります。例えば、西宮神宮福男選び（兵庫県、1月）は、多くの男女が神社の境内を200メートルほど競争し、その年の福男を決めます。西大寺はだか祭（岡山県、2月）では、まわし姿の男たちがその年の福男を競います。宇出津あばれ（石川県、7月）は、松明や神輿が水中や火中に投げ込まれる勇壮な祭りです。一方、笑い祭り（和歌山県、10月）は、道化に扮した人が人々に笑うように言いながら練り歩くというもの。新年の行事である男鹿のなまはげ（秋田県、大晦日）は、恐ろしい鬼の面をかぶった人が家を訪ね、怖がる子供にいい子になるようにと言います。岸和田だんじり祭（大阪府、9月）では、大きな神輿が町を疾走するという危険なもので、7年に1度開催される諏訪大社の御柱祭（長野県）は、人を乗せたままの大木を急な坂から落とすため、死傷者が出ることでも知られます。

御柱祭 下社木落し

Q: 花火大会は、いつから始まったの？

江戸時代の享保年間（1716-35）に疫病が流行し、犠牲者の供養と悪疫払いのために大川での水神祭で20発打ち上げたのが始まり。当時は和火といって、色数も少なく地味な花火でした。競技花火大会がはじまり、なかでも大曲の全国

Some of these festivals are termed "bizarre" (*kisai*). For instance, there is a race held as part of a festival at Nishinomiya Shrine (Hyogo prefecture, January), in which crowds of men (and women) sprint over 200 meters through the shrine compound to see who wins and is named the lucky man of the year. There is also the Naked Festival at Saidai-ji temple (Okayama prefecture, February), where loinclothed men compete for the "lucky man" honor. At Ushitsu on the Noto Peninsula (Ishikawa prefecture, July), there is an *abare* (violent) festival featuring bonfires, fiery lanterns, sacred palanquins being thrown into the sea, retrieved and then incinerated. On the other hand, there is the Laughing Festival (Wakayama prefecture, October), in which clown-like parishioners parade the streets, encouraging everyone to laugh and laughing themselves. In a New Year's ritual in Akita prefecture, men dressed as ogres (*namahage*) and wearing large, frightful masks go from house to house admonishing quaking children to be on good behavior. In the Kishiwada Danjiri Festival (Osaka, September), huge sacred palanquins careen dangerously through the streets, and in the Onbashira Festival in Nagano prefecture, held once every seven years, participants ride on huge logs shooting down a precipitous slope. Fatalities are not unheard of.

Q: When did fireworks displays first begin?

In the Kyoho era (1716-35) of the Edo period, an epidemic broke out, and 20 fireworks were shot off to console the spirits of the dead. The number of colors was small, and the overall effect was rather subdued. Later, competitive fireworks displays came into being, the most famous being

花火競技大会（秋田県）、土浦全国花火競技大会（茨城県）、長岡まつり大花火大会（新潟県）は有名です。

スカイツリーと隅田川

▶東京"三大"花火大会

最も古い歴史がある「隅田川花火大会」（7月最終土曜日）は約2万発、見物客90万人。「江戸川区花火大会」（8月第1土曜日）は約1万2000発、140万人。ベイエリアでの「東京湾大華火祭」（8月第2土曜日）は約1万2000発、70万人。

Q: 灯篭流しって、なに？

嵐山灯篭流し

「灯篭流し」は、お盆に死者の霊をなぐさめるために、木や竹の枠に和紙をはった灯篭の中のろうそくに火をともして川や海へ流す風習です。お供え物や花を一緒に流すケースもありますが、汚染につながるとして禁止する自治体もあり、昔ほど一般的ではなくなりました。

ピースメッセージとうろう流し（広島市）は、原爆ドームの対岸の元安川で被爆者などの慰霊と世界平和へのメッセージを書いた約1万個の灯篭を流します。灯篭流しは花火大会と一緒に行われることが多く、京都嵐山灯篭流し花火大会（桂川）が有名です。九州の長崎市内陸部、佐

the Omagari National Japan Fireworks Competition (Akita prefecture), the Tsuchiura All Japan Fireworks Competition (Ibaraki prefecture), and the Nagaoka Festival Fireworks (Niigata prefecture).

▶ Tokyo's Three Great Fireworks Displays

The oldest of the three is the Sumidagawa Fireworks Festival (last Saturday of July), where some 20,000 fireworks are shot off before 900,000 people. Then there is the Edogawa Ward Fireworks Festival (first Saturday in August) with 12,000 fireworks before 1,400,000 people, and the Tokyo Bay Grand Fireworks Festival (second Saturday in August) with 12,000 fireworks launched before 700,000 people.

Q: What is lantern floating?

"Lantern floating" (*toro nagashi*) refers to the custom during Obon (Festival of the Dead) when lanterns made of wood or bamboo and covered with Japanese paper (*washi*), with a candle inside, are floated down streams or in the ocean as a means of consoling the dead. Sometimes flowers or other offerings are included, but deciding that this might contribute to pollution, some local governments have outlawed the practice, with the result that it is not as common as it used to be.

In Hiroshima city, there is the tradition of floating lanterns for peace on the Motoyasu river, across from the Atomic Dome, to console the spirits of those who died from the bomb there. Some 10,000 lanterns are released containing messages for world peace. Often lantern floating is combined with a fireworks display, one famous example being Kyoto's

賀市・熊本市の一部では「精霊流し」と呼び、船を使うこともあります。

Q: かまくらって、なに?

秋田県や新潟県などの雪国で、雪を盛り固めてつくった家(雪洞)の中に祭壇を設けて水神を祀る、小正月(2月中旬頃)の伝統行事です。みちのく(東北)五大雪まつりの一つの「横手かまくら」(秋田県横手市)は400年以上の歴史を持ち、雪まつり期間中は100基ほどのかまくらが登場し、その中に入った子ども達が甘酒やお餅を振る舞います。横手より古い歴史を持つ「六郷かまくら」(秋田県美郷町)は、国の重要無形文化財に指定され、2月11日〜15日の間、神事が行われます。最終日の竹うちは、住民男性が2手に分かれ5mの長竹で打ち合って吉凶を占う、荒々しい行事です。

横手かまくら

Q: 学芸会って、なにをするの?

主に幼稚園や保育所、小学校などで開催される文化行事で、学習成果としての音楽・演劇を発表する場です。就学前の児童の場合は、家族を招待して開催します。

Arashiyama Lantern Floating Festival on the Katsura river. In the cities of Nagasaki, Saga, and Kumamoto this custom is called spirit floating (*shoro nagashi*) and includes boat-sized floats.

Q: What is a *kamakura*?

In often snow-laden Akita and Niigata prefectures, it is customary on the lunar New Year (mid February) to make igloo-like huts (*kamakura*) out of packed snow and erect therein altars to the gods of water. One of the Five Great Festivals of Michinoku (the Tohoku region), the Yokote Kamakura Festival (Yokote city, Akita prefecture) has a history of over 400 years. During the period of the festival, some 100 *kamakura* are built and occupied by children treating passersby to "sweet sake" (*amazake*) and rice cakes (*mochi*). Even older than the Yokote Kamakura Festival is the Rokugo Kamakura Event (Misato, Akita prefecture: February 11-15), which has been designated an Intangible Cultural Property. The last day of the event features the *take-uchi* ("bamboo-beating") competition, in which two teams of local men attack one another with 5-meter bamboo poles as a means of divining local prospects for the coming year.

Q: What is "performance day"?

Performance day (*gakugei-kai*) is a cultural event in which preschoolers, elementary school students, and others demonstrate what they have learned in school by putting on theatrical plays, playing music, and in other ways. In the case of preschoolers, the parents are invited to the event.

学芸会

1897年前後から自然発生的に始まり、やがて慣行として普及したとも言われます。近年、児童劇ではダブルキャストどころか主役がたくさんいる舞台が増えてきていますが、これは不平等にならないようにとの配慮からだそうです。親にしてみれば、わが子が主役というのは悪い気持ちはしませんが、たくさんの主役から同じセリフを聞かされる観客にとっては、はた迷惑な話です。

Q: 運動会って、どんな行事なの?

英国やドイツの体育行事が起源とする説もありますが、近代の日本で独自に発達したイベントの一つと言うべきでしょう。運動会は主に小学校、企業、地域での恒例行事になっていて、小学校の場合は家族参加の体育行事です。春（5月、6月）と秋（9月、10月）のいずれかか、年2回開催されることも多く、体育の日（10月の第二月曜日・祝日）には各地で運動会が行われています。紅白などの色別のチームで対抗試合をするのが一般的で、短距離走、リレー、騎馬戦、玉入れ、綱引きなどの競技やマスゲーム、ダンスなどの演技が披露されます。

運動会

Performance day seems to have come spontaneously into being sometime around 1897 and soon became a permanent fixture. In the case of theatricals put on by small children, the leading role is shared by a number of them, as this is apparently though to be the only fair way of seeing that each child gets a bit of the limelight. Naturally, parents are happy to see their child in the leading role, but it can become somewhat tiresome to hear the same lines repeated over and over.

Q: What is "sports day"?

Sports day (*undo-kai*) is said to have its roots in athletic meets held in the United Kingdom and Germany, but in Japan it has developed in some unique ways. For the most part, sports day is sponsored by elementary schools, companies, and local areas and has become a regular fixture. It is usually held one or two times a year, in spring (May or June) and/or autumn (September or October). Particularly on Health and Sports Day (second Monday of October, a national holiday), there are sporting events held throughout the country. Teams are customarily divided into the white and the red and compete for honors. There are short-distance races, relays, competitions between piggybacked riders, *tama-ire* (tossing balls into a basket), tug of war, as well as others, such as mass games and dance.

English Conversational Ability Test
国際英語会話能力検定

● E-CATとは…
英語が話せるようになるためのテストです。インターネットベースで、30分であなたの発話力をチェックします。

www.ecatexam.com

● iTEP®とは…
世界各国の企業、政府機関、アメリカの大学300校以上が、英語能力判定テストとして採用。オンラインによる90分のテストで文法、リーディング、リスニング、ライティング、スピーキングの5技能をスコア化。iTEP®は、留学、就職、海外赴任などに必要な、世界に通用する英語力を総合的に評価する画期的なテストです。

www.itepexamjapan.com

[対訳ニッポン双書]
日本まるごとQ&A
Everything You Should Know about Japan

2015年 8月18日　第1刷発行
2025年 1月11日　第7刷発行

著　者　　安部 直文
訳　者　　マイケル・ブレーズ

発行者　　賀川 洋

発行所　　IBCパブリッシング株式会社
　　　　　〒162-0804 東京都新宿区中里町29番3号 菱秀神楽坂ビル
　　　　　Tel. 03-3513-4511　Fax. 03-3513-4512
　　　　　www.ibcpub.co.jp

印刷所　　株式会社シナノパブリッシングプレス

© IBC パブリッシング 2015
Printed in Japan

落丁本・乱丁本は、小社宛にお送りください。送料小社負担にてお取り替えいたします。
本書の無断複写 (コピー) は著作権法上での例外を除き禁じられています。

ISBN978-4-7946-0358-6